Turkey's Water Diplomacy

Turkey's Water Diplomacy

Analysis of its Foundations, Challenges and Prospects

Aysegül Kibaroglu

ANTHEM PRESS

Anthem Press
An imprint of Wimbledon Publishing Company
www.anthempress.com

This edition first published in UK and USA 2025
by ANTHEM PRESS
75–76 Blackfriars Road, London SE1 8HA, UK
or PO Box 9779, London SW19 7ZG, UK
and
244 Madison Ave #116, New York, NY 10016, USA

First published in the UK and USA by Anthem Press in 2021

British Library Cataloguing-in-Publication Data
A catalogue record for this book is available from the British Library.

Library of Congress Control Number: 2024951170
A catalog record for this book has been requested.

ISBN-13: 978-1-83999-475-3 (Pbk)
ISBN-10: 1-83999-475-4 (Pbk)

Cover image: Kindlena/shutterstock.com

This title is also available as an e-book.

CONTENTS

ACKNOWLEDGEMENTS

I would like to thank Professor Shafiqul Islam for inviting me to contribute to his series with the Anthem Press. I also extend my gratitude to the staff concerned at the Anthem Press for their keen support throughout the publication process.

I thank Liam Murray and Dr Caroline Fell Kurban for reviewing the earlier versions of this volume.

I acknowledge the contributions of MEF University staff and students, namely Research Assistant Dr Cansu Gülec as well as students Ayse Deniz Ozturk, Bianca Isaoglu, Oguzhan Biderci and Ozge Bahar Coskun, in organizing the references section.

Last but not least, my heartfelt thanks go to my core and extended family for their patience, kind help and support all the through preparation process of the manuscript. I would like to specially thank my spouse Professor Mustafa Kibaroglu who has been enormously supportive and helpful in realizing this book.

ABBREVIATIONS

AFAD	Disaster and Emergency Management Presidency
CPET	Collaborative Programme Euphrates and Tigris
DGWM	General Directorate of Water Management
DSI	State Hydraulic Works
EIA	Environmental Impact Assessment
ET	Euphrates–Tigris
ETIC	Euphrates–Tigris Initiative for Cooperation
EU	European Union
FAO	Food and Agriculture Organization
GAP	Southeastern Anatolia Project
GAP RDA	Southeastern Anatolia Project Regional Development Administration
GOLD	General Organization for Land Development
HEPP	Hydro-Electric Power Plant
HSCC	High-Level Strategic Cooperation Council
ICMW	Islamic Conference of Ministers Responsible for Water
ILA	International Law Association
ILC	International Law Commission
IIWF	Istanbul International Water Forum
IWRM	Integrated Water Resources Management
JTC	Joint Technical Committee
TIKA	Turkish Cooperation and Coordination Agency
TMMOB	Union of Chambers of Turkish Engineers and Architects
MEF	Ministry of Environment and Forestry
MFA	Ministry of Foreign Affairs
MFWA	Ministry of Forestry and Water Affairs
MoU	Memorandum of Understanding
MWDF	Multi-track Water Diplomacy Framework
NATO	North Atlantic Treaty Organization
NGO	Non-Governmental Organization
OECD	Organisation for Economic Co-operation and Development

OIC	Organisation of Islamic Cooperation
ORSAM	Center for Middle Eastern Studies
OSCE	Organization for Security and Co-operation in Europe
PWC	Permanent Water Commission
RBMP	River Basin Management Plan
SDC	Swiss Agency for Development and Cooperation
SFG	Strategic Foresight Group
SIDA	Swedish International Development Cooperation Agency
SIWI	Stockholm International Water Institute
SUEN	Turkish Water Institute
TDA	Transboundary Diagnostic Analysis
UNDP	United Nations Development Programme
UNECE	United Nations Economic Commission for Europe
UNECE TWC	Convention on the Protection and Use of Transboundary Watercourses and International Lakes
UNEP	United Nations Environment Programme
UNESCO	United Nations Educational, Scientific and Cultural Organization
UNHCR	United Nations High Commissioner for Refugees
UNWC	United Nations Watercourses Convention
USAID	United States Agency for International Development
USSR	Union of Soviet Socialist Republics
WDF	Water Diplomacy Framework
WFD	Water Framework Directive
WWC	World Water Council
WWF	World Wide Fund for Nature
WWF3	3rd World Water Forum

INTRODUCTION

Diplomacy is a set of initiatives that aims at reaching agreeable solutions between parties who have diverging interests in potentially conflict-laden issues that might otherwise escalate into a hot confrontation. Diplomacy encompasses the processes and institutions by means of which national interests and identities of sovereign states are represented to one another (Wiseman and Sharp 2012) and is enshrined in international law, which states use to explain and justify their policies to actors concerned before the international system. Diplomacy brings state behaviour into the realm of logic and order, by explaining it in terms of existing international legal norms. It is thus a product of foreign policy, combined with international law (Hurd 2015). In line with these definitions, this book aims to assess 'the processes and institutions' in Turkey's water diplomacy framework with a specific focus on its evolving position vis-à-vis international water law.

Water is vital to many levels of human survival. It fluctuates both in space and time, and has multiple and conflicting demands in terms of its use. This means that flows crossing international boundaries can be a source of tension between states (Wolf 1998). While tension does not necessarily always lead to hot confrontation, early coordination and cooperation between riparian states through water diplomacy mechanisms can often help solve the problems that may arise thereof. Water diplomacy is a process of interactions between states that ultimately hope to prevent hostility through dialogue. The role of water diplomacy in the context of transboundary waters is to foster cooperation among riparians. A broader and more inclusive definition would posit that 'water diplomacy includes all measures by state and non-state actors that can be undertaken to prevent or peacefully resolve (emerging) conflicts and facilitate cooperation related to water availability, allocation or use between and within states and public and private stakeholders' (Huntjens et al. 2016, 13).

The main objective of this book is to elucidate Turkey's water diplomacy framework with its key actors and guiding principles. Thus, the analysis adopts an institutionalist approach, by presenting and emphasizing the role of the legal and institutional foundations upon which Turkey's water diplomacy framework rests. It carries systematic and accurate background information on Turkey's transboundary water relations from a historical and geographical perspective. It also includes a thorough analyses of Turkey's position towards international water law. Turkey's state practice in customary international water law, as well as treaty law, has been critically analysed.

The book also identifies non-state actors (i.e. Track II, NGOs, academia) and the salient processes in Turkey's water diplomacy framework. Identifying such actors and processes not only contributes to the existing academic body of knowledge, but also has the potential to bolster cooperation over Turkey's transboundary waters. Finally, the book comes up with policy-relevant recommendations for tackling with the growing challenges in Turkey's transboundary water relations.

A qualitative and normative methodology was adopted in analysing Turkey's water diplomacy framework. Legal documents, such as minutes of transboundary water negotiations, water treaties, protocols, memoranda of understanding, official reports, manuals and websites, were all held to scrutiny to this end. The author is a university professor who has been teaching the very subjects covered in this book for over twenty years, and regularly delivers conferences and seminars to high-ranking bureaucrats, diplomats, legal advisers and government officials – both in Turkey and abroad. She convenes extensive consultations with the representatives of the water bureaucracy in Turkey by attending various expert committee meetings. Her professional relations with the institutions that are involved in the making of Turkish water diplomacy enable her to have access to the decision-making circles and to discuss in detail various dimensions of both the past and the current water policies pursued by Turkey in the international arena.

On the other hand, the author's past advisory position at the water-based regional development agency, namely the Southeastern Anatolia Project (GAP in Turkish acronym) Regional Development Administration (RDA), gave her the unique opportunity to interact with water technocrats at a national and international levels. The GAP RDA strives to boost the benefits, and mitigate the social and environmental impacts, of water development projects, which comprises a number of large-scale dam and irrigation systems along the Turkish portion of the Euphrates–Tigris (ET) river basin. During her tenure at the GAP RDA, between 2001 and 2003, she had a chance to participate in the official delegations to negotiate the protocols of water-based development projects with the Syrian counterparts. There, the author enjoyed the chance to observe the perceptions, concerns as well as the needs of Syrian officials and technocrats concerning transboundary water resources use and management.

Moreover, since 2005, the author has acted as the co-founder of a Track II initiative, namely the Euphrates–Tigris Initiative for Cooperation (ETIC), together with her colleagues from Syria, Iraq and Turkey. ETIC has been a unique non-governmental entity founded in the region, acting towards government officials in a cooperative manner and transparent in all of its activities. Even in the midst of conflicts in Iraq and Syria, and despite the deterioration of bilateral political relations between any pair of the riparian states, the ETIC has managed to carry out research projects and training activities in these countries. Working for this distinct non-governmental entity has played a key role in building the author's knowledge and experience on emerging non-state water diplomacy actors.

Political rhetoric in Turkey emphasizes that only one-third of the country's water resources have been developed and that there is still a huge potential for development. Thus, at national level, water resources development for energy and food production has become the overarching aim, while an increasing amount of attention has also given to the protection of the water resources. Essentially, this developmentalist venture in water policy has shaped the institutional and legal foundations of Turkey's water diplomacy. It also brought complexities and challenges to the relations with her neighbours. Thus, the book begins by delineating the institutional and legal foundations of transboundary water policymaking in Turkey. To this end, major actors (institutions) in water diplomacy at the national, regional and international level have been identified and scrutinized. Specific attention has been paid to the evolution of transboundary water politics in the ET river basin, since Turkish water diplomacy and its basic principles have largely been shaped through state practices along this strategically important river basin.

Situated at the crossroads of the Middle East, the Caucasus and Europe, Turkey's transboundary water policy has been shaped by various geographical determinants. Interestingly, Turkey has taken her experience in one region (i.e. Europe) and implemented these practices in the other (i.e. Middle East). Therefore, the book also analyses how Turkey's harmonization with the European Union (EU) has had impacts on the transboundary water policy discourses and practices, and how these changes have been reflected on her relations with its Middle Eastern neighbours. A historical account of transboundary water relations in the ET basin can only be enriched by an analysis of the current state of affairs in the region, such as the Syrian conflict and its repercussions on water-related issues.

Chapter 1 elucidates the institutional setting in transboundary water policymaking in Turkey. Water became an issue in Turkish foreign policy in the early 1980s, when a series of large-scale dams and extensive irrigation schemes in the ET river basin were constructed. These took place as part of the GAP project, with a view to achieving social and economic development in the country.

With the increasing profile of the GAP in the international arena, a bureau-cratic structure has since evolved with determined principles and policies with regard to the transboundary waters. The Ministry of Foreign Affairs (MFA) became the main official body for formulating these principles, as well as exe-cuting Turkey's transboundary water policy. The relevant state institutions that provide technical information, such as the status of water resources in terms of quality and quantity, as well as those responsible for the develop-ment, management and preservation of water resources, have been entrusted to work in conjunction with the MFA in the formulation of the fundamental principles of foreign water policy. First and foremost, among these institutions is the State Hydraulic Works (DSI in Turkish acronym), which has been responsible for development and management of Turkey's water resources since 1954. Moreover, in 2011, within the restructuring process of the govern-ment, the Ministry of Environment and Forestry's mandate was reorganized under two new ministries. Thus, it is within this context that the Ministry of Forestry and Water Affairs (MFWA- Ministry of Agriculture and Forestry since 2018) was established. Under the MFWA, the General Directorate of Water Management was established as a relatively new public institu-tion to provide input to transboundary water policy. There is also a growing interest in conducting humanitarian water diplomacy through leading water agencies such as the DSI. Turkey's water infrastructure investments in Africa and water projects completed in Turkey and beyond its borders for Syrian immigrants constitute some of the country's main achievements in this regard. The auxiliary role of state institutions, namely the Turkish Cooperation and Coordination Agency (TIKA in Turkish acronym) and the Disaster and Emergency Management Presidency (AFAD in Turkish acronym) have been evaluated within the context of this new aspect of humanitarian water dip-lomacy. The first chapter concludes with an analysis of the GAP RDA as a regional coordination agency for socio-economic development in the Turkish portion of the ET basin.

The fundamental principles of Turkish water diplomacy are determined by the evidence of state practice. In Chapter 2, Turkey's state practice has been analysed by scrutinizing official manuals on legal questions and information notes published on the websites of the concerned ministries, namely those of the MFA and the MFWA, as well as statements made by the relevant author-ities present at international conferences. By reviewing these principles, one can observe that the ET river basin constitutes a reference point in Turkey's transboundary water policy. Not only the specific principles related to the basin, but also the first set of principles concerning Turkey's overall foreign policy posture are mainly generated from Turkey's transboundary water relations with Syria and Iraq.

It is observed that water diplomacy circles (diplomats, policymakers and decision makers) in Turkey have endorsed and practiced international customary water law, particularly its cornerstone principles, that is, 'equitable utilization' and 'no significant harm'. Accordingly, Chapter 3 delineates those customary water law principles and includes an in-depth analysis on how Turkey's state practices have developed in line with customary international water law. Turkey was one of only three countries that rejected the UN Watercourses Convention (UNWC) in 1997. Turkey's position towards the UNWC has constituted one significant aspect of its transboundary water policy. In this context, even though the reasons behind Turkey's rejection of the UNWC were officially stated during the Working Groups in New York in 1997, they have not been properly elaborated in such a way as to reflect its concerns and dilemmas to date. Hence, Chapter 3 aims to perform this task. Moreover, since the vote for the UNWC in 1997 there have been changes in Turkey's stance vis-à-vis the international water law. The chapter looks into those changes (e.g. bureaucratic reorganization process) and focuses on the evolving position of Turkey vis-à-vis the international water law. To illustrate, the main responsibilities of the Department of Water Law and Political Development, under the MFWA include making studies on national and international water law and legislation; scrutinizing international conventions and leading the harmonization efforts with regional and global water law instruments in coordination with concerned public institutions. Moreover, the newly established Turkish Water Institute (SUEN in Turkish acronym) under the MFWA has also been entrusted with the objective of conducting and supporting scientific research to strengthen Turkey's national and international water policy.

Turkey's water diplomacy practices regarding its individual transboundary river basins have faced complex and multifaceted challenges because of the discernible differences in terms of the hydro-geopolitical constellations, respective bilateral political relations and agreements, and the organizational approaches surrounding the areas of dispute. Hence, in Chapter 4, water diplomacy of Turkey in transboundary settings have been analysed by highlighting the issues peculiar to each river basin. Geography and history play a significant role in the formulation of transboundary water policy. In this context, the state of affairs in the relations with the neighbouring states since the first years of the Republic of Turkey (1923) determined the mainframe of the transboundary water policy of the country. In the ET basin, from the early 1920s until the late 1950s, Ankara enjoyed rather smooth relations with Damascus and Baghdad, when Turkey and its neighbours were simultaneously in the process of establishing their state bureaucracies and pursuing socio-economic development projects. Throughout this period, Turkey signed various bilateral treaties, which consisted of mostly the delimitation and use of transboundary rivers. The Cold War period also had a decisive impact on Turkey's regional and bilateral relations with its neighbours. Thus, as a NATO member, it was hardly possible for Turkey to develop fruitful relations with Syria, Iraq and Bulgaria over the waters of the Orontes, Euphrates–Tigris and the Meric Rivers, respectively. The geographical characteristics of Turkey have also played a key role in the determination of its transboundary water policy. Turkey is in upstream position in the Euphrates–Tigris, Coruh and the Aras rivers, while it is in downstream position in Meric and the Orontes rivers. The average water potential of these rivers flowing within Turkey is equivalent to 30 per cent of the overall water potential of the country. Moreover, Turkey has significant amount of arable and irrigable land in these river basins. In this context, ET basin alone constitutes 20 per cent of arable land. With the growing numbers as well as the needs of the urban and rural population in these basins, the role of geography stands out in the formulation of the transboundary water policy.

Since the early 2000s, Turkey's water policies towards its neighbours, and its role in the neighbourhood, have been changing considerably. Among these evolving relations, the one with the EU within the framework of accession negotiations deserves special attention. The Turkish foreign policy goal of joining the EU has required that Turkey adopt and implement the entire body of European Environmental Law, namely the EU Water Framework Directive with significant implications for the member states' international water cooperation, and a couple of international environmental agreements to which the EU is the contracting party. The fourth chapter, therefore, analyses how Turkey's harmonization with the EU has had impacts on the transboundary water policy discourses and practices, and how these changes have been reflected in her relations with Middle Eastern neighbours.

Previous chapters have intended to analyse Turkey's water diplomacy through an institutional perspective. The legal and institutional foundations of Turkey's water diplomacy discourse are thoroughly discussed within its historical and geographical context. The last chapter of the book delineates the 'non-state actors and the salient processes' in Turkey's water diplomacy practices. As the world affairs have evolved, diplomacy as the process of dialogue and accommodation among states, has adapted in response to various opportunities (Kishan 2011, 16–18). Along with official or Track I diplomacy – which is typically carried out by government officials who use bargaining, negotiation and other peaceful means to negotiate policies and treaties – unofficial or Track II diplomacy has also developed, which includes nontraditional diplomatic agents, including NGOs, academics and other private citizens who are typically conducting dialogue and problem-solving activities (Snodderly

2011, 19). With this in mind, Chapter 5 investigates how academia and NGOs contribute into transboundary water policymaking in Turkey. A particular attention is paid to a unique Track II initiative, namely the ETIC, which was established in 2005 by a group of scholars and professionals from the three main riparian countries in the ET river basin. The ETIC is forwarded as a Track II effort, meaning that it is voluntary, non-official, non-binding, not for profit and non-governmental. It is not affiliated with any government, but rather seeks to contribute positively to the efforts, be they official or unofficial, that enhance dialogue, understanding and collaboration among the riparians of the ET system.

Water diplomacy consists of the art and practice of understanding, negotiating and allocating transboundary waters in a sustainable and equitable manner. Thus, the final chapter also presents best practices and lessons learned in Turkey's water diplomacy framework. Keeping an open dialogue with neighbours over transboundary water issues, as well as signing of several bilateral water agreements, could be assessed as achievements (i.e. best practices) in Turkish water diplomacy. Yet, Turkey's (non-party) position towards regional and global conventions limits the chance to draw conclusions from practices in those contexts. The chapter offers a non-zero-sum approach to water negotiations and makes policy-relevant recommendations for tackling with future challenges in Turkey's water diplomacy.

Chapter 1

INSTITUTIONAL SETTING

Overview

This chapter delineates the institutional setting in transboundary water policy-making in Turkey. Water has become an issue in Turkish foreign policy in the early 1980s with Turkey's plan to build a series of large-scale dams and extensive irrigation systems in the upper reaches of the Euphrates–Tigris (ET) river basin within the context of the Southeastern Anatolia Project (GAP in Turkish acronym). With the increasing profile of the GAP in the international arena, a bureaucratic structure has evolved since then where the principles and policies with regard to the transboundary waters have been determined. The Ministry of Foreign Affairs (MFA) became the main official body for formulating as well as executing Turkey's transboundary water policy. In this context, a separate department/unit in charge of regional and transboundary waters was formed at MFA under the directorate general, which is responsible for issues pertaining to energy, water and the environment.

The relevant institutions within the state mechanism, which provide technical information, such as the status of water resources in terms of quality and quantity, as well as those responsible for the development, management and preservation of water resources, have been entrusted to work in conjunction with the MFA in the formulation of the fundamental principles of transboundary water policy. First and foremost, among these institutions is the State Hydraulic Works (DSI in Turkish acronym), which has been responsible for the development and management of Turkey's water resources since 1954. Moreover, in 2011, within the restructuring process of the government, the mandate of the Ministry of Environment and Forestry (MEF) was reorganized under two new ministries. It was in this context that the Ministry of Forestry and Water Affairs (MFWA) was established. Under the MFWA, the General Directorate of Water Management (DGWM) and the Turkish Water Institute (SUEN in Turkish acronym) were established as new public institutions to provide inputs to transboundary water policy.

There is also a growing interest in conducting humanitarian water diplomacy by the leading water agencies such as the DSI. Turkey's water infrastructure investments in Africa and water projects completed in Turkey and beyond borders for displaced people in Syria constitute main achievements in this regard. The auxiliary role of state institutions, namely the Turkish Cooperation and Coordination Agency (TIKA) and the Disaster and Emergency Management Presidency (AFAD), are evaluated within this new aspect of humanitarian water diplomacy. This chapter culminates with analyses of the GAP Regional Development Administration (RDA) as an integral component of institution-building in water diplomacy.

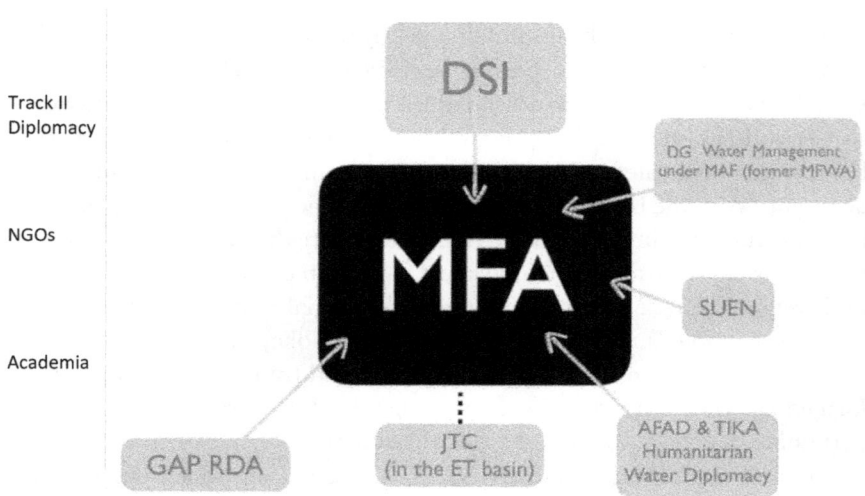

Figure 1. Turkey's water diplomacy framework: Institutional setting

The Defining Role of the Ministry of Foreign Affairs in Water Diplomacy

The MFA is the main state body to formulate and implement Turkey's transboundary water policy. Water diplomacy has been part of Turkey's bilateral political and economic relations since the formation of the Republic in the 1920s. Turkey signed historical treaties concerning boundary (waters) delimitation, water development and use with her neighbours, namely the former Soviet Union, Bulgaria, Greece, Syria and Iraq.

Later, in the 1960s, a series of diplomatic negotiations took place between Turkey, Iraq and Syria when Turkey declared that she was going to build the first large-scale dam, namely the Keban Dam across the Euphrates. Diplomats and technocrats coming from the concerned departments and directorates at the MFA and Ministry of Energy and Natural Resources conducted those historical diplomatic negotiations on an ad-hoc basis. Later on, in the late 1980s, a focused and specialized unit, namely the Department of the Regional and Transboundary Waters, was established at the MFA to pursue foreign policy interests for Turkey in the domain of transboundary waters.

In formulating water diplomacy, the MFA acted essentially in accordance with Turkey's national interests which were mainly defined by geographical conditions, socio-economic developmental needs, as well as historical and current bilateral and regional political relations with neighbouring countries. Thus, Turkey's state practices, that is, what Turkey says and does, were mainly conducted by the MFA relying on the main contours of Turkish foreign policy as well as the peculiarities of transboundary river basins.

However, in formulating transboundary water policy, the MFA was also influenced by developments in the international arena. Thus, since the early 1990s, the MFA has followed and contributed to global and regional water discourses developed by international organizations. Soft law principles adopted at international conferences as well as developments in international water law were also closely followed by the MFA. One example of this is the 'Helsinki Principles', which were codified by the International Law Association in 1966, as these were deemed suitable for supporting Turkey's stance in transboundary settings, particularly in the context of the ET river basin.

In the early 1990s, the MFA showed a keen interest in attending international conferences organized by the leading universities in Turkey. In this regard, the International Conference on Transboundary Waters in the Middle East: Prospects for Regional Cooperation, organized at Bilkent University in Ankara on 2–3 September 1991, provided a platform for MFA authorities to interact with leading scholars and experts in the field of transboundary water issues. Within the context of such conferences, MFA authorities had the chance to hear analyses by international water experts on pivotal transboundary river basins in the Middle East (Beaumont 1978; Anderson 1986) as well as thoughts regarding the evolution of international water law principles and rules (McCaffrey 1991a). They also had opportunities to present Turkey's position in transboundary waters, particularly in relation to the Euphrates, Tigris and Orontes Rivers.

In understanding and evaluating Turkish water diplomacy, primary sources such as memoirs of former ambassadors, and manuals, reports and articles prepared by experts from the Department of Regional and Transboundary Waters, MFA, are utilized. In this context, the memoirs reflect the perceptions and discourses of senior diplomats who participated in transboundary water negotiations in the ET river basin. These memoirs encompass first-hand information and insights on diplomats' perceptions and positions vis-à-vis Turkey's neighbours as well as international donor and development agencies. Kamuran Gürün, the late retired ambassador, wrote in his memoirs, about the details of the tough bargaining processes that occurred between Turkey and the United States Agency for International Development (USAID) on the one hand, and Turkey and the World Bank on the other. The result of this was conditional credits being extended to Turkey by those agencies for the construction of the Keban and Karakaya Dams, respectively (Gürün 1994). Under pressure from those donor agencies, through an agreement signed in Ankara in 1966 with USAID, Turkey guaranteed to undertake all the necessary measures to maintain a discharge of 350 cubic meters (m^3) per second immediately downstream from the Keban Dam, provided that the natural flow of the river was adequate to supply the above discharge. This was confirmed orally to Syria and Iraq the same year. USAID was the acting donor for the Keban project while the World Bank was the leading agency financing the Karakaya Dam further downstream. Both agencies insisted that guaranteed flows be released by Turkey to downstream riparians during the impounding and operation of the reservoirs.

Through her experience with the donor agencies during the construction of the Keban and Karakaya Dams, Turkey developed a negative stance towards the possibility of third-party mediation or so-called third-party intervention in the issue (Gürün 1994, 240–72). Turkey contended that the donors' intervention was solely in favour of protecting the rights of the downstream riparians and gave little recognition of Turkish rights to develop and use the river system. Donors did not give much weight to the essential Turkish view that a fair distribution of Euphrates waters could be made by taking into consideration the long-term projects and needs of the three countries along with the possibility of transferring water from adjacent rivers, namely the Tigris.

The MFA prepared official manuals, in Turkish and in English (MFA 1995), published articles (MFA 1996), and delivered talks (Rende 2004), which encompassed detailed information regarding Turkey's official approach concerning development, use and management of transboundary river basins. Those early publications contained information on geographical features of transboundary rivers, namely the Euphrates, Tigris and Orontes. They also underlined the socio-economic significance of transboundary rivers and provided information on the objectives and status of large-scale development projects, namely the GAP. Those publications also elaborated on the origin and evolution of international water law with specific references to its cornerstone principles, namely the 'equitable utilization' and 'no significant harm' to which Turkey adheres.

Over time, experienced staff of MFA took an active role in presenting Turkey's overall policies on environment and water. Mithat Rende, ambassador retired, who acted as the director general responsible for environment, water and energy at the MFA, explains: 'Turkish policies on the environment are directed towards satisfying the increasing demand for water supply, achieving food security, generation of energy, and conserving the environment in accordance with international standards, namely Sustainable Governance Indicators'. Moreover, he delineates that,

> Turkish water policy has four main dimensions: improvement of water resources for increasing agricultural production by irrigation, domestic use, flood control and power generation; water transfer from Turkey to water-stressed nations; EU accession prospects, which motivated adoption of the National Environmental Strategy and Action Plan; and studies on new water legislation and restructuring of institutions. Turkey's transboundary water policy depends on the following concepts: consistent and transparent, equitable and optimal utilization, efficient use, sharing of benefits, cooperation among riparian states, and sharing of information and data. (Rende 2004)

Hence, when it comes to transboundary water issues, the MFA played a guiding and defining role and provided a reference point for other technical government institutions, namely the MFWA and its affiliated institution, DSI.

The Department of the Regional and Transboundary Waters at the MFA is composed of a small cadre of career diplomats and advisers. Along with career diplomats, the technical advisers, who are trained as civil or environmental engineers, help to gather up-to-date scientific and technical information and data on issues related to water resources management at global, regional and national levels. They attend various national and international meetings and conferences to represent Turkey's position in transboundary water issues while also collecting data and information on the evolution of global water policies. The advisers' foreign posts included positions such as the Permanent Missions of Turkey to the UN, in New York and Geneva and to the United Nations Educational, Scientific and Cultural Organization (UNESCO) and the Organisation for Economic Co-operation and Development (OECD) both in Paris as well as to the Permanent Mission of Turkey to the European Union (EU) in Brussels. In each of these positions, advisers are instructed to follow water discourse and practices developing at these international organizations, and provide inputs to Turkey's approaches concerning transboundary and global water issues.

The MFA has adopted a balanced, consistent and predictable transboundary water policy approach, which has been clearly articulated in its official publications, and communicated orally during bilateral water talks as well as at the international platforms. However, at executive level, certain governments adopted pragmatic approaches, which had far-reaching consequences for transboundary water policy. In this context, Turkey's signing of the 1987 water allocation protocol (Protocol 1987) with Syria over the Euphrates waters constituted a deviation from the MFA's long-established approach to transboundary water issues in the ET basin. In 1987, the Turkish-Syrian Protocol on Economic Cooperation was the first formal bilateral agreement reached on regional waters, its conclusion made possible by simultaneous negotiations on security matters and water. Turkish prime minister Turgut Ozal, the decisive political actor at the time, promised a water flow of up to 500 m^3 per second, or about 16 km^3 per year, at the Turkish-Syrian border, with the intention of reaching an agreement with Syria on security matters. At the same time, a Mutual Security Accord was signed, setting out that each state would prevent activities against the other from originating in its territory and that criminals responsible for terrorist activities would be extradited. Ozal believed that the Kurdistan Workers' Party (PKK) would cease its attacks if Syria stopped supporting it. For a while, it seemed that Ozal's hopes had been fulfilled, but a dramatic upsurge in fighting between Turkish security forces and the PKK in 1988/1989 led to renewed Turkish concerns about Syrian support for the PKK (Scheumann 2003). That protocol was a deviation from the established transboundary policies of the MFA since, during the prolonged water negotiations over the Euphrates River, MFA authorities kept stating that an allocation agreement could only be reached upon the completion of joint objective studies on the water and land resources of the ET system. Moreover, MFA authorities paid utmost attention not to link water issues with the security (terrorism) issues, as water issues are a part of legal bilateral relations between Turkey and Syria and concerns regarding terrorism should be dealt separately in other realms (Interview 1996).

The Key Technocratic Role of the State Hydraulic Works (DSI) in Water Diplomacy

The relevant institutions within the state mechanism in Turkey which provide technical information, such as those responsible for the development, management and allocation of water resources, have been entrusted to work in conjunction with the MFA in the formulation of the fundamental principles of water diplomacy. First and foremost, among these institutions is the Directorate General of DSI (in Turkish acronym). The mission of the DSI is to utilize Turkey's water resources, safeguard against losses due to floods and droughts, and develop land and water resources which take into account scientific and technical principles, and the nation's interests.

The DSI is the primary executive state agency responsible for planning, design, construction and the operation of water structures in order to develop the nation's overall water resources in a sustainable manner. It constructed a series of dams and hydroelectric power plants, and built an extensive system of irrigation and drainage systems all over the country. It implemented large-scale projects for energy production, irrigation development, drinking water provision and flood control, inclusive of the GAP region.

The DSI, which was established by Law No. 6200 (18 December 1953), first operated under the Ministry of Public Works; later on, it functioned under the title Ministry of Energy and Natural Resources, and was affiliated to the MFWA between 2011 and 2018. It currently works under the title of the Ministry of Agriculture and Forestry, which was established by Presidential Decree No. 4, adopted on 15 July 2018, and published in the Official Gazette No. 30479. As a public agency, it is responsible for four major tasks: providing water supply for domestic and industrial use; taking necessary measures to prevent flood hazards from causing life and property losses; equipping all economically irrigable land with modern irrigation facilities; and developing technically viable capacity to generate hydroelectric energy. In order to achieve those tasks, the DSI primarily constructs dam projects, which are at the centre of the four tasks. Therefore, the DSI is mainly known as a public agency which develops dam projects (DSI 2012, 7).

The DSI carries out survey and planning for river basin development; collects data pertaining to the quality and quantity of the surface and groundwater resources; prepares master plans and feasibility reports to determine technically and economically optimal solutions for water resources projects in the river basin planning; where necessary, executes land expropriation as well as preparing resettlement action plans for people affected by dam constructions; and prepares Environmental Impact Assessment (EIA) reports. The DSI is the chief authority responsible for water allocation from surface and groundwater for single and multiple purposes.

Since the late 1980s, under economic liberalization programs, some of the tasks of the DSI have been transferred to the private sector, irrigation associations and other state institutions (Kibaroglu et al. 2009). Thus, the DSI prepares contract documents and implements bidding for works to be contracted out to private sector entities; proposes inclusion of projects in investment programs; supervises constructions; allocates water usage right to the private sector for the construction and operation of hydro-electric power plants (HEPP); and transfers hydraulic structures to the relevant agencies: HEPPs to the electricity authority, water treatment plants to the municipalities, and irrigation facilities to the irrigation associations (DSI 2012, 9–10).

Turkey is geographically divided into 25 river basins. These basins differ widely in terms of their respective water potential; the ET basin alone makes up about 28 per cent of the total water potential of all basins (DSI 2012, 7). The DSI conducts water management and investments with 26 regional directorates, which roughly settled up based on the river basin boundaries and dispersed throughout Turkey. Regional directorates execute their work on behalf of the DSI headquarters in accordance with annual and five-year development plans as well as investment programs (DSI 2012, 11).

Since 2010, the DSI has been in charge of preparing new Master Plans for 25 river basins in the country. Master Plans will constitute the basis of and are integral to the River Basin Management Plans (RBMPs), which have been in preparation in the hands of the MFWA since 2014, in accordance with the harmonization process with the EU Water Framework Directive (WFD) (Kimence et al. 2017). As of 2017, the DSI finalized Master Plans for 23 river basins. The remaining Master Plans are projected to be completed in due course including the transboundary river basins, namely the ET river basin (DSI 2017). The Master Plans and RBMPs prepared for the transboundary river basins, particularly for the ET basin, could be utilized in transboundary water negotiations as objective reference documents, which would clarify the status of water and land resources as well as water development and management practices in the Turkish portion of the transboundary rivers.

On the other hand, a Decree-Law came into effect on 2 November 2011, which brought changes, among others, into Law No. 6200, such as 'entrusting the DSI with conducting studies on transboundary or boundary rivers within its own sphere of competence' (DSI 2012, 8–9). Even before that legal stipulation change was brought into the establishment Law No. 6200, the DSI had systematically provided significant inputs to the formulation of transboundary water policy. In this regard, it has been supplying information and data to the concerned state institutions, namely the MFA, and report on physical, climatic and hydrological conditions of water and land resources in Turkey. The DSI provides up-to-date information on water supply and demand management policies and practices adopted in various administrative and hydrologic units such as cities, towns, villages and river basins. Moreover, time and time again, the DSI has briefed the MFA authorities concerning the objectives and progress of large-scale water development projects (e.g. GAP) which have been implemented in transboundary river basins with agricultural, industrial and overall socio-economic development purposes. Furthermore, the DSI's legal experts (advisers) have contributed systematically to the definition and interpretation of water allocation rules and water rights at local and national levels

(Ozbay 2006). In so doing, the legal experts specifically relied on the constitution, civil law and Law No. 6200. On the other hand, they also conducted comparative studies on national laws of several other developing states from different geographies, and scrutinized developments in international water law (Ozbay 2006). Furthermore, DSI legal experts shared their knowledge and experience in national and international water law with the MFA bureaucracy (Kibaroglu and Baskan 2011).

Since the 1960s, DSI officials (technocrats and legal advisers) have participated in transboundary water negotiations and provided essential technical background information to MFA staff in order to conduct transboundary water relations. In this context, the DSI significantly contributed to water diplomacy frameworks in the ET basin (Figure 1). When the DSI started the construction of the Keban Dam in the 1960s, the three riparians – Turkey, Syria and Iraq – entered a new phase of their relationship. The Keban Dam, which was an integral element of the overall Euphrates development scheme in Turkey, was designed for electricity generation and contained no features that would change the water balance of the basin. In fact, according to DSI experts, the Keban Dam had a very positive impact upon the water storage facilities of Syria and Iraq by ensuring regulation of the variance in the flow of approximately 70 per cent of the waters of the Euphrates (Bilen 2000). However, the downstream riparians, particularly Iraq, became anxious and insisted that guaranteed flows (350 m³ per second at minimum) be released by Turkey during the impounding period.

Hence, a first meeting was held on 22–27 June 1964 with the participation of Turkish and Iraqi experts. As an input to that meeting, the DSI engineers asserted that it was impossible to reach a single and final formula for the pattern of water to be released from the Keban Dam reservoir before impounding by the dam. This pattern, according to the Turkish delegation, depended upon the natural conditions that would prevail during the filling of the dam, and on the exact evaluation of the concerned countries' needs (DSI 1975). In order to provide the Syrian and Iraqi officials with up-to-date information on the Keban Dam, copies of the feasibility report on the project, prepared by the DSI, were submitted to the Syrian and Iraqi technicians. The DSI played a crucial role in providing all these technical data related to the Keban Dam during that early negotiation period of the ET basin.

Hence, in 1972 and 1973, with the participation of MFA diplomats and DSI technocrats, a series of technical meetings were held, albeit on an ad hoc basis. The major issue facing the tri-partite technical meetings continued to be ascertaining appropriate methods for filling the Keban and the Tabqa (Syria) reservoirs while simultaneously meeting the irrigation demands of the downstream riparians (Minutes 1972). However, during the meeting of the three delegations, a joint decision was taken to organise field trips to visit the main gauging stations and water resource development projects on the Euphrates. Three parties felt that observations gained through these trips would facilitate the development of an equitable method for filling the dams' reservoirs. In January 1973, a tri-lateral technical committee undertook field trips to the Tabqa project site in Syria to the discharge gauging stations on the Euphrates, and to major irrigation projects in Syria. Later, in February 1973, the committee visited Iraq. After completing these field trips, including a trip to the Keban Dam site, a subcommittee was formed to discuss and reach an agreement on the procedure and program for filling the dams so that the irrigation and energy requirements of the downstream riparians could be sustained (Minutes 1973a).

DSI technocrats were the backbone of the Turkish delegation during these field trips. Based on observations accumulated during these field trips, the Turkish delegation, mainly instructed by the DSI technocrats, submitted a report expressing extreme doubts on the accuracy of the figure of 18 billion m^3 that Iraq had presented as her water needs (Technical Delegation Report 1973). The Turkish delegation indicated that Iraq did not calculate her real water needs based on objective criteria, and that Iraq was insisting on exaggerated amounts so as to ensure her water rights before the upstream, and midstream riparians continued with their development projects. The Turkish delegation added that the Iraqi irrigation water demands could not be justified under the existing wasteful traditional water development and usage patterns.

Furthermore, during another technical meeting, the Turkish delegation proposed a joint study to gain objective data related to the water requirements of each riparian (Minutes 1973b). The DSI played a leading role in drafting that study, namely the Three-Stage Plan, which became Turkey's essential position during transboundary water negotiations in the ET river basin. During these negotiations, it emerged that the water potential was unable to meet the declared demands of the three riparians. And, more importantly, there had been rooted uncertainties and inadequacies relating to the data on water and land resources. In response to the Syrian and Iraqi demands for the formulation of urgent 'sharing agreements', depending on the criteria that they put forward, Turkey proposed the 'Three-Stage Plan for Optimum, Equitable and Reasonable Utilisation of the Transboundary Watercourses of the Tigris-Euphrates Basin' (Kibaroglu 2002). According to this plan, the inventory studies of water and land resources for the whole region, comprising the territories of the respective states, would be undertaken and evaluated jointly. Based on these studies, 'necessary means and measures to attain the most reasonable and optimum utilisation of resources would be defined' (Kibaroglu 2002).

The Three-Stage Plan was, in fact, first formulated in the 1960s by DSI technocrats. Its original version was more comprehensive than later versions and contained detailed descriptions of the responsibilities of the study groups and the work schedule that they were supposed to undertake. Three study groups, consisting of experts from Turkey, Syria and Iraq, were allocated to work on the three stages of the plan, consisting of 'hydrology', 'land resources' and 'engineering' study groups. The first version of the plan was entirely a product of the DSI engineers regarding its wording and content. In this plan, the engineers put a special emphasis on the economic concept of 'optimum utilization', along with criteria of equitable and reasonable use of the waters of the Euphrates and Tigris.

The DSI technocrats indicated that the problem in the basin basically stemmed from mismanagement as well as misallocation. However, by quantifying the problem through the implementation of the Three-Stage Plan, they indicated that the water issue would become more manageable. Within the plan, Turkey called for the establishment of a joint body for collecting, handling and exchanging data regarding water and land resources, so that annual and seasonal variations could be incorporated into the calculations being made in order to decide the allocations. Furthermore, it was stressed that the agreement on proper water allocation should be based on findings derived from a basin-wide planning process, and, furthermore, all negotiations should emphasise basin-wide planning as a goal. Such a plan depends on the collection, interpretation and evaluation of basic data relating to hydrology, soils, climate and other physical and socio-economic factors. DSI experts claimed that the presence of clear data anomalies in the available records concerning water and irrigable land resources in the ET river basin had been noted several times in various reports, and the question of data validity was pertinent to the formulation of any firm conclusions. Ozden Bilen, former director general of the DSI, underlines the fact that there has been conflicting data on the total irrigation project areas fed by the Euphrates in Syria and Iraq (Bilen 1994). Bilen asserts that a variety of local and foreign experts put forward different figures concerning the availability of irrigable land in each riparian country depending on expert observations and calculations (Bilen 1994, 98). Since irrigation is a major water consumer, and lack of consensus on irrigable land potential is an important issue, as such inconsistent figures can mislead analysts. Hence, data consistency and reliability, particularly on the land to be irrigated, is a major concern for all parties, and much work needs to be done to clarify the existing situation. The Three-Stage Plan would serve the end of data collection and survey of water and land resources of the ET river basin. This would be jointly performed by the experts from the three riparians so as to acquire a basis for water allocation questions.

Moreover, DSI engineers have asserted that the Euphrates and Tigris have to be considered as forming one 'single transboundary watercourse system', not only because they are connected by their natural courses when uniting at the Shatt-al-Arab, but also because Iraq uses the waters of both rivers interchangeably through its Thartar Canal Project which transfers the Tigris waters to the Euphrates. Consequently, all existing and future agricultural uses from the Euphrates, irrigation requirements of the same areas fed by the Euphrates, could be commanded by waters transferred from the Tigris.

During the fourth and the seventh meetings of the Joint Technical Committee, held in 1984 and 1986, Turkey proposed updated and revised versions of this plan. The plan was also reiterated in the tripartite meeting at a ministerial level on 26 June 1990 and during the bilateral talks with both Syria and Iraq in 1993. The DSI technocrats who were the main formulators of this plan were confident that its implementation would create a positive atmosphere that would be conducive to cooperation in the utilisation of not only water but also other natural resources. However, the plan was coolly received by Syrian and Iraqi authorities, and it was never put into practice.

Transboundary water relations in the ET basin were particularly influenced negatively by the building and filling of the dams. The first diplomatic crisis over the waters of the Euphrates River occurred between Syria and Iraq during the filling of the Keban (Turkey) and the Tabqa (Syria) Dams (Kibaroglu 2002). The controversy over the dams intensified in late 1980s as new, larger dams were introduced in Turkey, namely the Atatürk, Birecik and Karkamis Dams. Then, during the 1980s and 1990s, a number of crises occurred between the riparians due to the construction and filling of these dams, which were all conceived within the GAP. The DSI was the main actor in dealing with these crises by providing first-hand information to MFA diplomats concerning the benefits of dam construction as well as technical details about how the dams would be impounded by observing the needs of the downstream riparian states, namely Syria and Iraq.

Paradoxically, in the first decade of the 2000s, the riparian states started to consider building joint dams on the transboundary rivers as an element of cooperation. In this respect, the DSI played an essential role in developing all the technical details. These details included feasibility and investigation studies as well as project development for the joint dam projects, which were designated to be built and operated jointly with Syria (Friendship Dam across the Orontes) and Iraq (joint dams across the boundary river Tigris). This could be evaluated as a key contribution by the DSI to Turkey's water diplomacy approaches and practices in the ET basin.

At the first meeting of their High-Level Strategic Cooperation Council held in Damascus on 23–24 December 2009, Turkey and Syria signed fifty protocols, four of which concerned regional waters (Euphrates, Tigris and Orontes). In this context, the parties agreed to build a joint dam where the Orontes River crosses the Turkish-Syrian border (Memorandum of Understanding (MoU) 2009a). They agreed to share the cost of the dam, the aim of which was to produce energy for both sides and irrigate 20,000 hectares of agricultural land in Turkey and 10,000 hectares in Syria. The foundation stones were laid in February 2011, with the Turkish and Syrian prime ministers in attendance, just before the unrest broke out in Syria in the spring of 2011. Although the joint dam construction came to a halt due to the eruption of the Syrian civil war and worsening of high-level political relations between Turkey and Syria, this endeavour of joint dam building provided an impetus for rebuilding contacts and cooperation between Turkey and Iraq.

After years of deadlock in transboundary water relations, due to uncertainties imposed by the Syrian civil war, in 2014, Turkey and Iraq decided, at the ministerial level, to reopen dialogue on their transboundary water resources. In this context, the Minutes of the Bilateral Cooperation Meeting between Turkey and Iraq were signed on 15 May 2014 by the deputy undersecretary of the MFWA, Turkey, and the head of the unit for Neighboring Countries and Law of the MFA in Iraq, which encompass principles, modalities and issues of bilateral water cooperation. According to this protocol, both sides agreed in principle to continue to hold meetings aiming to further develop transboundary water relations. Both sides agreed, among others, to establish a joint working group with a mandate to conduct preparations for dam projects on the Hacibey Stream and the Lesser Zab (Tigris River tributaries). Hence, the parties agreed to form a joint expert committee to study and investigate the proposed Hacibey and Karadag friendship dam projects on the Turkish-Iraqi border. Once again, the DSI played a crucial role in developing all the technical details for these projects in collaboration with the Iraqi authorities.

In other areas, the DSI have contributed significantly to Turkey's recent efforts to pursue 'humanitarian water diplomacy' by extending aid in Africa and the Middle East to activities such as drilling wells and dam construction. The DSI has supplied water to more than 1,5 million people in Africa thanks to these bore drilling activities. To illustrate this, the DSI initiated construction work on a dam on the Ambouli River in order to provide domestic water to the capital city of Djibouti and to protect the city from potential floods. This rock-fill type of dam project, which cost 11 million Euros, was fully financed by the Turkish Government (MFWA 2017). Moreover, within the framework of an 'open-door policy', which facilitated the mobilization of Syrian war–victim civilians into Turkey, the DSI had dual functions in the implementation of this policy. The DSI has been working on increasing the water supply and sanitation capacities of cities that are hosting growing numbers of refugees, while also supporting infrastructure needs in the new refugee camps.

The unplanned population boom in smaller cities close to the Turkish-Syrian border also requires smart solutions coupled with urgent action. One significant case was Kilis; the city received so many refugees that the city's population doubled in a couple of years. In order to meet the surge in the domestic water needs of the city, the DSI contracted out a dam project in 2015, aiming to make it operational by 2018. The DSI also provided basic engineering solutions for the refugee camps, such as providing a drinking water supply, controlling rainwater and wastewater discharge, and by levelling the ground. The DSI has been active not only in Turkey but also in the Syrian towns of Azaz, Jarabulus, Cobanbey (Al-Rai), Al-Bab and Mari. In each of these cities, the DSI has provided emergency water provision activities such as water well drilling, maintenance and repair of the water distribution infrastructure (SUEN 2017a).

The Growing Role of the Ministry of Forestry and Water Affairs in Water Diplomacy

An institutional structure of environmental protection and water quality management has emerged over the past three decades in Turkey. This has been driven by domestic, social and economic change; the expansion of activity in terms of bilateral and multilateral international agreements; and the nation's efforts to meet the EU criteria towards full membership. The Ministry of the Environment, which was established in 1991 by Decree-Law (No. 443), replaced the Undersecretary for the Environment. This led to the diversification of the Ministry's responsibilities and to an expansion of its staff. This also led to the empowerment of administration concerning the implementation and enforcement of policies for the protection and conservation of the environment.

Despite its enhanced mandate, the Ministry of the Environment had limited resources and limited competence. Hence, with a governmental decree, the MEF was established in 2003, thus merging two central bodies: the Ministry of Environment, and the Ministry of Forestry. MEF had concerted aims regarding protecting and promoting the environment, and ensuring the most appropriate and most effective use and protection of the land and natural resources in both rural and urban areas. MEF also played a key role in the EU harmonization process. It was regarded as the key bureaucratic establishment to assume overall coordination and responsibility for adherence to the EU environmental legislation (Kibaroglu and Baskan 2011).

The declaration of Turkey as a 'candidate country' to the EU during the Helsinki Summit in December 1999 triggered a wave of changes in Turkey's water management policies. Turkey started to harmonize its domestic legislation with that of the EU in the field of environment and water resources. Beginning from the early 2000s, within the context defined by the Helsinki Summit, a number of steps were taken by Turkey in order to facilitate the harmonization process with the EU WFD and related EU level legislations (European Communities 2000). Moreover, the harmonization of the Turkish legislation and the restructuring of the institutions were accelerated by the accession talks that were launched in 2005. In this context, MEF led this harmonization process in close consultation with the MFA. With its technical competence on water quality management and environmental protection, MEF took charge of scrutinizing EU water law and transposing this body of legislation into national legislation. Within this framework, the MFA underlined Turkey's approach vis-à-vis transboundary rivers, making sure the adopted EU legislation were in line with Turkey's standpoint and priorities in transboundary waters. Thus, water diplomacy towards the EU was conducted jointly between the two ministries.

Turkey has made serious efforts to adapt the basic approach of the EU WFD to its specific needs. In this context, the main tasks that should be performed by Turkey in the framework of the WFD are summarized as follows: creating a reliable inventory of water data; establishing a proper monitoring system; setting up pricing systems for all sectors, taking into account the full cost recovery principle; realizing the participation of all interested parties in the processes of water management; and designating RBMPs with a view towards implementing the program of measures to reach the environmental objectives.

Hence, these new approaches developed by the ministries concerned, namely the MEF and the MFA within the framework of the relations with the EU, have played a key role in the MoU signed with Syria and Iraq in 2009 with respect to the use, development and protection of the water resources of the Euphrates, Tigris and Orontes Rivers (Memorandum of Understanding between Turkey and Syria (MoU 2009a, 2009b, 2009c); Memorandum of Understanding between Turkey and Iraq 2009). The general approach and the content of the MoU reveal that Turkey's first-hand experience with the EU's water policy and approaches to water management has been broadly translated into the principles envisioned in the protocols. Therefore, the staff of Turkey's MEF supported these protocols vigorously, as they felt that their implementation would be a useful practice for the implementation and extension of the new water legislation in Turkey transposed from the EU water legislation (Kibaroglu and Scheumann 2013). The EU's 'river basin level' water management approach in the form of its WFD of 2000 will be applied not only in Turkey's national river basins but also in transboundary river basins such as the Euphrates, Tigris and Orontes. Moreover, common standards for measuring quantities of water and monitoring the quality of transboundary water are among the MEF's main objectives in its cooperation with Syria and Iraq. In this context, one of the main aims of Turkish bureaucracy is to establish environmental quality standards and to implement the polluter-pays and cost-recovery principles at transboundary level, as the relevant MoU stipulates (Sümer 2011).

Later on, within the governmental reorganization process, MEF was restructured and its duties and responsibilities were undertaken by two different ministries, namely the MFWA and the Ministry of Environment and Urbanization. Thus, the leading government body that has dealt with management and protection of water resources since 2011 has been the MFWA. The main duties and responsibilities of the MFWA comprise, among others, creating policies for the sustainable protection and utilization of water resources; coordination of national water management; harmonization of the Turkish water legislation with the EU; protection, improvement and management of national and natural parks, wildlife reserves, wetlands and biological diversity; producing policies and strategies for the purposes of monitoring meteorological events and taking essential measures; crafting policies with regard to protection, improvement, managing and rehabilitation of the forestry; and prevention of desertification and erosion, continuation of reforestation. These responsibilities will be undertaken in collaboration with the concerned government institutions monitoring and contributing to studies on international water policy and law that are within the scope of the mandate of the ministry.

After the elections of 24 June 2018, under the new government system of Turkey, new ministries were formed by a presidential decree (*Hurriyet Daily News* 2018). Thus, the MFWA and the Ministry of Food, Agriculture and Livestock merged and the new Ministry of Agriculture and Forestry was established. In initial statements by the new minister, the importance of agriculture, forests and water resources were underlined (Ministry of Agriculture and Forestry 2019). The main tasks and responsibilities of the new ministry comprise, among others, food production safety, rural development protection, and efficient use of land, water and biodiversity. Water management has stayed as one of the main administrative units (directorate general) of this new ministry. Thus, 'water policy' has started to be handled together with other issues such as food, agriculture and forestry within the same ministry.

The General Directorate of Water Management

The DGWM, founded under the MFWA, is responsible for developing policies for protecting and sustaining water resources, and for coordinating and preparing RBMPs, together with relevant stakeholders, in accordance with WFD for 25 river basins to achieve their 'good status' (Kibaroglu 2020). Its main duties and responsibilities are determining water resources policies; providing coordination at national and international level; preparing RBMPs; conducting legislation studies on coordination of sectoral water allocation according to RBMPs; developing water quality standards and water quality monitoring systems for the whole country; developing policy and strategies related to flood control; preparing related legislation and flood management plans; preparing the National Water Database Information System; identifying and monitoring sensitive areas in terms of water pollution and nitrate; conducting studies on the effects of climate change on water resources; and, in collaboration with concerned institutions, namely the MFA, conducting studies on boundary and transboundary waters as well as following up on international water conventions (Delipinar and Karpuzcu 2017).

Turkey is making concerted efforts to prepare RBMPs for 25 river basins aligned with the WFD, with the main goal of reconciling economic development and ecosystem maintenance. In designing RBMPs, the transboundary nature of the river basin is specifically considered. Thus, according to Article 13 of the WFD,

> If transboundary effects occur within a river basin, the EU member states concerned must establish an international River Basin District (RBD) and coordinate the implementation of the EU WFD through a single RBMP. Where an RBD extends beyond the territory of the EU, the EU member states concerned must seek appropriate coordination with the non-EU riparians in order to achieve the EU WFD objectives. (European Communities 2000, 16)

Turkish authorities have underlined that Article 13 of the WFD, particularly with regard to the clauses related to 'transboundary coordination with the non-EU riparians', would be implemented when Turkey became a full member of the EU.

Through the initiatives of the DGWM, with an aim to improve water quality in river basins in line with the environmental objectives of the WFD, river basin protection action plans have been drafted for all 25 Turkish river basins since 2009 (Kimence et al. 2017). These plans are intended to function as models for the RBMPs. Thus, Turkey has adopted a stepwise approach to preparing the RBMPs (Republic of Turkey 2009).

Under the DGWM, the Department of Water Law and Political Development is also established as a new unit to provide new input to transboundary water policy. The main responsibilities of this department include studying national and international water law and legislation, scrutinizing international conventions, and leading efforts towards harmonization with regional and global water law instruments in coordination with concerned public institutions. In this context, the department is expected to contribute to the making of transboundary water policy.

The Turkish Water Institute (SUEN)

The SUEN was founded in 2011 as a national think tank under the MFWA. SUEN is entrusted with conducting and supporting scientific research to strengthen Turkey's national and international water policy (Kibaroglu 2015). SUEN works in cooperation with national and international water-related institutions on issues such as sustainable water management, developing water policies, sustainable energy, and capacity building for solving local and global water problems (SUEN 2018). The main tasks of SUEN include conducting scientific studies to develop and support national and international water policies; following the activities, innovations and statistics of national and international water organizations; organizing national and international education programs; and contributing to national and international fora, conferences, meetings, symposia, training programs and similar activities. Since its establishment, SUEN has organized training programs for more than seven hundred people from three continents in 30 countries. Delegates from the concerned ministries and research institutes attend training courses organized by SUEN with programs of lectures covering the planning of water resources, water and wastewater treatment, water quality management, and river basin planning (SUEN 2017b).

SUEN was founded as a think tank to realize the scientific experience and water vision of the team, which was brought together at the 5th World Water Forum Secretariat, in 2007. Multifaceted knowledge gained by the Forum became the basis of SUEN, which leads the organization of the Istanbul International Water Forum (IIWF) that brings together the global water community in Istanbul every three years one year prior to the World Water Forum, to discuss current international water-related issues.

The last decade has brought a significant increase in the number of people fleeing wars and conflict zones. The impacts of population mobility are felt in both conflict zones and host countries. Mass population mobility not only carries water issues to the global humanitarian agenda but also affects how water is used and managed. From this point on, the 4th IIWF, co-organized by SUEN and the DSI on 10–11 May 2017 in Istanbul, has focused on the current refugee issue under the central theme of 'Water and Peace'. The Forum addressed water-related issues that have arisen due to demographic pressures resulting from forced displacement with their humanitarian, theoretical, financial and legal aspects (SUEN 2017a, 3–4).

SUEN was able to interact with various leading international agencies, which have contributed to the 4th IIWF by either actively participating in the thematic panels or by holding side and special events. In this regard, organizations such as the World Water Council (WWC), UNESCO-IHE Institute for Water Education, the Stockholm International Water Institute (SIWI), the UN Environment Programme (UNEP), the UN World Water Assessment Programme (WWAP), UN-Water, UN High Commissioner for Refugees (UNCHR) and the OECD actively contributed to the Forum.

As it was emphasized by one of the keynote speakers at the 4th IIWF, this was the first time that an international event had been exclusively dedicated to water and the situation of refugees from a practical perspective. It was also underlined that the effects of population mobility are felt both in conflict zones and in host countries. The relevance of Turkey was expressed in terms of choosing such an important topic, as Turkey is the country that hosts the largest population of refugees in the world; currently over four million. It was also underlined that the challenges are numerous, and it is impossible to ignore that the provision of water to refugees or displaced people in camps goes beyond the mere supply of water for human consumption. It was stressed that although the problems are urgent and evident, to this date, little effort has been made to address these problems in a structured manner. Therefore, the 4th IIWF was designated as 'a sign of hope' as the Forum constituted the chance to share experiences among refugee-hosting countries, local administrations, IGOs and NGOs working in this field (SUEN 2017a, 7).

The Auxiliary Role of State Institutions in Different Aspects of Water Diplomacy

Turkey upholds its humanitarian responsibilities and provides financial and technical assistance in the water sector with a specific focus in the Middle East and Africa. The main target of the Turkish water aid is to ensure sustainable, safe drinking water and sanitation for vulnerable people living mainly in the crisis areas where there is no access to clean drinking water, and improvements in sanitation are required (MFWA 2017, 6–8).

Though, in a semi-fragmented manner, Turkey provides financial and technical assistance in the water sector with a particular focus on Africa and the Middle East. Institutions such as TIKA and AFAD carry out considerable aid programs individually and/or collectively in the water sector.

The Turkish Cooperation and Coordination Agency (TIKA)

TIKA is the main international development agency under the Ministry of Culture and Tourism and is charged with the coordination of all aid activities. TIKA's mission is to contribute to poverty eradication and sustainable development in partner countries. Turkey shares its own expertise and experience by tailoring these to fit the specific needs and development priorities of partner countries. In 54 partner countries, TIKA has 56 Program Coordination Offices. These play an important role in TIKA's direct communication with local stakeholders in the implementation of cooperation activities and the collection of country-specific first-hand information. TIKA's activities are not limited to these countries with overseas offices, but reach more than one hundred countries worldwide (MFWA 2017, 6).

The Disaster and Emergency Management Presidency (AFAD)

AFAD works under the Ministry of Interior to prevent disasters and minimize disaster-related damages, to plan and coordinate post-disaster responses, and to promote cooperation among various government agencies. AFAD has completed successful missions to provide humanitarian assistance to nearly fifty countries around the globe. The agency currently runs a network of 24 state-of-the-art refugee camps in Turkey where over 245,000 Syrians enjoy regular access to housing, healthcare, education and psychological support. AFAD remains committed to developing required strategies and to serving people in need at home and abroad (MFWA 2017, 6).

The Southeastern Anatolia Project Regional Development Administration (GAP RDA)

While Turkey intends to develop water resources all over the country, the GAP is of particular importance for generating hydropower and producing agricultural commodities in the Turkish portion of the ET basin. GAP region includes nine Turkish provinces, which faces many of the problems that are typical of underdeveloped regions in the world. Compared with the rest of Turkey, the region has had higher fertility rates and lower literacy rates. The region has also experienced net out migration – both seasonal agricultural migration and permanent rural-to-urban out migration, as a response to high unemployment in the region. The region's economy is based largely on agriculture, but productivity historically has been low. The region also has several urban centres that are experiencing rapid growth, and that have had problems keeping infrastructure development in pace with rural–urban migration. Thus, the region presents challenges in terms of both rural and urban development (Ünver 2001).

In response to these disparities in the southeast, and in recognition that strengthening this region socially and economically will benefit Turkey as a whole, GAP was originally created as a water resources development package for the construction of 13 main irrigation and energy projects on the Euphrates and Tigris river basins. The project includes 22 dams, 19 hydropower plants, and irrigation networks which irrigate 1.7 million hectares of land.

GAP's focus on sustainable human development in the region builds upon the concept of integrated regional development of the GAP Master Plan of 1989. In order to implement the principles set out in this Master Plan, GAP RDA was created to coordinate the implementation, management, monitoring and evaluation of development-related activities, in a concerted effort to respond to the problems. GAP RDA focused on particular themes in sustainable development, such as environmental protection, gender issues and the preservation of cultural assets. These themes in turn were translated into specific projects. In realizing these projects, the GAP RDA collaborated with various international organizations and agencies. For instance, GAP RDA, together with the United Nations Development Programme (UNDP), implemented a project for assisting in the resettlement of more than 30,000 people from 43 villages in the Halfeti area along the Euphrates River; areas which had been affected by the creation of the Birecik Dam and reservoir (Ünver 2001). In addition to developing partnerships with local and national government institutions, the GAP RDA also built partnerships with international agencies, likewise to create entrepreneurship support and guidance centres as well as community-based women's centres.

Moreover, since the early 2000s, the GAP RDA has built close relationships with the international water NGOs, namely the WWC, Global Water Partnership and the International Water Resources Association. GAP RDA officials took part in the decision-making bodies of these international water NGOs while a series of delegations from Turkey participated in the international gatherings of these global NGOs, namely the World Water Forum and World Water Congress.

The GAP RDA led the representation of GAP as a sustainable human-based development project, which, in turn, contributed largely to Turkey's water diplomacy initiatives within the ET basin. In other words, project partnerships with the UN agencies as well as active participation in global water organizations enabled Turkish diplomatic circles to present GAP with its multi-faceted development aspects that could contribute to regional socio-economic development in the entire ET basin. However, those initiatives occurred in parallel with the harsh criticisms of downstream riparian states, Syria and Iraq, as well as global environmental NGOs, such as the International Rivers Network, concerning the negative environmental impacts of dam building in Turkey within the context of the GAP. All in all, the GAP RDA's activities could be interpreted as providing invaluable contributions to Turkey's water diplomacy practices, particularly at the level of the concerned UN agencies and global water NGOs.

Chapter 2

WATER DIPLOMACY PRINCIPLES

Overview

Turkey's fundamental foreign policy principles with respect to transboundary waters have been shaped by physical as well as human geography, and influenced by global, regional and bilateral political, economic and social interactions. In this chapter, Turkey's water diplomacy principles will be analyzed by scrutinizing the official manuals and information notes published by the concerned ministries, namely the Ministry of Foreign Affairs (MFA) and the Ministry of Forestry and Water Affairs (MFWA), as well as from speeches and statements delivered by concerned authorities at international gatherings and in the press.

An analysis of the MFA's standpoint on 'sustainable water management', through the documents posted on its official website, demonstrates that Turkey's overall water policy and water diplomacy principles are closely connected (Table 1). The MFA's observations on the global water predicament are informed by international scientific studies issued by UN agencies (UN-Water 2018). In this respect, the MFA highlights that more than half of the world's population will be living with a water shortage within 50 years due to the worldwide water crisis. The MFA also draws attention to related global statistics and scientific information: 'While the world's population grew threefold, water use increased sixfold during the twentieth century, and the problem is further aggravated by the uneven water distribution on earth'. Moreover, the MFA to ask the critical question regarding 'what governments and international organizations should do to reverse the situation and avert a water crisis at the global level'. The MFA has, indeed, been attentive to the global water situation and has developed discourses on issues such as ensuring global food security for over eight billion people by providing adequate supply of water for irrigation and agriculture. Furthermore, the MFA underlines the importance of the adoption of a more efficient water management system so that governments can meet the most basic human needs (MFA 2018a).

The MFA underlines that 'water resources are essential for satisfying basic human needs, alleviating health problems, promoting social and economic development in general, and conserving ecosystems'. The MFA stresses the importance of sustainable water resources management in the context of socio-economic development. The MFA also recognizes the multiplicity of interests and tradeoffs in utilizing water resources for water supply and sanitation, hydropower generation, agriculture, industry, urban development, fisheries, transportation and recreation. The MFA equally emphasizes the need for the adoption of appropriate national integrated basin management strategies to protect water resources and reduce water pollution. Thus, the MFA adopts a comprehensive water policy approach, which necessitates coordination of the related institutions and genuine cooperation among riparian countries on transboundary waters.

The MFA describes key determinants of Turkey's transboundary water policy and water diplomacy principles mainly by highlighting the physical characteristics of water resources in Turkey. To this end, the MFA describes Turkey's water potential as follows:

> Contrary to the general perception, Turkey is neither a country rich in freshwater resources nor the richest country in the region. Furthermore, given its growing population, rapid urbanization and industrialization it is anticipated to become a water-stressed country by 2030. Turkey is situated in a semi-arid region, and has only about one fifth of the water available per capita in water rich regions such as North America and Western Europe. Water rich countries are those, which have 10,000 m³ of water per capita yearly. This is well above the 1,500 m³ per capita in Turkey.

> Another point is that Turkey's water is not always in the right place at the right time to meet present and anticipated needs. Certain regions of Turkey such as the Black Sea region have ample but unusable freshwater, while some of the more heavily populated and industrialized regions such as the Marmara and the Aegean regions lack sufficient fresh water. (MFA 2018a)

On the other hand, the MFA stresses the fact that Turkey is dependent on water for energy, that is to say, 'Turkey, which is neither oil nor natural gas producer, plans to meet the rising energy need in several ways, including the increasing use of its indigenous sources and in that respect, hydropower'. Turkey's dependence on water for food is also emphasized by highlighting that rain-fed agriculture in Turkey is being realized almost to the maximum level. As a result, increasing agricultural productivity has become primarily dependent upon irrigation by using modern techniques. In this respect, Turkey has made great strides in water resources development for irrigation. The dams and reservoirs built have enabled Turkey to save water from its brief seasons of rainfall to use throughout the year for various purposes, agriculture in particular (MFA 2018a).

The MFA underscores the evolutionary and flexible character of Turkey's water policy, which has been developed as a response to the growing needs at domestic level as well as to keep up with the global policies, namely the UN Millennium Development Goals and the subsequently adopted Sustainable Development Goals. In this respect, the MFA refers to the transformation of the Southeastern Anatolia Project (GAP in Turkish acronym) from a straight-forward engineering and water resources development project in the 1970s to a sustainable human-based socio-economic development project in the 1990s. According to the MFA, the GAP stands as an outstanding accomplishment in the field of water development with its great engineering achievements in irrigation, sanitation services and hydropower, however, the uniqueness of the GAP lies in its strategies of fairness in development, participation, environmental protection, employment generation, spatial planning and infrastructure development (MFA 2018a).

The MFA clearly states that Turkey's transboundary water policy has a motto:

> Water should be utilized among riparian states in an equitable, reasonable and optimal way. Each transboundary water has its own specific characteristics and peculiarities and reflects its own regional, economic, social, cultural and historic aspects. Turkey believes that transboundary water resources can present a real opportunity for collaboration rather than a source of conflict and a constraint for development. Moreover, efficient use of water in a transboundary context requires a proper and detailed information exchange between the riparian states. Such an exchange is also essential for a sound integrated basin management. The riparian states should adopt a comprehensive approach to the matter. Such an approach calls for determination to discuss all water-related issues in a transboundary context. It entails sharing of responsibility as well as the benefits. (MFA 2018a)

In addition to these overall principles, the MFA also stresses that as a candidate country to the EU, Turkey acts in compliance with the WFD. To this end, Turkey has been building monitoring stations for each basin and standardizing the parameters and monitoring frequency. Turkey has also been constructing wastewater treatment plants to diminish water pollution, and constructing facilities for wastewater reuse and prevention of water losses and leakages. Water saving efforts are promoted among stakeholders, especially farmers by training them on suitable crop patterns versus water demand (MFA 2018b).

Main Principles

Turkey's water diplomacy could be properly scrutinized by delineating its fundamental principles, which, all in all, constitute primary sources and evidences of Turkey's state practice. The MFA declares that Turkey's policy regarding the use of transboundary rivers is based on the following principles:

1. Water is a basic human need.
2. Each riparian state of a transboundary river system has the sovereign right to make use of the water in its territory.
3. Riparian states must make sure that their utilization of such waters does not give 'significant harm' to others.
4. Transboundary waters should be used in an equitable, reasonable and optimum manner.
5. Equitable use does not mean the equal distribution of waters of a transboundary river among riparian states. (MFA 2018a)

On 21–23 March 2013, the National Consultation Council on Forestry and Water was gathered with the participation of officials from the concerned ministries as well as academics. After consultations with the concerned ministries, the Working Group prepared the Report on Basin Management and Water Information Systems, which included, among other things, the following principles related to Turkey's water diplomacy:

1. Transboundary water disputes should be solved between the riparian countries, third party involvement for mediation should not be supported.
2. The variable natural hydrological and meteorological conditions must be taken into account in the allocation and use of transboundary waters. These variable conditions make it necessary to share the risks of the droughts among all riparian countries. Thus, it is not possible to share waters through fixed quantities or quotas.

3. Turkey is ready to share its experiences in building hydropower-stations, dams and other water structures such as drinking water supply networks and irrigation systems as well as its potential in technology and human resources. (MFWA 2013, 33–34)

In review of these principles, one can observe major influences of core norms of customary international water law (see Chapter 3) as well as Turkey's upstream dilemma specifically as it relates to the Euphrates–Tigris (ET) basin. The first principle that Turkey adopts, 'water is a basic human need', aims at expressing Turkey's understanding that to respond to the basic needs of the downstream riparians, Turkey will always have the good intention to release as much of the available water as possible under the given hydrological and meteorological conditions. In this respect, the MFA stresses that 'Since the 1970s, Turkey has paid the utmost attention to releasing water from the Euphrates during the filling as well as the operation of the dams. Turkey is committed to doing this in conformity with an international customary law principle of equitable utilization' (MFA 1995, 19).

In a recent interview with *Daily Sabah*, ambassador retired, who acted as the director general responsible for environment, water and energy at the MFA, Mithat Rende said that,

Turkey has never overlooked the needs of the downstream riparian states, even during drought periods. For example, 1988 and 1989 were the driest years of the past 50 years. At the height of the summer, the flow of the Euphrates was around 100 m^3 per second. In spite of that unexpected low natural flow, Turkey was able to go on releasing water to downstream neighbors at a rate of more than 500 m^3 per second. This proves that Syria and Iraq benefit from the water infrastructures that Turkey has built on the Euphrates. (Ersen 2018)

Rende also stressed that even in dire circumstances Turkey had fulfilled its commitment to the agreement of 1987 between Turkey and Syria that guaranteed the latter a minimum flow of the Euphrates of 500 m^3 per second throughout the year (Protocol 1987). He stressed upon that 'Turkey's transboundary water policy has always been consistent and transparent. Turkey's policy is aimed at efficiently utilizing and sharing the benefits of water resources through cooperation among riparian states'.

Moreover, in the midst of the unrest in Syria and in the process of the worsening of bilateral political relations between Turkey and Syria, the former minister, MFWA, Veysel Eroglu was interviewed by a group of reporters from Iraq on water issues, where he said, 'We have never considered water as an instrument of threat. We will never cut off the water we supply for Syria regardless of the state of our relations because Syrian people need water. Turkey believes that water resources should be shared fairly'. Eroglu added that 'Turkey had agreed to release 500 m^3 of water per second from the Euphrates river and at times of drought in Iraq we even released more water than the amount we had pledged' (Anatolian Agency 2012).

Furthermore, Turkey completed the construction of the Ilisu Dam across the Tigris River in early 2018 and began filling the reservoir behind the dam in June 2018. Yet, because of increasing objections from Iraq, Turkey and Iraq have since agreed that Turkey would allow the river's natural flow to continue until 1 November 2018. The decision came amid a drought in Iraq, which affected farmers, leading to violent protests against the government in the country. The protesters blamed Baghdad for poor management of water resources, including the lack of modernization of infrastructure and methods. Turkey's step of goodwill would reportedly continue until the winter months. Delegations from Ankara and Baghdad met on 2 November 2018, for further discussions (Tastekin 2018). During a press conference, Hassan al-Janabi, Iraq's minister of Water Resources, said meetings would continue between the two countries on how to ensure enough water flows to Iraq during and after the filling of the reservoir behind the Ilisu Dam (*Daily Sabah* 2018).

First principle also reflects the official Turkish position that 'needs' rather than 'rights' enable the 'equitable use' principle is operational. In this contention, by calculating the objective needs of domestic water users, major sectors of the economy – namely agriculture – as well as taking into consideration the demands of the riparian countries at an international level, it would be possible to turn the right to equitable use into tangible practices. In this context, Turkey has been advocating the necessity of adopting a common set of criteria based on objective needs in allocating the waters of the ET basin. Accordingly, Turkey's 'needs-based' approach was expressed in the Three-Stage Plan put forward by the technocrats of its central water agency, DSI, in 1984. That plan involves that an inventory studies of water and land resources throughout the region, comprising the territories of the various states, would be undertaken and jointly evaluated by Iraq, Syria and Turkey. On the basis of these studies, the means and measures needed to attain the most reasonable, optimum utilization of resources would be defined (Minutes of the Fifteenth Meeting of the Joint Technical Committee 1990).

Time and again, the MFA authorities emphasized that 'Turkey views water as a catalyst for cooperation rather than a source of conflict'. Traditionally, Turkey has also stressed the principle of 'good neighborliness' which considers other riparians' interests in dealing with 'transboundary' or 'international' rivers. However, Turkish official discourse explicitly distinguishes between the terms 'international rivers' and 'transboundary rivers', and considers international rivers only to be those that constitute a border between two or more countries, such as the Meric River which forms the border between Turkey and Greece, and the Arpacay River (Aras basin) where it forms the border between Turkey and Armenia. In the Turkish official contention, while such boundary rivers are to be shared equally between the riparian countries, the water of transboundary rivers should be allocated equitably (MFA 1996, 2–9).

While endorsing the 'equitable utilization' and 'no significant harm' principles, Turkey intends to reassure that 'sovereign right to the use of water', as well as 'equitable, reasonable and optimum use' rather than simply 'equal use' are the defining principles of Turkish transboundary water policy. Yet, Turkey objects to the claim of the downstream countries that they should have the right of co-sovereignty on the waters of the upstream country or vice versa (Kibaroglu 2002, 228). In order to explore upstream dilemma for (mainly) upstream states like Turkey, Patricia Wouters identifies the concept of the 'sovereignty paradox', which is a challenge posed by the local/international interface in international relations among riparian states (Wouters 2013, 374–75). Turkey's strong argument in claiming its sovereign rights over the portion of the transboundary rivers that are situated on its territory basically originates from the foundational principles of international law as codified in the UN Charter as 'the principle of the sovereign equality of all its members' as well as 'territorial integrity of the members'. However, similar to numerous UN resolutions and international instruments (hard and soft law), including treaties and transboundary water agreements, Turkey attempts to balance the issues arising out of the sovereignty paradox by putting forward a bunch of cooperation initiatives over its transboundary waters, such as concluding bilateral water allocation treaties, establishing joint water mechanisms and initiating joint projects such as joint dams and joint technical trainings on water use and efficiency (Turan 2011).

Turkey's state practice demonstrates that she has preferred direct negotiations as a basic diplomatic mechanism to settle disputes over transboundary water resources. Through its experience with donor agencies during the construction of the Keban and Karakaya Dams, Turkey developed a negative stance towards the possibility of third-party intervention in transboundary water issues (Gürün 1994, 240–72). In the early 1960s, Turkey submitted the copies of the feasibility report of the Keban Dam project to Syrian and Iraqi officials in order to provide them with up-to-date information on the dam. Hence, the first diplomatic meeting on the Keban Dam was held in 1964 between 22 and 27 June , with the participation of Turkish and Iraqi experts. In that meeting, the Turkish delegation asserted that it was impossible to reach a single and final formula for the pattern of water to be released from the Keban Dam reservoir before impounding by the dam. This pattern, according to the Turkish delegation, depended upon the natural conditions that would prevail during the filling, and on the exact evaluation of the concerned countries' needs (DSI 1975). However, under pressure from the donors through an agreement signed in Ankara in 1966 with the US Agency for International Development (USAID), Turkey guaranteed to undertake all necessary measures to maintain a discharge of 350 m^3 per second immediately downstream from the dam, provided that the natural flow of the river was adequate to supply the above discharge. This was confirmed orally to Syria and Iraq the same year.

USAID was the acting donor for the Keban project, while the World Bank was the leading agency financing the Karakaya Dam further downstream. Both agencies insisted that guaranteed flows be released by Turkey to downstream riparians during the impounding and operation of the reservoirs. International donors did not give much weight to the essential Turkish view that a fair distribution of Euphrates waters could be made by taking into consideration the long-term projects and the needs of the three countries along with the possibility of transferring water from adjacent river, namely the Tigris. Turkey contended that the donors' intervention was solely in favour of protecting the rights of the downstream riparians and gave little recognition of Turkish rights to develop and use the river system.

Turkey's negative attitude towards third parties' interventions in transboundary water diplomacy did not change in its essentials. The preferred method of dispute settlement by Turkey in practice is direct negotiations, which leave her as much as possible in control of the outcome of the process. This official stance has been specifically articulated in the MFA's official notes and publications (MFA 1996).

One clear observation is that transboundary water problems, particularly in relation to the ET basin, often cannot be solved, because the positions of the parties have been simply irreconcilable. However, with the new institutions that have recently emerged in the Turkish water bureaucracy, such as the Turkish Water Institute (SUEN in Turkish acronym), third parties, such as international development agencies, international research institutes and think tanks, have become partners with Turkish institutions in joint projects encompassing transboundary waters.

SUEN, founded in 2011 as a national think tank under the MFWA, collaborated with the Strategic Foresight Group (SFG), a Mumbai-based think tank to facilitate dialogue between Iraq and Turkey; this involved meeting of policymakers and experts from the two countries (SUEN 2016). With the support of the Swiss Agency for Development and Cooperation (SDC), the SFG organized a series of meetings in 2013–14, with stakeholders from both countries deciding to focus on the Tigris River, as the situation in Syria did not allow any basin-wide cooperation on the Euphrates River. As a culmination of its efforts, in June 2014, the SFG organized a meeting between senior representatives from Iraq and Turkey. The delegations, comprising senior advisors of the prime ministers, former cabinet ministers, members of parliament, officials of water ministries and water authorities, and experts from Iraq and Turkey, established consensus on a plan of action to promote exchange and calibration of data and standards pertaining to Tigris River flows. The plan was expected to contribute significantly to transforming water from a source of crisis into an instrument of peace. Such a change in the role of water in a challenging region such as the Middle East requires institutional arrangements. On several occasions, the governments of Iraq and Turkey agreed, in principle, to promote exchange and harmonization of water data. The SFG initiative intended to help both countries take the agreement to the next level of an operative plan of action. That facilitative role of the SFG became possible thanks to the enabling political atmosphere created by the concerned state institutions, namely the MFWA. This led to various other actors of transboundary water governance taking initiatives to foster cooperation between Turkey and Iraq.

Moreover, recently, the SFG also led the establishment of a new regional initiative to increase cooperation and coordination on transboundary water resources in the Middle East. This new regional initiative, announced on 31 August 2018, in Stockholm, is supported by the Swedish International Development Cooperation Agency (SIDA) and SDC, and has come about as a product of a nearly decade-old effort by Blue Peace in the Middle East – an initiative steered by the SFG since 2009 among pivotal countries of the Middle East.

SUEN has been chosen to be the host of the regional initiative's coordination office until the end of 2020. The structure of the new regional initiative will include water experts and decision makers from Turkey, Iraq, Syria, Jordan, Lebanon and Iran to increase the use of water as a tool for cooperation and for minimizing the conflict over transboundary water resources in the Middle East region. Hasan Sarikaya, former undersecretary at the MFWA, following the two-day meeting on the new initiative told the Daily Sabah in the Swedish capital that 'As a member of the [Blue Peace] initiative, Turkey has aimed to contribute in a way that would change perceptions on water "as a source of conflict" to water "as a reason for peace"' (Celik 2018).

Sarikaya said the new initiative, which will ensure that decisions on the future of water will be decided by countries in the region, will also receive support from international donors on water projects, such as Sweden and Switzerland, and that the new establishment would include a coordination office, thematic activity centers, a managing committee and also a policy advisory committee. 'The new initiative will also act as a platform for Turkey to better explain itself on water-related projects that have received criticism', he said, and added that while 'Turkey has always been in coordination with bordering countries on water-related issues, the new initiative will also expand cooperation with countries like Jordan and Lebanon, as well' (Celik 2018).

Furthermore, SUEN has acted as a country partner in another international research project, namely the Collaborative Programme Euphrates and Tigris (CPET), a five-year project (2013–18) that aims to assist countries in the Euphrates and Tigris region to make progressive steps towards improving water management through dialogue, trust building, information exchange, analysis and regional investment prioritization. This project is funded by the SIDA. The following organizations are part of implementing this project: The International Center for Biosaline Agriculture (ICBA) together with the Stockholm International Water Institute (SIWI), basin country partner representatives and four implementing partner institutions such as the American University of Beirut (AUB), the International Center for Agricultural Research in the Dry Areas (ICARDA), the Stockholm Environment Institute (SEI) and the Swedish Meteorological and Hydrological Institute (SMHI). The CPET aims to provide a rigorous evidence base to evaluate transboundary impacts and enable the identification of a range of water management options and a regional investment program in the ET basin. The country partners, including SUEN, jointly develop and periodically steer the program. The CPET provides a number of important building blocks that support future cooperative efforts in the region where there has been a low level of cooperation to date. The anticipated outcomes of these cooperative efforts for a more efficient and productive use of transboundary water resources in the Euphrates and Tigris region include contributing to improved (1) water security for small and large water users; (2) efficiency and productivity of water use, and generation of additional socio-economic benefits per unit of water; (3) management of ecosystem goods and services at the regional scale and restoration options of deteriorated marshlands; (4) livelihood security in rural communities and reduced rural-urban migration; (5) participation of stakeholders, including women, in decision making on cooperative action in water management at the regional level; and (6) accountability and communication. CPET provides a platform for dialogue, exchange and trust building by building up the trust, momentum, and progress generated among the partners of the project (Ammar and Chaisemartin 2014).

Water Diplomacy Principles Specific to the Euphrates–Tigris River Basin

A significant portion of the water diplomacy principles relate to the ET basin regarding its peculiarity among five major transboundary basins that Turkey shares with its neighbours. The MFA declares these principles as follows:

1. The two rivers constitute a single basin.
2. The combined water potential of the Euphrates and the Tigris rivers is, in view of the Turkish authorities, sufficient to meet the needs of the three riparian states provided that water is used in an efficient way and the benefit is maximized through new water saving irrigation technologies and the principle of 'more crop per drop' at basin level. Riparian states should carry their obligation of preventing pollution of water.
3. The variability of natural hydrological conditions must be taken into account in the allocation of the waters of the Euphrates and the Tigris rivers.
4. Turkey is ready to negotiate the waters of the Euphrates and Tigris with all its aspects. In this context, as a sign of good will, data and information requested by neighboring countries will always be provided. Yet, exchange of data and information should be basin-wide and reciprocal.
5. The principle of sharing the benefits at basin level should be pursued. (MFA 2018a)

The principles adopted pertaining to the ET basin are the accumulation of years of experience and practices that Turkey developed during the endured diplomatic negotiations with its southern neighbours. Since the 1970s, through bilateral and trilateral negotiations with Iraq and Syria, as well as paying visits to water and land resources development projects in downstream countries, Turkish authorities concluded that there would be an increasing pressure on the Euphrates due to the magnitude of the planned irrigation projects of all three riparians in the Euphrates region. Hence, to deal with this pressure, Turkish negotiators kept advocating that the Euphrates and Tigris Rivers constitute a single basin 'due to the fact that they are linked by their natural course when merging at the Shatt-al-Arab in the Gulf, and also because of the Thartar

Canal built to connect the two rivers inside Iraq'. Therefore, they suggested that 'all existing and future agricultural water uses need not necessarily be derived from the Euphrates' and that 'irrigation water for areas fed by the Euphrates may also be supplied from the Tigris' (MFA 1996, 1–15). This principle has, in a way, without any substantial revision since the mid-1990s, become an established and predominant principle of Turkish water diplomacy.

In this context, ambassador retired Mithat Rende stressed that,

> The combined water potential of the Tigris and Euphrates rivers is sufficient to meet the needs of the three riparian states to achieve sustainable development, provided that water is used in an efficient way and the benefits are maximized through new irrigation systems and technologies throughout the basin, Syria and Iraq included. From 1984 onward to 2009, Turkey, Syria and Iraq had been negotiating the management of transboundary waters. In 1984, Turkey proposed a Three-Stage Plan for the optimal, equitable and reasonable utilization of transboundary waters of the ET basin. Yet, the plan was rejected by Syria and Iraq since there were diverging opinions concerning the definition of the basin area. While Turkey considered the ET basin to be a single system, the other two wanted to categorize it as two separate basins.

Rende added that 'Turkey has scientifically proven its stance during the Joint Technical Committee meetings. Even the historical trajectory confirms that the ET basin is a single system; however, the downstream riparians Syria and Iraq insisted on their positions' (Ersen 2018).

Rende underscored that 'at a time when the international arena was talking about water wars due to rising conflict between Turkey and its neighbors, upstream Turkey developed water resources both for its own benefit and for the benefit of its neighbor, Syria, which is situated in a semi-arid region and exposed to precipitation only five to six months a year'. Rende stressed that 'the billion-dollar dam projects of Turkey, including the Keban, Karakaya, Birecik and Atatürk, impounded water and the benefits of the reservoirs were shared with downstream neighbors', adding, 'Had Turkey not built these dams, it would not have been possible to regulate the unbalanced fluctuations in the flows and ensure the equitable share of water'. Rende explained,

> On one occasion, the snow in the highlands of the Euphrates melted in a very short period of time – in 10 days instead of three months – because of a southwester. Such incidents in the past had caused massive flooding,

but after the construction of the dams, flood water had been regulated. Even the pledged 500 m³ per second for Syria was increased during that period and Syria was notified of the situation. (Ersen 2018)

More than a quarter century of living with a water-sharing agreement, which has put Turkey under obligation to release a certain amount (i.e. 500 m³ per second) of water from the Euphrates River to Syria, has led Turkish decision makers to be overly cautious about hydro-meteorological conditions in the river system. This obligation urges Turkey to provide the promised amount of water even in dire conditions such as prolonged, severe droughts. Thus, a series of water diplomacy principles were adopted through that state practice. Likewise, Turkey's emphasis on the principles of achieving 'efficiency in water use', 'prevention of pollution', and 'basin wide data exchange' are the products of those perceptions which were developed over the years during the futile negotiation processes in the ET basin, which did not pave the way to efficient and equitable use and management in the basin.

Turkish authorities adopted a progressive understanding in dealing with the transboundary water issues, namely the 'benefit sharing' approach, thanks to their increasing participation in the global water fora, such as the World Water Forum organized every three years by the World Water Council and the World Water Week conducted annually by the Stockholm International Water Institute, as well as through their growing understanding and perceptions about the evolving global water management paradigms.

Rather than sharing the waters through simple arithmetic, as suggested by Iraq and Syria, Turkey suggested sharing the benefits of water-based development projects and water structures by way of conducting joint inventory studies for water and land resources as a basis for a trilateral, final allocation agreement in the ET basin (MFA 1996, 15–20). Turkish policymakers argue that the 'benefit-sharing approach' fits with Turkey's historical position and it provides opportunities for win-win solutions. In this respect, Turkey has come up with more concrete proposals, such as the joint dam development projects in the river basins, as initiatives for enhancing mutual benefits related to hydropower and irrigation. Examples of Turkish initiatives for joint development of scarce water resources driven by a pragmatic and workable approach to transboundary cooperation in these river basins include joint water storage projects, such as the Serdarabad Regulator (already in operation) on the Aras River (Arpacay), the Suakacagi Dam (in planning and negotiation stage) across the Meric River (Tunca tributary) and the proposed Friendship Dam across the Orontes River (an item discussed in the Turkish-Syrian technical talks between 2009 and 2011).

It has been observed that Turkey did not demand any preconditions to be fulfilled before entering into water negotiations. This was even valid for water negotiations with Syria with whom Turkey had had severe political problems concerning border security issues. Turkish foreign policy circles regarded the transboundary water relations with Syria and Iraq in the context of political and legal relations; relations governed by official treaties, diplomatic correspondence and contacts. Even though the terrorism issue marred bilateral relations with Syria, the official policy of the Turkish authorities, particularly that of the MFA, was to deliberately separate the terrorism issue from water-related matters. However, one significant deviation from this official stance was the signing of two protocols with Syria at prime ministerial level, which linked security and terrorism issues with water sharing arrangements in 1987 (see Chapter 1).

Turkey's position on transboundary water issues is characterized by proposals to jointly investigate water use and water needs in respective countries, instead of merely negotiating water rights. This paradigm shift is probably best illustrated by the Turkish offer to build joint dams with Georgia, Bulgaria, Syria and Iraq that could serve the energy needs of both countries, and the proposed Three-Stage Plan for the ET river system. The latter would contribute to water allocations that would take into account water needs for agriculture, population and industry and the basin-wide costs and benefits of different management options. Taking this Turkish proposal seriously, the offer could have contributed to a sustainable water management strategy. However, basin-wide and needs-based coordination is highly challenging in political terms regarding open questions of distribution and institutionalisation. Yet, in the long term, the shift from water-rights negotiation to a needs-based approach will be highly relevant in the context of water scarcity in international basins (Kibaroglu et al. 2005).

Turkey is also open to international cooperation concerning environmental issues, such as the protection of nature. This is illustrated by the water diplomacy initiatives relating to cooperation on nature protection between Turkey and its Caucasian neighbours. Potentially, such initiatives could serve as starting points for broader cooperation in the basins, and the development of a more integrated management perspective.

Emerging Water Diplomacy Principles

A new trend has developed in Turkish water diplomacy, which could be defined as 'humanitarian water diplomacy'. Turkey undertakes humanitarian responsibility by providing financial and technical assistance in the water sector with a specific focus in the Middle East and Africa. The main target of Turkish water aid is to ensure the provision of sustainable, safe drinking water as well as sanitation for vulnerable people living mainly in crisis areas without access to clean drinking water and in need of improved sanitation. Concerned institutions in Turkey, namely the Disaster and Emergency Management Presidency (AFAD), Turkish Cooperation and Coordination Agency (TIKA), DSI, SUEN, and the Municipalities and Water and Sewerage Administrations, carry out considerable aid programs individually and/or collectively in the water sector (see Chapter 1).

Turkey's water aid perspective envisages a model for an international water fund that focuses on urgent water-related issues particularly in Africa and the Middle East. In line with an analysis of the leading international agencies (e.g. UNHCR, WHO, UNICEF), Turkey identified the following main water-related priority and emergency issues, namely, water scarcity and famine, waterborne diseases and the needs of refugees that require rapid global response (MFWA 2017). Through its first-hand experience, Turkey identified country cases in the Middle East and North Africa, namely Syria, South Sudan, Yemen and Somalia who were also facing these emergency issues and in urgent need of water aid. Syria is a particular case in point since over 3.6 million registered Syrian refugees are living in Turkey. Over 245,000 Syrians live in 21 government-run temporary protection centres, while the majority of the Syrian population lives outside the protection centres in rural and urban areas (AFAD 2017). The rise in water demand which arises due to migration inevitably puts more stress on already scarce water resources. Investment requirements soar both for maintenance of the existing infrastructure and also for wastewater management. With extensive infrastructure investments made by the government and municipalities, and with appreciable efforts paid for by institutions working in the field to provide water and sanitation services to Syrians living both in temporary protection centres and in cities, Syrian refugees have equal opportunities with Turkish citizens at the point of access to water and sanitation services. Between 2012 and 2017, Turkey allocated 25 billion USD to humanitarian relief actions for Syrians registered in Turkey. It is estimated that 4 per cent of this amount has been spent for water-related activities (AFAD 2017).

Moreover, since the second Islamic Conference of Ministers Responsible for Water (ICMW), Turkey has initiated a process to establish a fund allocation system towards solving water problems in the least developed countries of the Organisation of Islamic Cooperation (OIC). After the UN, with 57 member states, the OIC is the second-largest intergovernmental organization. A significant number of OIC member states are facing several water problems, especially in Africa and the Middle East, which are part of the Asian region of the OIC. The second ICMW underlined the significance of international cooperation for addressing water issues and challenges. By consensus, OIC member states adopted a Common Water Vision to increase the capacity of Islamic countries for solving water issues and to implement the strategy that the third ICMW recently approved – the establishment of a body entitled the OIC Water Council. Turkey has been elected as one of the members of the OIC Water Council until 2022, to act as a pioneer for establishing the council and to host the ICMW meetings from 2009 to 2016. Creating a new funding mechanism led by the Turkish government to solve water issues is still on the agenda of the OIC Water Council (MFWA 2017).

To create synergies both nationally and internationally, Turkey suggests establishing an International Water Fund (IWF) with a particular focus on Africa and the Middle East regions' urgent water-related issues. Turkey suggests this is done by joining forces and collaboratively expanding ongoing water aid activities on a global scale. Any country is welcome to contribute to this joint collaborative action.

The working principles of the Fund should be transparent, flexible, operational, accountable, economic, effective, efficient, catalyzing, financially sustainable and allocated based on needs. The Fund should be accompanied with a case-specific high-level group that works in close cooperation with the Fund leadership to facilitate the use of the Fund effectively.

Supporting projects to solve urgent water problems in the field may be based on grants from developed countries. Each willing developed country is expected to commit a certain amount of aid under the Water Fund. Turkey, for instance, granted 11 million Euros in Djibouti in order to build a dam for water supply as well as a flood protection. Turkey also elaborated on possible sources of finance as well as the organizational structure of the suggested IWF.

Table 1. Turkey's Water Diplomacy Framework

Main Principles

- Water is a basic human need
- Each riparian state of a transboundary river system has the sovereign right to make use of the water in its territory
- Riparian states must make sure that their utilization of such waters does not give 'significant harm' to others
- Transboundary waters should be used in an equitable, reasonable and optimum manner
- Equitable use does not mean the equal distribution of waters of a transboundary river among riparian states
- Transboundary water disputes should be solved between the riparian countries, third-party involvement for mediation should not be supported
- The variable natural hydrological and meteorological conditions must be taken into account in the allocation and use of transboundary waters. These variable conditions make it necessary to share the risks of the droughts among all riparian countries. Thus, it is not possible to share waters through fixed quantities or quotas
- Turkey is ready to share its experiences in building hydropower-stations, dams and other water structures such as drinking water supply networks and irrigation systems as well as its potential in technology and human resources

Principles Related to the Euphrates–Tigris Basin

- The two rivers constitute a single basin
- The combined water potential of the Euphrates and the Tigris Rivers is, in view of the Turkish authorities, sufficient to meet the needs of the three riparian states provided that water is used in an efficient way and the benefit is maximized through new water-saving irrigation technologies and the principle of 'more crop per drop' at basin level. Riparian states should carry their obligation of preventing pollution of water
- The variability of natural hydrological conditions must be taken into account in the allocation of the waters of the Euphrates and the Tigris Rivers
- Turkey is ready to negotiate the waters of the Euphrates and Tigris with all its aspects. In this context, as a sign of good will, data and information requested by neighbouring countries will always be provided. Yet, exchange of data and information should be basin-wide and reciprocal
- The principle of sharing the benefits at basin level should be pursued

Chapter 3

TURKEY'S EVOLVING POSITION
VIS-À-VIS INTERNATIONAL
WATER LAW

Overview

Water law, especially at the international level, has been relentlessly criticized as vague, useless and impotent. Yet, whenever a dispute arises at local, national or international level, water law has often been instantly resorted to as a panacea to lead negotiations to settlements between competing stakeholders. And thus, despite its many ambiguities, the overriding view is that by levelling the playing field for all stakeholders and permitting the consideration of all relevant factors, international water law still constitutes a valuable tool in providing the necessary framework to set the fundamental principles, priorities, approaches and objectives of integrated water resource management at the river basin level (Wouters et al. 2003).

It is generally observed that water diplomacy circles, namely diplomats, legal advisers and decision makers in Turkey have endorsed and adopted customary international water law, particularly its cornerstone principles, that is, 'equitable utilization' and 'no significant harm'. Hence, this chapter first depicts how and to what extent Turkey's state practices follow and contribute to the principles of customary international water law.

Turkey's position towards the Convention on the Law of the Non-navigational Uses of International Watercourses (hereinafter, United Nations Watercourses Convention – UNWC) has constituted a significant aspect of how its transboundary water policy have been perceived by relevant external actors. It is striking, for instance, that Turkey was one of only three countries who rejected the UNWC in 1997 (Convention 1997). Although the reasons behind Turkey's rejection of the UNWC were officially stated during the Working Groups in New York in 1997, they were never properly elaborated upon in such a way as to reflect its concerns and dilemmas. Hence, it falls to this chapter to shed some light on just these concerns.

It pays to recall in the meantime that since the UNWC vote in 1997, there have been many changes to Turkey's stance vis-à-vis international water law. The chapter will also look into those changes (i.e. the bureaucratic reorganization process) and focus on the evolving position of Turkey vis-à-vis international water law. To illustrate, the main responsibilities of the Water Law and Policy Department, under the General Directorate of Water Management (DGWM) of the MFWA (Ministry of Agriculture and Forestry since 2018), include making studies on national and international water law and legislation, scrutinizing international conventions and leading harmonization efforts with regional and global water law instruments in coordination with the relevant public institutions. Moreover, the Turkish Water Institute (SUEN in Turkish acronym) has been also entrusted with the objective of conducting and supporting policy-relevant research to strengthen Turkey's national and international water policy.

Customary International Water Law and Turkey's Standpoint

A basic understanding of the fundamental concepts and principles of public international law is necessary in order to appreciate fully the issues that arise in the context of the law governing transboundary water resources. For example, it is important to know that the rules of international law apply to sovereign states and thus it falls primarily on states themselves to ensure compliance with international commitments (Malanczuk 1997). There is no supra authority to enforce such rules, except in very specific circumstances, such as when a failure to abide constitutes a threat to international peace and security. Law enforcement is a central issue of concern, but first, one must identify the applicable rulings themselves (Wouters 1999).

The rules regarding water law are based on a scattering of treaties, international customary law, general legal principles and the texts of various learned publicists. Treaties usually provide the most immediately accessible legal requirements, but other sources cannot be ignored. It is worth noting that not all treaties apply to all states. First, it must be ascertained whether the state concerned is a party to the treaty in question and, second, whether the latter has come into force and thus has become legally binding on the state (Malanczuk 1997).

Customary international law is defined as the customary practices that states follow out of a sense of obligation. It has the same legal force under international law as treaties. It provides interpretive presumptions, it extends treaty norms to non-signatories and it influences efforts to expand treaty regimes. It has always regulated important elements of international relations such as territorial sovereignty, laws of treaty, laws of war, human rights. It has always been multilateral in the sense of purporting to bind all or almost all states.

Customary international law emerges from state practice; however, this is predominantly determined by state interest and the distribution of state power. Much of customary international law coincides with state interests. Compliance with customary international law is driven by a sense of obligation (*opinio juris*), or because it reflects morally valid procedures or consent or internal value sets. On the other hand, the motive behind most state behaviour falls to self-interest, and thus the resulting pattern emerges due to the more cynical dynamics of international relations (Goldsmith and Posner 2005, 225).

Customary international water law did not emerge substantially until the end of the First World War. Before this time, human consumption, industrial waste and diversions for irrigation were not deemed major issues. Rivers were used primarily for navigation and log floatation, both of which were covered for Europe in the Congress of Vienna of 1815. With the development of international water use for purposes other than navigation and, in particular, for consumptive uses such as irrigation and domestic purposes, a number of potential or actual disputes have emerged among riparian states (Kibaroglu 2002).

In the evolution of customary international water law, the theoretical foundation of the law of international water resources relates to the state practice. That is to say, legal framework doctrines emerged from controversies between states, their claims and counter-claims over the rights to use of transboundary rivers Consequently, state practice, scholarship and jurisprudence have produced three basic legal doctrines, namely 'absolute territorial sovereignty', 'absolute territorial integrity' and 'limited territorial sovereignty'. By means of categorizing the legal framework doctrines, one could comprehend the approaches of the riparians to the allocation and management of transboundary water resources. Initially, upper riparian states claimed 'absolute territorial sovereignty' entitling themselves to use the transboundary water resources as they pleased within their boundaries and without regard to the demands or wishes of the lower riparians. In response, lower riparians claimed 'absolute territorial integrity', a doctrine, which justified the demand of an undisturbed flow from upstream. These mutually exclusive claims raged back and forth across diplomatic channels until the international community moved gradually towards the more reasonable middle-ground doctrine of 'limited territorial sovereignty', which is expressed in terms of the principle of equitable utilization (Kibaroglu 2002).

The doctrine of limited territorial sovereignty strikes a golden mean between the two preceding theories – by recognizing a state's sovereignty over the waters of a transboundary river under its jurisdiction, but limiting the exercise thereof in such a manner as to ensure other riparians a reasonable share of the waters. Under this doctrine, all states are equally sovereign, hence, the sovereignty of one state is limited by the sovereignty of the others. In other words, every state is free to use its territorial water, provided that in no way prejudices the rights and the uses of the other states. This doctrine is supported by the principles of reasonable and equitable use and the obligation to avoid significant harm (Kibaroglu 2002).

To illustrate, Turkey has been advocating the necessity of common criteria in the allocation of the waters of the Euphrates–Tigris (ET) basin, based on the principle of equitable utilization, which is grounded in the doctrine of 'limited territorial sovereignty'. Turkey's needs-based approach is simply a reflection of the limited sovereignty doctrine which combines the two cornerstone principles of international water law in an effective way: (1) equitable right to use, and (2) obligation not to cause significant harm. In order to operationalize this doctrine, the needs of each riparian have to be determined through the exchange of reliable and accurate data. In addition, Turkey recognizes that all riparians in the basin have correlative entitlements and obligations regarding their use of water resources. To this end, Turkey embraces the principle of equitable utilization as the primary rule governing the allocation of the waters of the basin. Hence, each state's obligations should be shared, just like the benefits. Each riparian must pay attention to the criteria of efficiency and equity when making use of its portion (MFA 1996).

The period following the Second World War was one marked by massive reconstruction efforts all over the world, as well the emergence of more and more independent states – particularly in Africa and Asia. With these events, the need to develop water resources through the construction of large-scale dams and extensive irrigation networks became widespread. Projects aimed at economic growth intensified competition and disputes over rivers crossing international boundaries.

International legal rights regarding the use of the waters of transboundary rivers became a thorny issue, with upstream states holding a view of the law that directly opposed those held by downstream states. This divergence of views clearly indicated the urgent need for an authoritative statement on international rivers, which went beyond the legal framework doctrines (Bourne 1996). To this end, in 1966, the International Law Association (ILA) adopted the Helsinki Rules on the uses of the waters of international rivers. This set of articles represented a significant attempt by a private international professional organization to allow for a complete codification of laws regarding international watercourses (McCaffrey 1991a). In drafting the Helsinki Rules, the ILA's main objective was 'to clarify and restate existing international law as it applies to the rights of states to utilize the waters of an international drainage basin'. The Helsinki Rules were completed, later on, by various additional texts dealing in particular with environmental problems and with the status of groundwater (Bourne 1996).

In its state practices, Turkey has referred to the Helsinki Rules by highlighting that the ILA considered the principle of equitable and reasonable utilization as a guiding rule, while the no-harm rule was one among a series of elements to be considered in determining whether a given use was 'equitable and reasonable' (Belül 1996).

Main Principles of Customary International Water Law and Turkey's State Practices

International water law, just as in international law, is based on general legal principles such as, inter alia, the equality of states, good neighbourliness, peaceful settlement of disputes, achieving international cooperation in solving international problems. Two principles, in particular, are considered cornerstones of customary international water law: the principle of equitable and reasonable utilization and participation in the development of the watercourse by all riparian states, as well as the obligation not to cause significant harm to another watercourse state through the use of the international watercourse (Brunnée and Toope 1997).

Where there are insufficient amounts of water to meet competing demands, adjustments must also be made on the basis of equity to accommodate the respective water needs of the co-riparian states. The principle of equitable and reasonable utilization determines the riparian rights to water with a view to arriving at an equitable resolution of a conflict over use. In so doing, it entitles 'each basin state, within its own territory, to a reasonable and equitable share in the beneficial uses of the waters of an international drainage basin' (International Law Association 1966). Derived from the theory of limited territorial sovereignty this substantive principle has gained considerable support in state practice, international treaties and judicial decisions (McCaffrey 1986). Its customary status was confirmed by the authoritative decision of the International Court of Justice in the Gabcikovo-Nagymaros case (Case Concerning Gabcikovo-Nagymaros Project 1998) with a particular reference to article 5 of the UNWC (Convention 1997). Although it rests on the principle of 'equality of rights', equitable utilization should not be confused with 'equal division' of waters, but rather taken to construe that 'all states riparian to an international waterway stand on a par with each other' (Lipper 1967).

The principle of equitable utilization is the most widely acknowledged principle in international water law when it comes to negotiating the allocation of the waters of a transboundary river. In order to arrange for an equitable and efficient allocation of disputed waters, the relevant countries must take certain factors into consideration, such as socio-economic, hydrological and geopolitical conditions. The list of these factors is not exhaustive and, if other national and natural resources are available to meet the needs of the co-riparians, these resources have to be considered as well. Both article 5 of the 1966 ILA Helsinki Rules and article 6 of the 1997 UNWC provide a useful list of all relevant factors and circumstances to be taken into account in each particular case when determining the meaning of what an equitable and reasonable entitlement may be.

To illustrate, in the dispute surrounding the utilization of the Euphrates and Tigris Rivers, Turkey incorporated the doctrine of equitable and reasonable utilization as part of customary international law for transboundary water allocation in its proposal of the Three-Stage Plan (MFA 1996). The plan aims to determine the equitable and reasonable uses of Turkey, Syria and Iraq in a technical framework for a common criterion, based on riparian interests to allocate the available water to cover the needs of each party in a mutually satisfactory way. However, the implementation of such an elaborate plan called for a whole set of considerations, closely associated with the notions of water uses being beneficial, efficient, historical, acquired, existing or contemplated to be taken in relation to their harmful consequences – an issue that essentially bears on compatibility with another principle, harmless use (Kibaroglu et al. 2008).

The parallel fundamental principle, that is, the obligation not to cause significant harm to other watercourse states (no-harm rule) covers a whole range of neighbourly relations including issues pertaining to the protection of the environment. It is relevant, in particular, for two aspects of the law of international watercourses; the allocation and utilizations of such watercourses and the protection of their environment. Regarding the second aspect, environmental protection, the no-harm rule remains fully valid. Concerning the first aspect, however, that rule is of little use today. Most international watercourses are at present fully exploited or even over-used (Kibaroglu et al. 2008). Accordingly, Lucius Caflisch (1998) argues that the issue is no longer one of aim to prevent harm caused in situations of full or overuse, because every new or increased activity is harmful to existing utilization. This is why the negative no-harm rule had to be superseded by a positive rule which would make it possible to affect such an apportionment. In the same vein, Turkey's standpoint, as reflected in the official Manual prepared by the Ministry of Foreign Affairs (MFA), stresses that

The principle of not causing significant harm also enjoys wide support. According to this principle, riparian countries of a transboundary river should mutually abstain from causing any significant harm in their utilization of a watercourse. Turkey has never perceived of or used the water of the ET basin as a tool to put pressure on downstream riparian countries. Turkey has paid utmost attention to releasing an amount of water from the Euphrates that is in conformity with the principle of equitable utilization. (MFA 1995, 19)

Another main principle of customary international water law is the 'general obligation (duty) to cooperate'. As Christina Leb (2019, 95) articulates, the 'duty to cooperate' is integral to the implementation of other general principles in international water law. Cooperation allows for the equitable and reasonable utilization of transboundary watercourses and processes related to the prevention of or compensation for harm. Cooperation may take the form of, inter alia, exchange of data and information, notification, communication, consultations and negotiations. Cooperation in the basin can sometimes begin at a minimal level. In determining the manner of their cooperation, riparian states have the option of establishing joint mechanisms, as they deem necessary, to facilitate cooperation on relevant measures and procedures in the light of experience gained through cooperation in existing joint mechanisms and commissions in various regions. For instance, establishing and empowering of the Joint Technical Committee had been, in fact, an affirmative step to materialize cooperation among the riparians in the ET basin (see Chapter 4).

The basic idea behind this principle is that in order to achieve a regime of equitable and reasonable utilization, riparian states often have to cooperate with each other by taking affirmative steps, individually or jointly, with regard to the watercourse. Its acceptance as a part of the 1997 UNWC (article 8) is welcome, because it helps to convey the message that a regime of equitable utilization of an international watercourse system, together with the protection and preservation of its ecosystem, cannot be achieved solely through individual action by each riparian state acting in isolation; again, affirmative cooperation as a necessity in many cases (McCaffrey 1998). On the other hand, the same leading commentator argued that, although the supporting evidence cited in treaty practice and the practice of states was significant, 'duty to cooperate' was seen as a practical necessity rather than customary legal requirement for the implementation of the principle of equitable and reasonable utilization as well as for the proper functioning of other pertinent procedural requirements in part 3 of the UNWC (McCaffrey 1987). Indeed, the fundamental obligations of customary international water law, such as the obligation of prior notification, as formulated in part 3 of the 1997 UNWC, are directly related to this general principle. Riparian countries can benefit from implementing the duty to cooperate by coordinating the respective uses, planning and management of these resources to optimize sustainable use and mutual benefits that can be derived therefrom (Leb 2019, 95).

All in all, the general duty to cooperate is an established principle of international water law. Together and in combination with the other general principles of customary international water law, it guides the way towards achievement of sustainable and peaceful transboundary water resources management for the benefit of all (Leb 2019, 107).

On the other hand, 'duty of prior notice' also constitutes a substantial part of customary international water law and is defined as the 'duty to give prior notice where possible significant harm exists'. Even though Turkey agreed with general state practice regarding this principle, it also strongly argued that the 1997 UNWC did not serve to provide for the principle of a cooperative regime framework in the case of transboundary river basins. The main sticking point that Turkish diplomats contended represents part 3 of the Convention, which outlined procedural arrangements such as determining the appropriate period responses to notifications to take place. Essentially, it was argued that each transboundary watercourse possesses specific characteristics, and thus time limits ought to be determined according to the specific circumstances of each watershed with the consent of the riparians. In this context, in the ET basin, starting from the early 1960s, as the three riparians started to implement their unilateral water resources development plans, the bilateral and trilateral talks and the technical meetings held on ad hoc basis allowed the three riparians to exchange information on the stages they had achieved in their various development projects, namely the dams. The continuation of these meetings at a technical level, in particular, would evidently provide the necessary platform to exchange the unilateral development plans of the three riparians and possibly to harmonize them at the well-advanced stages of cooperation (see Chapter 4).

UN Watercourses Convention and Turkey's Position

The Convention on the Law of the Non-navigational Uses of International Watercourses (UNWC) was adopted on 21 May 1997 with the basic objective of establishing general principles for the use and management of international watercourses and to assist state parties in the resolution of disputes (Convention 1997). It encourages states to enter into specific agreements concerning the watercourses they share. It contains 37 articles dealing with the obligations of riparian states in utilizing international watercourses in an equitable and reasonable manner, while taking all appropriate measures to prevent the causing of significant harm, to consult with each other, to protect the environment and to resolve disputes.

The UNWC entered into force on 17 August 2014, marking the beginning of a new era of legally binding codes (Convention 1997). Three countries, namely Turkey, China and Burundi, had voted against the UNWC back in 1997. As the Convention has started to take effect, a fundamental question remains as to whether these opposing states will ever consider becoming party and, if not, how they will get along with neighbours without the guidance of the document (Chen et al. 2013). Turkey, like China, was seen as a 'hegemon' (Zeitoun and Warner 2006) in its riparian settings. Therefore, it is useful to look deeper into the factors that led to Turkey's rejection of the UNWC in 1997, and how its transboundary water policy discourse and practice have evolved dramatically ever since (Kibaroglu 2015).

Turkey's position towards the UNWC has constituted one significant aspect of its transboundary water policy. In this context, even though the reasons behind Turkey's rejection of the UNWC were officially stated during the Working Groups in New York in 1997, they were not properly elaborated in such a way to reflect its concerns and dilemmas to date. Hence, this section aims to perform this task. From its outset, Turkish officials argued that the UN has contributed significantly to the codification and progressive development of the rules of customary international law that apply to transboundary water resources (MFA 1995, 25–26).

Indeed, a thorough analysis of Turkey's state practice reveals that, since particularly the second reading of the Draft Articles on the Law of the Non-Navigational Uses of International Watercourses (UN General Assembly 1994), drafting of international water law has become a serious matter for Turkey, which is an upstream country in respect of several transboundary watercourses (MFA 1995, 25). That is to say, Turkey was actively interested in the drafting as well as making of the UNWC and paid particular attention to how the scope and substantive rules have evolved in drafting the Convention (Kibaroglu 2015).

Turkish authorities were confident that the idea of regarding transboundary water as a 'shared resource' would not be widely supported in the codification exercises on transboundary waters (The Yearbook of the International Law Commission 1987, 19). In this context, during the negotiations in the 1980s which took place surrounding the ET basin, the concept of 'sharing common water resources' through a mathematical formula has been proposed by Iraq in order to guarantee the utilization of water for its projects in the Euphrates River. Syria supported this idea in terms of approach. However, that concept turned out to be in contradiction with the principle of 'equitable utilization', which is the core idea of codification exercises in customary international water law (MFA 1995, 18).

Moreover, it was also acknowledged by the Turkish authorities that, 'the historical and acquired rights' claimed by Syria and, especially, Iraq were inadequate in the sense that, article 6 of the Draft Articles denotes that prior uses of water by downstream countries would represent only one of many factors to be taken into account in reaching an equitable utilization of a transboundary river (MFA 1995, 18). Furthermore, Turkish diplomats, as well as legal advisers (Personal correspondence 1997), considered it to be a 'very important development' (MFA 1995, 26) when the key concept of 'appreciable harm' (Draft Articles, first reading 1991) was changed to 'significant harm' in the second reading of the Draft Articles (1994). Thus, the level of accountability of upper riparian state, which may have caused damage to the lower riparian state raised the threshold from 'appreciable harm' to 'significant harm'. In this respect, Turkish officials expressed the view that a considerable improvement was achieved in the determination of reciprocal responsibilities of all riparians (MFA 1995, 26). In line with this reasoning, the Three-Stage Plan mainly used the terminology developed by the International Law Commission (ILC) of the United Nations entrusted with the codification of the law of non-navigational uses of international watercourses. Hence, an overview of the Turkish official stance with respect to the ET river basin leads one to the conclusion that it is in conformity with the essence of the Draft Articles (1994), namely with part 2: General Principles (Kibaroglu 2002).

Even though Turkey endorsed the primacy of the rule of 'equitable and reasonable use' during the discussions in the UN Sixth (Legal) Committee related to the Draft Articles (The Statement of Turkey 1997, 1–2), representatives from Turkey expressed serious dissatisfaction with the text of the draft Convention in New York in 1997 (The Turkish Government's Observations 1997). Most of the comments with regard to the UNWC relate to its key procedural provisions. During the discussions in the Working Group of the Whole, which was convened by the UN to consider the ILC Draft Articles of 1994 as the final draft, Turkey was particularly active in advancing its views on the governing rules of law applicable to the transboundary watercourses in order to ensure that the rights of upstream states are better protected.

Turkish officials asserted that the main purpose of the UNWC should be to achieve an equitable and reasonable arrangement regulating water utilization among the watercourse states: 'Any other approach turns the UNWC into a document which unilaterally restricts, in terms of both quantity and quality, the utilization rights of states in which watercourses originate; due attention should also be paid to establishing an equitable balance of rights and obligations among all watercourse states' (The Statement of Turkey 1997, 5). Yet, according to Turkish representatives, while these requirements were taken into account to a certain extent in the general principles set forth in part 2 of the UNWC, the same could not be said of part 3 and part 4 of the document.

Stephen McCaffrey (2018) underlines that 'Article 7(2) should be read in light of Articles 5 and 6, if harm is caused the overall objective must be the achievement of an equitable balance of uses'.

'It may be that, the balance is equitable even though uses in one State result in some harm in another. If not, however, the State causing the harm is to do its best to restore an equitable balance of uses including possibly curtailing its own uses and, where appropriate, providing any compensation necessary to complete restoration of the equitable balance. But it is clear that the relativity of the States' rights means that the State causing the harm may itself have to bear a portion of it itself, even if that means scaling back harm-causing projects'. (McCaffrey 2018, 164)

Turkey held that article 5, the 'most fundamental principle of the draft', must be understood 'in light of the fundamental principle of the sovereign rights of States over their territory'. Essentially, Turkey strongly endorsed article 5 as the 'governing principle' and suggested factors favourable to their particular situation be added to article 6 (The Statement of Turkey 1997, 36, 37–40). It should also be applied by taking fully into account all the particularities of the watercourses, including the distinction of whether they are transboundary by nature, or international (forming a boundary) between states. In relation to the first paragraph of article 5, Turkish officials suggested that the principle of 'optimal utilization', which comprises both protecting the watercourse and optimizing the interests of riparian states in a way that avoids water waste, ought to be added to article 5. From the Turkish standpoint, the first paragraph of article 5 did not clearly state that 'equitable utilization' should not be restricted to the protection only but should be seen also as comprising the concept of 'efficient use' (The Turkish Government's Observations 1997, 3).

In Turkey's view, the draft failed to establish the primacy of the principle of equitable utilization over the obligation not to cause significant harm. Turkey claimed that the no-harm rule was unbalanced and favoured downstream states. Thus, Turkey's concern that the contribution of each watercourse state be included in the formula so that an assessment of a reasonable use could be met in line with the principle of equitable utilization (The Turkish Government's Observations 1997).

The most dramatic change that the Turkish government officials proposed on the UNWC was deleting article 7 (the 'no harm rule') altogether. The Turkish delegation indicated that this deletion would not eliminate the no-harm rule altogether, but would, rather, subordinate it to the principle of 'equitable utilization' as outlined in the ILA's Helsinki Rules. To this end, the delegation of Turkey requested that it should be made explicit in the text that the no-harm rule would be 'without prejudice to the principle of equitable and reasonable utilization' (The Turkish Government's Observations 1997, 3).

Ambassador retired Mithat Rende, who acted as the director general responsible for environment, water and energy at the MFA, underscored that Turkey had always been committed to the article 5 and article 7 of the 1997 UNWC, despite the country having not signed the Convention. He emphasized that Turkey abides by article 5, which stipulates that watercourse states shall in their respective territories utilize an international watercourse in an equitable and reasonable manner in its water management operations with Iraq and Syria. In compliance with article 7 of the UNWC, Turkey claims that it engages in water management by taking measures to prevent causing any significant harm to other riparian states (Ersen 2018).

A leading learned writer, Patricia Wouters is of the opinion that the 'duty to cooperate' provides the legal foundation at the core of the UNWC (Wouters 2013). This broad principle is articulated in article 8. Thus, the Convention formulates the principle as a general obligation of watercourse states to 'cooperate on the basis of sovereign equality, territorial integrity, mutual benefit and good faith in order to attain optimal utilization and adequate protection of an international watercourse' (Convention, 1997). Turkey favours article 8 in its wording as well as its objectives because of its emphasis on concepts such as 'sovereign equality', 'territorial integrity', 'mutual benefit' and 'good faith' in order to attain 'optimal utilization' that is highly embraced by Turkey's water diplomacy cadres (MFA 2014).

Turkey also reserved its position on 'procedural rules': articles 12–19 proposed that those rules should be replaced with provisions referring primarily to consultations and other methods of cooperation. Turkey claimed that the Convention became more specific than had been intended in General Assembly resolution 51/206 of 17 December 1996; it should have merely established general principles, the application of which would be determined by means of specific agreements taking account of the particular characteristics of each watercourse (Working Group of the Whole 1997). Contrary to what should be the case with a framework convention, the UNWC established a mechanism for prior notification on planned measures which had no basis in general and customary principles of international law, and which created an obvious imbalance among states by setting up an obligation to obtain prior approval on planned measures from other riparians. Yet, the learned writer and former rapporteur of the ILC Stephen McCaffrey asserts that,

> Compliance with procedural obligations is necessary for the mainten-ance of a regime of equitable and reasonable utilization of an inter-national watercourse. Thus, whether these procedural obligations are seen as free-standing under customary international law or as part and parcel of equitable and reasonable utilization or environmental impact assessment, it seems undeniable that they are applicable and binding, whether or not they are found in a relevant treaty. (McCaffrey 2018, 171)

In a similar vein, Turkish government officials totally disagreed with the inclusion of article 33 (rules of dispute settlement) in the UNWC on the grounds that 'it would be more appropriate not to foresee any compulsory rules as regards the settlement of disputes, and to leave this issue to the dis-cretion of the concerned States'. Moreover, Turkish officials argued that 'a framework agreement should not attempt to set forth detailed rules in this respect, since it is virtually impossible to respond to the pressing needs of spe-cific and more often than not very complex cases of water disputes'. In this respect, Patricia Wouters found that in terms of practices in this field, 'there are distinctive regional differences on approaches to dispute settlement', and that 'what is important is the commitment to peacefully resolve any disputes that arise' (Wouters 1999). In that manner, Turkey is committed to the fun-damental tenet of international law that international disputes be resolved peacefully.

Turkey's cautious attitude towards the ILC 1994 Draft and its rejection of the 1997 UNWC arise from deep concerns about the fact that certain art-icles, especially in part 3 of the UNWC, have the potential to constrain its official stance in future negotiations for the allocation and management of the ET river basin. Turkish officials at the time were very keen on the point that the UNWC ought to maintain its original aim of constituting a frame-work document. Objection thus arose given the UNWC clearly comprises provisions, which go far beyond that scope. The Turkish contention is that the UNWC should be confined to setting forth a conceptual framework and principles regarding international watercourses. As to specific watercourses, bilateral and regional arrangements between watercourse states should be concluded by taking into account of the specific characteristics of each river system itself.

The official discourse developed by Turkish diplomats and legal advisers towards the UNWC rested, in fact, on the knowledge and experience that had been gained by monitoring developments in international water law through their interactions on various multilateral and bilateral platforms. Academics were also consulted at certain stages to comment on the Draft Articles (Kibaroglu 2015).

Turkey's negative stance towards the UNWC could also be a result of misconceptions and misperceptions regarding the interpretations of the UNWC, especially as they relate to the issue of dispute settlement and notification processes (Salman 2013). Turkish authorities have time and again emphasized that Turkey is geographically located in close proximity to one of world's most volatile regions. Hence, complex regional politics have constituted a serious obstacle to the nurturing of basin-wide cooperation and treaty-making, and this remains the case (Personal correspondences with officials at the MFA 2018).

Owing to these experiences and perceptions, Turkish officials have preferred to steer clear of the UNWC accession process and have not considered revising their position. Instead, in due course, since 1997, official discourse has focused on arguments aiming to justify and explain the country's stance. Furthermore, Turkish authorities have stated that the UNWC has lost credibility in light of the fact that it has taken so long to enter into force (Rende 2002, 8; Personal correspondences with officials at the MFA 2002, 2010, 2011, 2014).

Contrary to the legal interpretation that the UNWC has codified and progressively developed customary international water law, Turkish diplomats have claimed that Turkey has been a 'persistent objector' – particularly with regard to the rules on notification and dispute settlement as formulated in the UNWC. Even though Turkey has rejected certain provisions of the UNWC, it has also frequently expressed its adherence to the core norms of international water law, such as the obligation to prevent harm and equitable and reasonable utilization. Hence, as Adele Kirschner and Katrin Tiroch put forward, on the basis of such express commitment, it would be far-reaching to regard Turkey as a persistent objector (Kirschner and Tiroch 2012). Moreover, to be able to act as a persistent objector, it is also necessary for the members of the international community to accept this claim. In this particular case, there is no satisfactory evidence showing that Turkish argument is supported by states at regional or global levels.

On another front, the NGOs, namely the water- and environment-related associations, foundations, water user organizations, as well as chambers of various professions in Turkey, have not displayed an informed and systematic attention towards global legal instruments such as the UNWC. Their attention has mostly been directed towards legal developments at home and the harmonization process with the European Union (EU) pertaining to water policy and law (Kibaroglu et al. 2009).

With the entry into force of the UNWC, Turkey's position towards the Convention came back on the agenda of concerned circles in Turkey. Experts from the Turkish NGOs examined the UNWC from the perspectives of prevailing paradigms and urgent issues: they argue that the UNWC has a narrow scope and objectives which ignore the complex implications of climate change on freshwater resources. Moreover, in their contention, the increasing linkages between water, food, energy and environmental security have not been dealt within the UNWC sufficiently (Yildiz 2014).

UNECE Environmental Conventions and Turkey's Position

As part of the United Nations Economic and Social Council (ECOSOC), the United Nations Economic Commission for Europe (UNECE) was established in 1947 to encourage economic cooperation among its member states in pan-European region. The broad aim of UNECE's environment activities is to safeguard the environment and human health, and to promote sustainable development in its member countries in line with Agenda 21. UNECE has negotiated five environmental treaties, all of which are now in force:

- Convention on Long-range Transboundary Air Pollution (Geneva, 1979)
- Convention on Environmental Impact Assessment (EIA) in a Transboundary Context (EIA/Espoo Convention, 1991)
- Convention on the Protection and Use of Transboundary Watercourses and International Lakes (Helsinki Convention, 1992)
- Convention on the Transboundary Effects of Industrial Accidents (Helsinki, 1992)
- Convention on Access to Information, Public Participation in Decision-making and Access to Justice in Environmental Matters (Aarhus Convention, 1998)

Of all these Conventions, Turkey has only been party to the Convention on Long-range Transboundary Air Pollution since 1983 (Kramer and Kibaroglu 2011).

UNECE Convention on the Protection and Use of Transboundary Watercourses and International Lakes and Turkey's Position

The UNECE Convention on the Protection and Use of Transboundary Watercourses and International Lakes (hereinafter, UNECE TWC) provides an example of how regional legal framework, especially when assisted by a well-developed institutional mechanism, can bolster transboundary water cooperation at various levels – basin, regional and global. This instrument is aimed at limiting transboundary impact in all transboundary basins in the UNECE area. Endorsed by 43 states, the conventional regime is supported institutionally by the Meeting of the Parties (MoP), Secretariat and a number of subsidiary bodies created under the UNECE TWC (UN Treaty Collection 2019). Its participants are urged to:

> Cooperate on the basis of equality and reciprocity, in particular through bilateral and multilateral agreements, in order to develop harmonized policies, programs and strategies covering the relevant catchment areas, or parts thereof, aimed at the prevention, control and reduction of transboundary impact and aimed at the protection of the environment of transboundary waters or the environment influenced by such waters, including the marine environment. (Art. 2(6))

Now into its third decade of existence, the Convention is open for universal accession. On 28 November 2003, parties to the UNECE TWC adopted amendments to articles 25 and 26 that would allow accession to the Convention by states which are not members of the UNECE (UNECE Helsinki Convention 2003). On 8 November 2012, the conditions for the entry into force of the above-mentioned amendments were met, entering into force on 6 February 2013 (UN Treaty Collection 2019).

The UNECE TWC plays an important role in encouraging and supporting river basin and transboundary cooperation in the pan-European region, including Central Asia. Being a framework document, the Convention provides a set of basic obligations and general guidelines, which must be operationalized through watercourse-specific agreements to be concluded by the states sharing the same watercourse. Given the prominence of the regime established by the Convention and its subsidiary instruments (protocols and guidelines) and institutions, it may be sensible for the riparian states of the ET river basin to carefully examine the UNECE TWC in practice and its possible applicability within their particular regional context.

In this regard, the 25 years of relatively successful transboundary cooperation across Europe under the umbrella of the UNECE TWC offers an important reference point for Turkey. With the Convention now open for universal application, it is appropriate to explore possible lessons learned from its continuous implementation. On several occasions, the UNECE TWC MoP has reiterated its support for extending the Convention's impact around the globe, aimed at 'strengthening national measures and transboundary cooperation for the protection and ecologically sound management of transboundary surface waters and ground waters' (UNECE 2012). Since 2009, over twenty non-UNECE countries have participated in activities under the Water Convention, recognizing its relevance and role beyond the UNECE region. Eighteen non-UNECE States took part in the sixth MoP in Rome on 28–30 November 2012. During that meeting, Iraq and Tunisia expressed a strong interest in joining the UNECE TWC as soon as possible. To support these objectives, the MoP has then appointed an Implementation Committee, a 'simple, non-confrontational, non-adversarial, transparent, supportive and cooperative' mechanism to support implementation of the Convention.

Turkey has been consistently advised by the European Commission, through its regular progress reports, to become party to those international conventions, UNECE environmental conventions, in particular those to which the EU is a party (Sümer 2013). Communication between the EU and Turkey constitutes, in fact, an obligation which Turkey needs to fulfil before the membership to the EU (Saner 2006). Turkey's relevant institutions, namely the Department of Water Law and Political Development, under the DGWM of the Ministry of Agriculture and Forestry, has been studying and analyzing the UNECE conventions particularly by comparing and contrasting them with the national legislation. The conventions have also been under review particularly with respect to their possible impacts or pressures on Turkey's official stance vis-à-vis transboundary waters by the MFA.

An official comprehensive presentation by the Department of Water Law and Political Development indicates that the general provisions of the UNECE TWC includes ambiguous legal wording which emphasizes 'any transboundary impact' in article 2/1: 'The Parties shall take all appropriate measures to prevent, control and reduce any transboundary impact'. Accordingly, 'any transboundary impact' does not constitute an objective or scientific concept or a relation thus constituting a major legal uncertainty' (Ministry of Forestry and Water Affairs n.d.).

Turkish experts go on to stress that the wording of the UNECE TWC 'is not clear, particularly regarding as to how transboundary waters can be used in a reasonable and equitable way' (article 2/c). Moreover, 'the Convention (1992) does not make necessary the differentiation between 'boundary' and 'transboundary waters', whereas Turkey's water diplomacy practices uphold the position that those two types of resources should be treated differently when water allocations are decided upon' (Ministry of Forestry and Water Affairs n.d.).

Turkish experts see the inclusion of transboundary groundwater along with surface water as another problematic area of the UNECE TWC. They assert that 'technically river basin boundaries do not always overlap with borders of the transboundary aquifers, and add that, those two types of water resources have distinct hydrological cycles causing complexity in determining their physical relationships' (Ministry of Forestry and Water Affairs n.d.).

It seems evident that one of Turkey's major concerns about the UNECE TWC has been not just its focus on environmental regulations, but its content as a dispute resolution mechanism. The UNECE TWC, in article 22, states that 'if a dispute arises between two or more Parties about the interpretation or application of this Convention, they shall seek a solution by negotiation or by any other means of dispute settlement acceptable to the parties to the dispute'. The Convention also adds in paragraph 2 that,

> When signing, ratifying, accepting, approving or acceding to this Convention, or at any time thereafter, a Party may declare in writing to the Depositary that, for a dispute not resolved in accordance with paragraph 1 of this article, it accepts one or both of the following means of dispute settlement as compulsory in relation to any Party accepting the same obligation: (a) Submission of the dispute to the International Court of Justice; (b) Arbitration in accordance with the procedure set out in annex IV. (Convention 1992)

Turkey has been traditionally averse to third-party involvement in dispute settlement (see Chapter 2). Thus, Turkish experts at the Department of Water Law and Political Development interpreted the UNECE TWC clauses on adjudication as compulsory, and advised the Turkish government about the negative repercussions they may cause along with other articles such as article 9/h 'exchange of information on existing and planned uses of water and related installations that are likely to cause transboundary impact' on Turkey's national interests in transboundary settings. By referring to article 9/j 'participation in the implementation of environmental impact assessments relating to transboundary waters, in accordance with appropriate international regulations', Turkish experts have often cautioned that in the event Turkey becomes party to UNECE environmental conventions, their implementation may have negative consequences for Turkey's future plans regarding water supply, irrigation and hydropower development in various transboundary river basins (Ministry of Forestry and Water Affairs n.d.).

While in Europe, the pollution of transboundary watercourses represents the most serious challenge, this is not necessarily the case in other regions, such as the Middle East, where competition over increasingly scarce water resources overshadow all other concerns. Turkish experts emphasize that each transboundary watercourse possess sui generis technical, socioeconomic and political characteristics. Additionally, most of the Middle Eastern countries face frequent instabilities and hot conflicts, which further

complicates transboundary water cooperation. Under these abnormal political circumstances, Turkish experts assert that it is not possible to prepare joint
EIA reports with Iraq and Syria for the dams across the Euphrates and Tigris
as stipulated by the 1991 Espoo Convention (Ministry of Forestry and Water
Affairs n.d.).

On the other hand, Act. 4982 on the Right of Information Acquirement,
which was adopted in 2003 at the Turkish parliament, may be evaluated as
being in the scope of the UNECE Aarhus Convention (1998) to the extent
that it lays down the guidelines and procedures for individuals to exercise
their right of information acquirement in accordance with the principles of
equality, neutrality and openness which are the fundamentals of democratic
and transparent administration However, the Turkish experts point out that
Aarhus Convention (1998) encompasses more comprehensive rights than the
Turkish legislation pertaining to right of information and document acquirement; public participation in decision making and access to justice in environmental matters. It is pointed out that if Turkey becomes party to the Aarhus
Convention, then it will have to undertake further arrangements in domestic
legislation. For instance, Turkey would have to adopt more inclusive legislation
for participation by involving the public directly in environmental planning
and policy, along with professional and NGOs (Ministry of Forestry and Water
Affairs n.d.).

The fact that the amendments were adopted by the UNECE Helsinki
Convention (2003) and the EIA/Espoo Convention (2001), which allow
accession by countries outside the UNECE region that are not members of
the UNECE, also seemed to be another complicating factor for the Turkish
authorities in their deliberations of membership to these conventions. The
possibility that Syria and Iraq may become parties to these conventions in the
future adds further thorny questions in balancing the transboundary water
strategy with the stipulations of these conventions (MFA 2010).

Chapter 4

THE ROLE OF HISTORY AND GEOGRAPHY IN TURKEY'S EVOLVING WATER DIPLOMACY

Overview

While the assertion that 'geography and history play a significant role in foreign policy-making' (Cohen 2015) is a point that has been well contested, in the case of the Republic of Turkey, the country's own state practices demonstrate that its geographical characteristics have played an important role in the determination of at least its transboundary water policy. Turkey lies at the upstream of several transboundary rivers – namely, the Euphrates–Tigris (ET), Coruh and Kura; it is considered at least one source of the many transboundary tributaries of the River Aras, and is in a downstream position regarding the Orontes and Meric Rivers.

The total surface area of the drainage basins of these rivers comes to 256,000 km^2, which constitutes around one-third of Turkey's total surface area. The average water potential of these rivers within Turkey is 70 billion m^3 per year, equivalent to 30 per cent of the overall water potential of the country. Transboundary rivers form the basis of 22 per cent of Turkey's borders, constituting at least some of the dividing markers with all neighbours – namely, Greece, Bulgaria, Georgia, Armenia, Azerbaijan, Iran, Iraq and Syria. Moreover, Turkey presides over a significant amount of arable and irrigable land in these river basins; the ET river basin alone constitutes 20 per cent of the country's arable land. Considering the growing demands of the increasing urban and rural populations of these basins, geography clearly lies at the fore in the formulation of transboundary water policies (Kibaroglu 2015).

Since the first years of the Republic of Turkey (established in 1923), the changing nature of relations with various neighbours has determined the subsequent evolution of transboundary water policies. Hence, from the early 1920s until the late 1950s, when Turkey and its neighbours were all engaged with establishing state bureaucracies, their aligned concerns and similar need for socio-economic development paved the way for an overall productive relationship to ensue. Throughout this period, Turkey signed various bilateral treaties, which mostly concerned the delimitation and the nature of use of boundary rivers (Kibaroglu et al. 2011). Also significant is that, at the time, none of the relevant countries pursued any major development projects which would have resulted in utilization of water by one to the detriment of the others (Kibaroglu et al. 2012). From the 1950s onward, however, Turkey, along with her neighbours, had built up the technical and financial capabilities needed to carry out large-scale water development projects, putting many at odds with others, particularly regarding the ET river basin, where uncoordinated and competitive transboundary water policies became the norm.

Furthermore, the geopolitical dynamics of the Cold War period began to have a decisive impact on Turkey's regional and bilateral relations with its neighbours – no less in its transboundary water policies than in other spheres of foreign policy. Although Cold War conditions were not conducive for Turkey – as a NATO member – in fostering fruitful transboundary water relations with Syria, Iraq, the Soviet Union (USSR) and Bulgaria as members of the 'enemy camp', Turkey pursued transboundary water policies which centred around the building of institutional structures with neighbours through diplomatic mechanisms and the instruments of international law, whether by negotiations, treaties or the peopling of technocratic water committees. In this context, the Arpacay Dam, which was constructed jointly with Armenia (Protocol 1964), the 1987 protocol signed with Syria as an (interim) agreement for sharing the waters of the Euphrates (Protocol 1987) and a series of protocols and agreements signed with Bulgaria, are testaments to Turkey's determination to solve the disputes with its neighbours over the transboundary water resources in a peaceful manner through diplomatic mechanisms, as envisaged in the UN Charter, as well as through customary international law.

However, the outstanding issues which remained concerning Turkey's various transboundary rivers were overlaid, or at least influenced, by multifaceted interstate conflicts involving other core political issues, such as terrorism, recognition of borders and territorial disputes. River basins in general, seem to be found located in areas inseparable from those traditionally characterized by political tensions. These political circumstances aggravated disputes, such as those concerning water policy, which, in a more favourable political climate, would have been solved with relative ease (Kibaroglu et al. 2005).

There exist variations concerning the precise nature of these disputes. While, for instance, those related to the ET, the Sarisu (Aras basin) and the

Orontes Rivers mainly concern guaranteed river flow, the issue at hand pertaining to the Coruh River has been sediment flow. Between the Meric riparians, flood protection is a matter of concern, in addition to water quantity and quality issues. However, water quality generally plays a minor role, while quantity/water flow issues still dominate, mirroring respective weak national water quality provisions or their weak enforcement measures (Kibaroglu et al. 2005).

In addition, where Turkey represents the upstream country, classical upstream-downstream conflicts have occurred, characterized by the divergent interests of the riparian states. The respective cases of the Meric and Orontes Rivers are important exceptions with Turkey as a downstream riparian. The knowledge that Turkey lies upstream at several important transboundary rivers (ET, Coruh, etc.) goes hand in hand with the widespread international perception of (powerful) upstream states aggravating conflicts, or being reluctant to cooperation, and has also clearly contributed to Turkey's rather dubious 'international water cooperation reputation'. However, Turkey's water diplomacy practices in both constellations illustrate that cooperation can principally be developed in upstream-downstream constellations too, and that location is not the only or necessarily decisive factor in explaining whether and when cooperation takes place (Kibaroglu et al. 2005).

Turkey's water diplomacy practices in many of the transboundary basins must be understood in the context of the limited water availability suffered by several (or even all) riparian countries, making the allocation of water quantity, that is, agreements on guaranteed river flow, an important and potentially discordant issue. Because of natural conditions and basic political decisions on national development, Turkey, as well as its neighbours, relies heavily on water for irrigation and hydropower production – with water being an important and, in some respects, strategic resource for the national economy. Consequently, regional water negotiations are frequently exacerbated and dominated by states insisting on their sovereign right to water due to economic needs. Although a number of bilateral protocols and other arrangements have been successfully agreed upon and signed, they are mostly outdated and fail to respond to current needs and associated issues regarding usage and protection. Bilateral negotiations at various levels have failed to blossom into comprehensive transboundary agreements or treaties that could help regulate potentially inharmonious claims by riparian states. Similarly, the water diplomacy practices of the relevant riparian states have not been successful in creating a comprehensive river basin organization or committee that might serve as a permanent forum for the accommodation of water disputes or in fostering healthy cooperation over water.

Water Diplomacy Frameworks in Turkey's Transboundary River Basins

Turkey's water diplomacy practices regarding its individual transboundary river basins have faced complex and multifaceted challenges because of the discernible differences in terms of the hydro-geopolitical constellations, respective bilateral political relations and agreements and the organizational approaches surrounding the areas of dispute. Below, water diplomacy frameworks of Turkey in transboundary settings are analyzed by highlighting the issues peculiar to each river basin.

Meric River Basin

To the northwest, Turkey shares the Meric river basin with Bulgaria and Greece. The Meric River (Maritsa in Bulgarian and Evros in Greek), a major Balkan water source, flows from Bulgaria along the Turkish Greek border into the Aegean. At the point where the Meric approaches the tri-border between Bulgaria, Greece and Turkey, it first forms a natural boundary between Bulgaria and Greece for around 15 km, then, for about 187 km, it forms the border between Turkey and Greece, continuing through the Thrace region before finally entering Aegean Sea. Shortly following its course along the three-way border, close to the Turkish city of Edirne, the Meric is joined by the Arda River from the south and the Tunca River from the north. The Ergene River springs forth from the Istranca Mountains in Turkey and joins the Meric around 30 km north of the mouth of the river (Kibaroglu et al. 2005). As the Meric River forms the border between Greece and Turkey, Turkish authorities consider it to be an 'international river', and a 'transboundary river' where it crosses the border between Bulgaria and Turkey (see Chapter 2). The founding treaty of the Turkish Republic, the Treaty of Lausanne (1923), even includes a regulation recognizing the Meric River as the basis of the border between Greece and Turkey.

Compared to other transboundary river basins (e.g. ET river basin) which Turkey shares with its neighbours, the Meric River has a relatively smaller drainage basin and provides only a limited amount of water resources for Turkey. However, there is a burgeoning water demand in the basin due to the intensive agricultural practices of the riparian countries. The basin is also highly industrialized and densely populated with cities. Thus, water quality in the basin suffers from agricultural run-off and the discharge of untreated industrial effluents and urban wastewater. Moreover, there are high seasonal and annual variations in flow.

Several main dams and regulators operate in the basin, particularly in its upstream state, Bulgaria, mainly for irrigation and hydropower production. Turkey and Greece have complained about Bulgarian dams regarding their effect on the quantity of water that ends up on the downstream parts of the basin. Furthermore, the way Bulgarian dams operate has been another source of contention, conflicting as they do with flood protection requirements regarding flow retention in their reservoirs (Eleftheriadou et al. 2015). However, poor water management and the operational status of Bulgaria's dams are joined by the capacity of dikes and the land use regime in the flood plains of the river network of all three riparian countries as a key factor behind the repeated flooding suffered in the area (Skias et al. 2011).

The delta of the river, protected by the Ramsar Convention and also a Natura 2000 site, is known for its rare ecosystem and is considered an important natural resource (Mylopoulos et al., 2008) the maintenance of which remains another major challenge.

Water Diplomacy Frameworks

The water diplomacy framework in the Meric basin must be considered within the broader context of the political relations of the riparian countries. Relations between Greece and Turkey, in particular, have been far from friendly over the past century. Since the Turkish War of Liberation (1919–22) fought mainly with Greece, a number of major issues have cropped up, not least the Cyprus dispute and conflicting territorial claims made over the Aegean Sea. In addition, the Meric basin is situated in Thrace, an area home to diverse communities, with Turkish minorities living in both Greek and the Bulgarian parts of Thrace as well as Greek minorities who used to live in Turkey. The minority conflict is the oldest such issue between Turkey and Greece and has been the main problem affecting Bulgarian-Turkish relations since the end of the Second World War (Kibaroglu et al. 2005).

Historically, political distrust between the three countries hampered any cooperation. However, in the 2000s, rapprochement between Turkey and Greece, Bulgaria's joining of the European Union (EU) and the prospect of EU membership for Turkey had positive effects on transboundary water management. Bilateral relations in the Meric basin have improved over the last decades, providing a political context for negotiations and for the settling of major water-related conflicts. On the one hand, membership in the EU provides a general framework for cooperation between Greece and Bulgaria. On the other, the Accession Partnership between the EU and Turkey has further provided opportunities for cooperation between Turkey and its European neighbours.

The EU's main legislative instrument, namely the Water Framework Directive (WFD) explicitly requires Member States to assign transboundary river basin districts for basins lying within the EU's territory and to coordinate in particular all programmes to achieve the WFD's environmental objectives. Where international river basins extend beyond the territories of the EU, the WFD requires Member States only to 'endeavor' to establish appropriate coordination and to produce a single river basin management plan with the relevant non-Member States, with the aim of achieving the objectives of the WFD throughout the river basin district (Kibaroglu et al. 2005). However, no such full-fledged coordination has yet taken place between the Meric's riparians (Yildiz 2019a).

With regard to potential water cooperation, it can be observed that the water management systems of each of the three riparians have been undergoing a transition period moving towards the European acquis communautaire, though each case has unfolded in a unique way (Kramer and Schelling 2011). Similar water management systems and approaches in line with the EU framework directives may facilitate transboundary water cooperation among the three riparians in the future (Kibaroglu et al. 2005).

Water Treaties and Water Diplomacy

The water diplomacy practices in the basin have produced historical interstate agreements, albeit on purely a bilateral basis, which cover the issues of flood protection and joint infrastructural projects as well as general environmental cooperation including conservation of protected areas. Issues of water allocation, on the other hand, remain unsettled.

The first agreement formalized between Greece and Turkey was signed in 1934, followed by an agreement in 1955 regarding the construction of flood protection works – only a small number of which were eventually realized (Bilen 2000). In an additional attempt to mitigate the effects of flooding, the two countries agreed on the Protocol on the Improvements of the Meric River Watercourse Constituting a Significant Portion of the Turkish-Greek Thracian Border. In 2000, the two countries signed the Memorandum of Understanding Concerning Cooperation on Environmental Protection aiming at the exchange of scientific, technical and legal information (Kramer and Schellig 2011). In 2006, a cross-border cooperation agreement was signed for the prevention and control of floods in the riparian region of Meric. More recently, a flood forecasting and early warning system was implemented between Turkey and Bulgaria, by which alarm levels were defined at certain water level forecast locations along the Meric River (Tuncok 2015).

Conflicting interests over the development of water resources along the Meric basin mainly exist between Bulgaria and Turkey. Turkey's plans to increase irrigation in the Meric basin has the potential to aggravate the situation. In order to make more water available for irrigation in Turkey, it was proposed, as a compromise, however, that Turkey should consider the possibility, despite the additional cost, to unilaterally construct off-stream storage facilities which may collect excess winter outflow from Bulgarian and Greek dams (Ozis et al. 2002). In addition, Turkey has proposed joint dam projects with Bulgaria which would also serve as a means for flood control.

The issue of climate change has also emerged as a potential impediment to effective long-range policies and management of water resources in the Meric basin. Climate change puts a layer of uncertainty over the effectiveness of existing water resources management practices. This is especially troubling for the future of transboundary water agreements. Turkey has been severely affected by climate change–induced floods in Meric river basin. The principles of Turkish water diplomacy provide for the shifting nature of meteorological and hydrological conditions along transboundary river basins by adding considerations over the risks posed by climate change in transboundary water agreements (Yildiz 2019a).

Although historical agreements exist between Turkey and Bulgaria, Turkey and Greece, and Bulgaria and Greece, the exchange of information – early warnings, for instance – and the operation of dams during floods have not been satisfactory. International support, extended particularly by the EU, to the three riparian countries supporting the establishment of a joint programme for flood warning and control have the potential to provide for such effective transboundary water management as is needed, however.

Existing agreements do not cover legal provisions on water quality standards. Likewise, arrangements on the exchange of data and information mainly focus on information on flooding, while cross-border availability of data on water quality is reported to be a problem (Mylopoulos et al. 2004). In addition, no agreement exists that would provide for a minimum inflow of freshwater into the delta, satisfying the water needs of the ecosystem and prevent salt water intrusion and siltation.

While there are several technical projects between Bulgaria and Turkey as well as between Bulgaria and Greece that are ongoing, none of these water-related initiatives involve all three riparians. However, relations between local governments that aim to promote cross-border cooperation among the three countries exist (Skias et al. 2011). These networks, an innovative component of water diplomacy frameworks, deal mainly with issues such as tourism, labour, health and culture, but also facilitate cooperation on humanitarian assistance during flooding. While they have no mandate to take actions with regard to water management, they may provide a stepping stone towards tri-lateral projects with regard to managing the water resources of the Meric basin. Papayannis (2004) states that while the population in the border region is open to cross-border cooperation, there are reservations at the state level, especially from military authorities. However, such local networks may pro-vide the pressure needed on a national level to facilitate transboundary cooperation on issues of importance for the local population (Kramer and Schellig 2011).

Irrigated Agriculture, Droughts and Water Diplomacy

The major use of water in the basin is agricultural irrigation in both Bulgaria and Turkey. The diversion and storage of water for irrigation purposes, mainly in Bulgaria, has resulted in reduced river flows downstream. On the other hand, due to the subsequent water shortages caused by this, Turkey has on occasion, been deprived of irrigation needed for its paddy fields (Ozis et al. 2002).

In 1993, Turkey's water diplomacy cadres were forced to take effective measures in response to a severe drought in the Meric basin. The relevant authorities, namely the Ministry of Foreign Affairs (MFA) and State Hydraulic Works (DSI) recognized the need for cooperation in order to alleviate the severe consequences suffered as a result of this on both the Turkish and the Bulgarian side of the river basin. Turkish diplomats negotiated and signed the Agreement on Assistance and Cooperation in the Field of Water for Reducing the Negative Effects of the Drought with Bulgaria. The agreement stated that Bulgaria, on a one-off basis limited to 1993, should provide add-itional water to Turkey from the Tunca River (a main tributary of Meric river basin). In turn, Turkey would pay 0.12 USD per m^3 of water provided by Bulgaria. Accordingly, Turkey purchased 15,866,000 m^3 of irrigation water from Bulgaria at a cost of 1,903,904 USD. This agreement represents one of the rarest cases in transboundary river management literature, in that a downstream riparian country (Turkey) was obliged to purchase water from an upstream neighbour. International water law upholds the principle of equit-able utilization for sharing transboundary waters, and state practices regarding this principle fail to support any agreement which would involve a monetary trade-off for water between upstream and downstream riparian countries.

Conflicting claims by Turkey and Bulgaria over water for the purpose of irrigation constitute an impediment to the implementation of effective Turkish irrigation projects. On the other hand, promoting joint riparian efforts to increase the efficient use of water for irrigation would not only help to reduce pressure on available water resources, but also foster broader cooperation in water resource management. The same applies to efforts on reducing pollution by agricultural run-off.

Floods and Water Diplomacy

Flooding is a major problem in the Meric basin. Floods in the basin over the last decade have caused significant damage. Due to the increasing frequency and magnitude of these floods, transboundary collaboration in flood protection requires concerted attention. Although experts from Bulgaria, Greece and Turkey all concur that the major flooding has been primarily caused by coincident string of unfavourable flow patterns and extreme meteorological conditions due to climate change, they disagree on how water management, or the lack thereof, also contributes (Kramer and Schellig 2011). According to Turkish and Greek experts, the management of Bulgarian reservoirs is not sufficient: maintaining high water levels in reservoirs close to the border (e.g. Ivailovgrad Dam) increases the risk of uncontrolled flooding, they argue, because, in cases of heavy rainfall and snow melt, Bulgaria ends up flooding agricultural land downstream in order to prevent dams from breaking (Yildiz 2019a). On the other hand, experts emphasize that inappropriate floodplain management in Greece and Turkey, such as changing land use patterns and intensification of agriculture as occurred since the 1970s and 1980s, also increases risk and vulnerability for downstream riparians. Furthermore, the impact of floods was exacerbated by the lack of an appropriate early warning system between Bulgaria and downstream riparians (Kramer and Schellig 2011).

Thus, one of the most urgent fields of action in Turkey's water diplomacy has long taken the form of initiatives for flood protection. Although bilateral water agreements exist between Turkey and Bulgaria, adherence to them has not been satisfactory in the past. After the severe floods of March 2005, Turkey is reported to have sent Bulgaria a note of protest due to her alleged failure to abide by these bilateral agreements (Kramer and Schellig 2011). Likewise, Greece also blamed Bulgaria for the incidents. Subsequently, several gauging stations were installed along the Meric, Arda and Tunca Rivers in Bulgarian territory. These allowed warning downstream riparians 15 hours in advance of the occurrence of the 2006 spring flooding. Likewise, the prime ministers of Greece and Bulgaria signed an official declaration in April 2006 that outlined a new framework for bilateral partnership regarding, among others, 'policy measures and actions to avert floods in Evros River basin' and decided that the first step should be the construction of monitoring and early warning systems (Kramer and Schellig 2011). Bilateral technical projects such as those funded under the Poland and Hungary Assistance for the Restructuring of the

Economy-Cross Border Cooperation (PHARE-CBC) programme have since worked to improve early warning capacities of the basin countries. However, the monitoring system is still considered insufficient for effective flood risk management (Darama 2009).

Turkish water diplomacy cadres have mainly focused on encouraging better control methods, such as improving the operation of dams, management of floodplains and improvement of early warning systems as crucial ways to avert flooding. Moreover, the construction of additional dams upstream is often considered favourable by Turkish authorities. This becomes obvious, for example, in the planning of an extensive dam project on the Tunca River close to the Bulgarian-Turkish border: The Suakacagi dam project has been in the planning phase since 1968. In the aftermath of the 2005 floods, however, Ankara and Sofia agreed to advance the project in order to mitigate flood problems in Turkey. The two sides agreed on appointing experts to develop the project and to establish a Turkish-Bulgarian joint technical commission for the implementation of the project. The dam was expected to not only serve as flood protection, but also serve further benefits for both countries. It could, for example, also provide irrigation water for the area around Edirne and Kirklareli in Turkey (Kibaroglu et al. 2005). In April 2005, a technical delegation from Bulgaria paid a visit to the DSI Regional Directorate in Edirne. Consensus was reached regarding the dam site and a protocol was signed. However, the project did not pass the planning stage and could not be realized due to disagreements between Turkey and Bulgaria over land rights.

Turkey's diplomatic interventions did not materialize into joint projects aimed at coping with flooding effectively, all the while as flood protection measures became increasingly urgent. Thus, Turkey decided to take measures into its own hands, building a by-pass channel to protect Edirne province and its agricultural areas, at a cost of around 10 million USD. But, as experts, such as Dursun Yildiz, stressed, despite flood protection structures being built and methods such as dredging being widely implemented in Turkey, Greece and Turkey still need basin-wide preventive flood management measures (Yildiz 2019a). In this regard, it is essential for Bulgaria, Greece and Turkey to cooperate in the planning of flood prevention and protection measures together. This is of extra importance when one considers that the Turkish and Greek reaches of the river basin are located only just above sea level and therefore are unsuitable for efficient engineering measures for flood prevention (Yildiz 2019a).

It is unfortunate that the three riparian states, two of which are currently members of the EU, have not taken any measure to prevent the floods collaboratively and that a basin-wide flood protection cooperation between the riparian states has not been achieved. So far, the three countries have only been able to establish an 'early-warning system' in the basin through an EU project (Angelidis et al. 2010). This system has allowed the reduction of casualties, but has not prevented serious economic losses and social problems resulting from devastating floods.

In the future, not just infrastructure but also the development of an integrated basin-wide management approach should be considered when addressing problems of flood control and water allocation. While transboundary cooperation on the issue of flood protection has proven to be complicated on a trilateral as well as bilateral level, existing bilateral work on flood forecasting should still be considered a launch pad for broader cooperation in pursuit of further water resources management and initiatives. Transboundary flooding induced by climate change and dam operation has meant that this issue requires more attention than ever before. Experts argue that a paradigm shift from classical hydro-diplomacy to a more proactive one is needed (Yildiz 2019a). The adopted coping strategies in the Meric basin, however, remain rather more technocratic than management-oriented. With regard to a more integrated approach to flood risk management, the EU Floods Directive provides orientation for long-term developments in the basin. It explicitly states that Member States shall coordinate their flood risk management practices in shared river basins, including third counties, and shall in solidarity not undertake measures that would increase the flood risk in neighbouring countries (European Commission 2007).

Water Quality Control, Environmental Protection and Water Diplomacy

Water quality remains an unsolved issue. No agreements yet exist regarding the water quality of the basin, and upstream water pollution is increasingly perceived as an issue by Turkey and Greece. EU-membership for all three riparian countries offers a good incentive to increase transboundary cooperation (Kramer and Schellig 2011). The prospect of joint nature conservation activities and a legal framework for the protection of wetlands provides further incentives for collaboration in water resource management. Such collaboration could also contribute to good neighbourly relations between the riparian countries, and among the communities living along the border regions. Any solution to this problem, arising, to a significant degree, from insufficient wastewater treatment, would need large investments in infrastructure (Kibaroglu et al. 2005). Ongoing EU-cooperation programmes with accession countries may lead to some alleviation of the problem by supporting the construction of wastewater treatment plants upstream. The Instrument for Pre-Accession Assistance for Turkey, for example, which replaces earlier programmes such as PHARE, includes a priority axis on improved water

supply, sewerage and wastewater treatment services with a financial contribution from the EU. However, EU member countries, as well as the accession
country Turkey, are obliged to implement the EU Urban Wastewater Directive,
which would result in a significant improvement of the river water quality
(Kramer and Schellig 2011).

High sediment loads – a consequence of erosion in the catchment areas –
causes siltation in the river delta and the forming of sand islets. Turkey has
launched a programme to clean up the sand islets in order to maintain regular
flow. However, technical cooperation by the other riparians is deemed necessary to fully address this issue (Yildiz 1999a). Yakup Darama (2009) reports on
a cooperation project between Bulgaria and Turkey with regard to the issue
that is yet awaiting implementation.

A joint programme for transboundary cooperation on hazard prevention
could, for example, be the scope of an EU Twinning project. Several initiatives
touch the issue of transboundary cooperation in the basin. Building on these
initiatives or providing technical or financial support to them could improve
the status of ecosystems and biodiversity in the basin area and foster cooperation between the riparian countries in water management.

Aspirations for EU accession require Turkey to adopt the WFD and the
United Nations Economic Commission for Europe (UNECE) Helsinki
Convention (1992). Using the Meric river basin as a pilot area, Turkey could
be assisted in implementing the relevant legislation, thus providing an agenda
for transboundary cooperation. Such an initiative could finally aim at the
establishment of a trilateral river basin commission, in the same way as exist
in other European transboundary basins.

Coruh River Basin

The Coruh River is located in north-eastern Turkey and shared by two countries: Turkey and Georgia. It is of high economic importance for Turkey
because of its largely undeveloped but economically exploitable hydropower
potential. The dams in Turkey, operational and planned, have become a major
issue of water diplomacy between two riparian countries.

Because of climatic conditions, the river carries plenty of water throughout
the year, albeit with remarkable seasonal variations (Yildiz 1999a). At present,
water quantity is not a relevant transboundary issue. The current allocation
rule (50:50) is not under dispute. Since the proposed dams will predominantly be used for hydropower generation, the impact of the infrastructure on
annual water flows from Turkey to Georgia is rather limited and, unsurprisingly, transboundary water quantity questions are therefore not at the centre
of political debates. Furthermore, Georgia is not dependent on the Coruh

River for energy and water; which clearly reduces the potential for conflict (Klaphake and Scheumann 2011).

The main outstanding issue regards the potential negative impact Turkish dams will have on the sediment regime and on coastal zones in the environs of Batumi, Black Sea coastal erosion. The fact that the dams will change the sediment flow in one way or another is largely acknowledged by both Turkey and Georgia; however, the expected and precise impact on the Georgian coastline and the possible acceleration of erosion in the Batumi region are not clear. Typically, it is not easy to foresee the direct effects of the planned Turkish infrastructures, because coastal erosion is a multifaceted issue with a variety of causes and effects generated by a variety of human intervention. Thus, even within Georgia, estimates have come to widely varied results when it comes to attempts to calculate the costs of additional coastal protection (Klaphake and Scheumann 2011).

Insufficient data exchange and a lack of a comprehensive approach for protection of freshwater ecosystems also constitute main items of transboundary water diplomacy.

Sediment Management, Erosion Control and Water Diplomacy

This 'sediment dispute' was bilaterally addressed in the late 1990s through the establishment of several technical committees, and some cooperative moves were made, however, at least from the new Georgian government's point of view, an agreement acceptable to both sides is yet to be reached.

As early as the 1980s, the Soviet government expressed concerns, via diplomatic channels, about the possible environmental impact of the planned dams and requested a joint investigation. The Soviet Union (USSR) repeated this request in 1990, but, in light of the subsequent collapse of the state, diplomatic channels inevitably ceased to function. When Georgia expressed concerns about the Coruh River Development Program later, in 1994, both countries entered a phase of bilateral technical cooperation in the form of a series of technical meetings in 1994 and 1995 (Yildiz 1999b). Even at this stage of consultation and negotiation, divergent problems emerged due to differing priorities of the two parties. Turkey proposed to plan future dams in a bilateral manner and invited Georgia to enter into a broader cooperation relating to joint energy projects over the Coruh and Kura Rivers. These joint developments were designed in such a manner that Georgia could receive compensation for potential damages from the already planned Coruh River development.

In fact, the Turkish government was apparently unwilling to consider a renunciation of the disputed dams across the Coruh River, but proposed a broadening of negotiations. Georgia's government, in contrast, put the main emphasis on the negative environmental impacts of the already proposed Turkish dams, and was neither prepared nor willing to negotiate bilateral cooperation on future joint dams, inter alia, due to its different energy priorities.

The Coruh issue then entered a higher tier of the bilateral political agenda, being discussed during several political consultations on a ministerial level between 1997 and 1998. During an official visit by a Georgian delegation to Ankara in 1998, Turkish officials acknowledged Georgia's concerns. On that occasion, the Turkish delegation also stated that conditions were unconducive for the signing of an agreement concerning the environmental impact of the dams due to a lack of sufficient information. Moreover, the Turkish side renewed the idea of broadening water cooperation and embracing projects that would potentially produce mutual benefits.

According to Georgian representatives, a possible solution may present itself in the involvement of a neutral third party who might facilitate and mediate the joint environmental impact studies. Prevention and/or miti-gation measures could then be designed accordingly and the right costs allocated.

Despite a rather unsatisfactory situation from a Georgian perspective, it is not likely that the country would risk damaging political relations with such a strategically important neighbour on this basis. Thus, water cooperation on the Coruh River benefits from generally good political relations between the two riparians.

In addition, an escalation of ill will is unlikely, given Turkey is also interested in a stable political and economic climate. In spite of the absence of an effective bilateral agreement, Turkey has already taken on the obligation of financing the monitoring of, and compensating for, the effects of dams on the other side of its border; a fact that points to particular caution being exercised in her relations with Georgia.

However, in order to tackle the 'sediment dispute' and to ensure sustain-able management of the river, transboundary water cooperation is essential. Referring to EU regulation, Turkey should be assisted in carrying out a state-of-the-art environmental impact assessment for the planned dam cascade on the Coruh River. In this context, the sediment question has to be addressed and studied carefully (Klaphake and Scheumann 2011).

However, aside from a number of outdated and now-obsolete agreements between the USSR and Turkey (e.g. Kars Protocol 1927), there remains no adequate legal or organizational (institutional) approach to water manage-ment in place. Despite good relations, water cooperation between the two countries still suffers from a weak legal foundation and an absence of organ-izational support. A permanent bilateral cooperative structure should be established to strengthen bilateral monitoring of the proposed infrastructure (Klaphake and Scheumann 2011).

Since both countries already cooperate in a number of ongoing activities aimed at improving the ecological state of the Black Sea, the Coruh River dispute and the assumed effects of the infrastructure on the coastal zones could be addressed within this framework. In addition, the issue of erosion on the Georgian coast demands a comprehensive and long-term approach for which multilateral Black Sea Cooperation may provide an adequate platform (Klaphake and Scheumann 201).

Although bilateral cooperation between Turkey and Georgia benefits from good political relations and extends to water-related fields such as nature protection, the ecological state of the Coruh River and the related coastal ecosystems should be subject to supplementary scientific studies and analyses. International support may be helpful in developing sufficient capacity and in supplying adequate resources (Klaphake and Scheumann 2011).

Based on a careful assessment of the sediment issue, various technical cooperation measures could be designed and implemented in order to reduce negative downstream effects. The transfer of international experience coupled with a technical approach to sediment management in the context of dam-building should be analyzed.

Current cooperation suffers, inter alia, from a lack of reliable data. Activity could be targeted on the exchange of water flow and water use data, water quality and so on. Although there are already several projects ongoing, the set-up and/or the improvement of a working and well-adapted monitoring infrastructure is urgently required (Klaphake and Scheumann 2011).

Water Diplomacy for Benefit-Sharing

There is no comprehensive bilateral agreement between Turkey and Georgia over the transboundary river system, but establishing a regional electricity market could facilitate coordination to this end (Scheumann and Tigrek 2015). The river system has high potential for hydropower generation due to the conditions of climate and topography, in particular, the steep gradient of the river sloping from high mountains to sea level. Both Turkey and Georgia are eagerly pursuing the exploitation of this potential in both parts of the river basin. Characteristic of both governments' endeavours is that they take place in a liberalized and deregulated electricity market with an increase in trans-border activities which aim to establish a regional electricity market, namely the Black Sea Electricity Ring (Scheumann and Tigrek 2015). When Turkey joined the European transmission network in 2011, it provided Georgia with the opportunity to sell into the lucrative European energy market after

Georgia, and Turkey signed the Cross-Border Energy Trading Agreement in January 2012 (USAID 2012).

Similar to Turkey, the Georgian government has been promoting hydro-power development by means of liberalizing the energy/electricity sector from 2004 onwards and has created attractive incentives for investors, Turkish companies among them. Turkey is seen as the most attractive market for Georgian electricity exports because 'the price of electricity in the Turkish private wholesale market is among the highest' (Ghvinadze and Linderman 2013).

Dispute resolution between Turkey and Georgia benefits from overall good political, economic and trade relations, and neither Georgia nor Turkey wishes to run the risk of spoiling them. Economic exchange between both countries has increased to an impressive level since late 1990s: In terms of exports Turkey is the number one trade partner of Georgia with a 17 per cent of the total share in international trade volume of the Georgian economy while Turkey constitutes number three in terms of imports with a share nearly 8 per cent (World Bank 2017). Thus, Turkey is not only a principal political and a strategically important partner for Georgia, but also a very important trading partner and a favourable market for investments, including hydro-power projects.

The Georgian government, which is interested in maintaining close political and trade relations, is already unilaterally implementing mitigation means and bears considerable costs: It annually deposits 200,000 m^3 of sand and gravel from another river delta as a means of technically compensating effects from a reduced sediment regime 200,000 m^3 is assumed to be only 10 per cent of the amount needed to counteract sea erosion (Scheumann and Tigrek 2015). Turkey is also interested in a stable political and economic climate, and has therefore taken on the obligation of funding the monitoring of the impacts of dams, and is willing to compensate for them, a fact that points to the particular caution being exercised in its relations to Georgia.

Looking at the one subject of the interstate conflict, the sediment regime, technical means can successfully be applied, at least to a certain degree, and compensation payments can be made even though this may not be acceptable from an environmental point of view. In this respect, collaboration has been successfully exercised in diplomatic negotiations of high-level bureaucrats, although disputes prevail relating to the extent of impacts and how to share the costs of mitigation means.

Yet to be settled are issues which relate to the changed water regime caused by the many power plants built both in Turkey and in Georgia on which the regional electricity market relies. This concerns the harmonization of plant operations, the regular exchange of hydrological and meteorological data, and the installation of an early warning system.

A major shift in the degree cf cooperation can be expected as a result of the Agreement between Georgia and Turkey Concerning Cross-Border Electricity Trade Via Borcka-Akhaltsikhe the Interconnection Line (CBETA), which was signed on 20 January 2012 by both Ministers of Energy and Natural Resources (USAID 2012) and ratified by Turkish Parliament in 2013. Both countries agreed to strengthen cooperation in general and commercial electricity trade in particular, giving priority to electricity produced from renewable energy sources. A joint committee was established (Article 10) 'to cooperate in the proper implementation of this Agreement, exchange information, resolve disputes, and conduct meetings and consultations...' (USAID 2012).

It is reasonable to assume that the issues related to hydropower plant operations will be dealt with in the context of electricity trade consultations, for which the joint committee serves as a platform. It can also be assumed that motivations to collaborate are high in both countries: Turkey can satisfy its energy needs (it already relies on 70 per cent of imported energy/electricity), while Georgia will be able to export its surplus (Ghvinadze and Linderman 2013, 3–6).

Kura–Aras River Basin

The Kura–Aras basin includes five countries, namely Turkey, Iran, Armenia, Georgia and Azerbaijan. It is located in the south Caucasus and is an important transboundary river basin in the region in terms of surface area, water flow and socio-economic importance of water resources and preservation of fresh-water ecosystems (Klaphake and Kramer 2011).

The river basin consists of two main branches: the Kura and Aras Rivers contributing 55 per cent and 45 per cent, respectively, to the total discharge (Revenga et al. 1998). Both rivers rise in Turkey and flow to the Caspian Sea after joining in Azerbaijan. The Kura River rises in Turkey and enters Georgia after some 210 km. After winding 390 km through mountainous terrain, the river flows over the Azerbaijan steppes and finally discharges into the Caspian Sea. The source of the Aras is also located in Turkey, and for a distance of around 300 km, forms the basis of several borders: namely, between Armenia and Turkey, for a very short distance between Azerbaijan and Turkey, between Azerbaijan and Iran, between Armenia and Iran, and finally again between Azerbaijan and Iran (Klaphake and Kramer 2011).

The Kura–Aras River basin is influenced by a much more complicated political constellation than, for instance, the Coruh River, due to the larger number of riparians who share, in some cases, considerably tenser political relations. Contrary to the high importance that the management of the transboundary waters of the Kura–Aras basin has for its downstream south Caucasian riparians, the topic does not receive much political attention in upstream riparian Turkey, and the interest in water conflict matters is rather low (Klaphake and Kramer 2011). At present, Turkey has little involvement in ongoing international efforts to bring riparian states together and to improve coordination within the basin. While this appears somewhat justified given the minimal transboundary impact caused by current Turkish water use (i.e. on the Kura River) and expected political impediments caused by tension between Turkey and Armenia, increasingly diverging interests between Turkey and other basin countries cannot be completely ruled out in the long term. Several riparian states, in particular Turkey and Iran, have plans to develop water infrastructure for hydropower generation and irrigation. However, Turkey is interested in long-term cooperation in the basin, and political relations with the riparian states are expected to improve through small-scale confidence building measures (Klaphake and Kramer 2011).

The Joint Dam Diplomacy

From the Turkish perspective, the Arpacay River in the Aras basin, which is located in Turkey and Armenia, is of particular importance for the two countries. It is formed through the merging of the Kars River, which originates in Turkey, and the Ahuryan River, which begins in Armenia. An important text signed between Turkey and the USSR in this regard is the 'Protocol on the Joint Construction of the Arpacay Dam', which dates back to 1964. This protocol provides a set of rules concerning the construction of a joint dam project, the waters of which would be shared on a 50:50 basis. The agreement holds that states are free to use their water for irrigation purposes and may build a hydropower plants on their respective territories. Issues such as the allocation of construction costs and the compensation for land losses are addressed in the protocol; the same being true for the founding of a joint dam commission to operate the infrastructure.

In 1973, the USSR and Turkey signed the Cooperation Agreement on the Construction of a Dam on the Bordering Arpacay River and the Constitution of a Dam Lake (Klaphake and Kramer 2011). Accordingly, the two countries agreed to construct a dam and a dam lake with a volume of 525 million m^3 on the shared Arpacay/Akhuryan River, as well as to share the water that would be allocated from the Arpacay/Akhuryan Dam and Aras River equally. Per the 1973 agreement, the USSR was put in charge of building the

Arpacay/Akhuryan Dam, while Turkey was given the responsibility of overseeing construction. The parties agreed on equally contributing to the construction expenses. They also reached consensus on establishing the Permanent Water Commission (PWC) – composed of three members from each country – for managing the joint use of water and the operation of the dam. In addition, the parties agreed to establish a subcommission to execute the decisions of the PWC. The USSR and Turkey also agreed that, without violating the rights of the other party, both parties could use their internal water resources at any place, in the time and quantity that they found suitable.

It is noteworthy that these Protocols were signed during the height of Cold War, regardless of the fact that USSR and Turkey were part of otherwise rival alliances. For decades, the Arpacay Dam and its Regulator (Serdarabad) operated smoothly – first by Turkey and the USSR, and then by Turkey and Armenia following the dissolution of the USSR in 1991. The countries distributed responsibilities for the design and construction of the dam and reservoir – the USSR preparing detailed design studies and ensuring construction of the dam, while Turkey oversaw the construction (Altingoz et al. 2018). The Joint Water Committee, established on the basis of the 1964 Protocol, managed the joint construction of the Arpacay Dam. It was also charged with preparing the annual operation schedule of the dam and overseeing its implementation; this responsibility was later delegated to the PWC in 1973. Altingoz et al. (2018) effectively outlines the water diplomacy frameworks which have been operational between the two parties since the 1960s:

> Once the dam had been built, the parties used the following tools to implement the agreements:
>
> • International Treaties: a bilateral agreement that specifies the rules for managing the dam and the dam lake was signed in 1973.
> • River Basin Organizations, Authorities or Commission: the PWC, a joint entity to manage the rivers as well as dam operations, was established based on the 1973 agreement.
> • Executive Functions: the PWC established a sub-commission to carry out its decisions.
> • Technical Entities: a joint inspection commission carries out regular site visits and subcommittees on both sides gauge the water usage of the other party.
> • Negotiations: the PWC is charged with negotiating disputes that arise between the two sides; if it cannot resolve the conflict in question, the governments of both countries are notified.

Turkey's Water Use and Development and Water Diplomacy Mechanisms

It is necessary to distinguish between the two main branches of the Kura–Aras River system when looking at Turkish plans to build new dams in the region (Polat 2004). The Kura River is planned to require less water infrastructure. Some 3,000 hectares of land (6 per cent of the irrigable land in the basin) is irrigated by individual farmers with spring waters and by the former General Directorate of Rural Services. However, the Durancam, Besikkaya and Burmadere Dams are under construction. Thus, 50,670 hectares of land are planned for irrigation. In addition, there are plans to develop the Koroglu Dam for hydropower generation.

The Arpacay and Demirdoven dams were built in Turkey on the headwaters of the Aras River and its tributaries. The Serdarabat Regulator, located where the Aras River enters into the Igdir Plain, diverts water both to Turkey and Armenia and with a regulated flow, will provide for agricultural irrigation throughout the Igdir Plain (Yildiz 1999a). The waters of the Aras River are vital to the livelihoods of residents of the Igdir Plain and to the eastern Anatolian lowlands, which often experience dry climates.

At present, the total irrigated area in the basin is equivalent to 49,000 hectares. Additionally, construction of the Bayburt Dam and of irrigation systems fed by the Kars River continues and will irrigate 33,300 hectares. The Bayburt Dam is the largest and most vital of these, as it provides water supply for domestic and industrial purposes in the dry Kars region, whereby the associated irrigation target is rather modest. Furthermore, there are 13 other dam projects in the pipeline (Polat 2004; Yildiz 1999a). These and other planned irrigation projects will irrigate, all in all, a total of 185,458 hectares of land.

The Aras basin plays a much more important role in Turkey's agricultural irrigation. Although the transboundary effects of the current and proposed Turkish development projects across the river basin have yet to be systematically assessed, one can expect a negative impact on water quality and quantity (Polat 2004). In principle, the impact of Turkish activities on both water quality and quantity is more relevant in the Aras river basin, while the hitherto proposed activities on the Kura River are less important.

It is anticipated that Turkey will cause only a minor share of the pollution in the river, given that its provinces of Erzurum, Ardahan, Kars and Igdir, which lie upstream in the basin, enjoy comparatively good environmental conditions, even despite concerns over watershed degradation, erosion and agricultural pollution (Polat 2004). Proposed developments in Turkey may change this picture, as intensive agriculture on irrigated land usually has an impact on water quality due to salinization and the use of fertilizers and pesticides.

In the face of such challenges, coordination and cooperation between the five basin countries is rudimentary. There is neither an agreement nor joint body covering the entire Kura–Aras river basin, and few bilateral agreements exist. In fact, only rudimentary agreements between Turkey and its neighbours have been ratified (Polat 2004). The history of Turkish cooperation within the basin goes back to the 1920s and the early days of the USSR. The most important boundary rivers shared between Turkey and the USSR were the Posof (which now forms the border with Georgia), the Arpacay and the Aras (now shared with Armenia). All these rivers used to form boundaries between Turkey and the USSR. There are bilateral agreements between Turkey and USSR, and Turkey and Iran, which address border issues, water infrastructure development and respective water withdrawals at border rivers. Yet, comprehensive agreements on transboundary water issues are clearly lacking. For instance, questions over water quality and preservation of the freshwater ecosystem have not been addressed. In addition, existing agreements lack when it comes to implementation and monitoring structures, while the same is true for procedural rules, such as transboundary (environmental) impacts assessments, information sharing, notification and so on.

Water Quality Management and Third-Party Involvement in Water Diplomacy

The Kura-Aras river basin, particularly the downstream portion, suffers much in terms of water quality. With support from international donor projects, progress has been made towards the development of water quality monitoring standards and practices in three downstream countries: Azerbaijan, Georgia and Armenia (Altingoz et al. 2018). In this context, one of the most impactful projects in the basin has come in the form of the UNDP-GEF Reducing Transboundary Degradation in the Kura-Araks River Basin Project. The initial formation of the project involved all three riparians, who conducted a Transboundary Diagnostic Analysis (TDA) that culminated in the Strategic Action Program (SAP), providing foundational support to national and transboundary efforts over management of the basin. However, the current iteration of the project only involves the Kura basin within Azerbaijan and Georgia; both countries having signed letters of endorsement for the SAP (Leummens and Matthews 2013). The TDA included discussions with stakeholders and highlighted the deterioration of water quality as one of four main transboundary issues in the basin. Furthermore, water quality assessments have been carried out through third-party assistance from the UNECE, USAID, NATO, EU and the Organization for Security and Co-operation in Europe (OSCE).

In fact, such existing transboundary water quality management frameworks in the basin are mainly based on the principle of parallel bilateralism. That is to say, given the political conflict between Armenia and Azerbaijan, cooperative agreements on the environment have only been signed bilaterally between Georgia and Azerbaijan, and between Georgia and Armenia (Altingoz et al. 2018).

It is evident that the sustainable, long-term development of the river basins and the preservation of freshwater ecosystems demands multilateral cooperation between the basin states. Long-term efforts and initiatives aimed at overseeing the Kura–Aras basin and coordinating the riparian states would certainly also require the involvement of Turkey to guarantee any significant degree of success (Klaphake and Kramer 2011). Current programmes and initiatives largely focus on the three south Caucasian states of Georgia, Armenia and Azerbaijan, with Turkey as a marginally (if at all) involved partner. Clearly, water quality is a prime transboundary issue between Georgia and Azerbaijan, but is relevant along the Turkish-Armenian and the Turkish-Iranian border, too. Here, bilateral measures to control emissions from point and non-point sources could serve as a basis from which to start. In addition, Turkey and Iran should be invited to join ongoing transboundary efforts in hazard prevention. In general, there is a need to work towards a joint platform which includes all riparian countries, and to establish consultation mechanisms to harmonise basin-wide water quality management efforts. This would also mean taking an integrative perspective on water development, use and protection, including in-stream flows (Klaphake and Kramer 2011).

Orontes River Basin

The transboundary water politics in the Orontes basin involve a number of entrenched complexities. For decades, Syria and Turkey have held starkly divergent views over the use and management of the waters of this river basin. However, in the first decade of 2000s, a high level of rapprochement and political will enabled a number of initiatives for transboundary water cooperation to take root. A series of Memoranda of Understanding (MoU) were signed between Syria and Turkey over transboundary water resource management, including one on building a joint dam on the Orontes River along the boundary between the two countries. Yet, since the eruption of conflict in Syria, the then proposed joint dam (The Friendship Dam) project came to a halt, while Turkey–Syria relations deteriorated across all domains.

The Orontes River (known in Turkish as 'Asi Nehri', in Arabic as 'Nahr-al Asi') originates in the northern Bekaa region of Lebanon. The Orontes is the only river in West Asia which has a northward flow, discharging west into the

Mediterranean Sea (UN-ESCWA and BGR 2013). The Orontes enters Syrian territory northeast of the town of Hermel (Lebanon) and passes through the cities of Homs and Hamah. It then crosses the fertile region of Al-Ghab where intensive irrigation systems have been established and constitutes 56 km of the Syrian-Turkish border before entering into Turkey, where it turns southwest passing through Antakya, and discharging into the Mediterranean Sea near Samandag, in Turkey's Hatay province (Korkmaz and Karatas 2009).

Data concerning the total length and catchment area of the Orontes varies according to sources. Most sources provide figures in the range of 448–571 km. One local study, conducted using satellite images at an altitude of 2,000 m, calculated the total length as 556 km, 40 km of which are in Lebanon, 366 km in Syria and 98 km in Turkey (Korkmaz and Karatas 2009). The waterway has a catchment area of 24,745 km² (Comair et al. 2013), with two main tributaries: the Afrin River, larger in terms of water flow, and the Karasu. Originating in Kartal Mountains in Turkey, the Afrin River first crosses into Syrian territory, passing through the town of Afrin, before re-entering Turkey and draining into Amik Lake. The Karasu River runs almost entirely through Turkey, except forming a small section that runs along the Turkish-Syrian border (Kibaroglu and Sümer 2016).

The combined mean annual discharge potential of the Orontes River, including its tributaries, is estimated at 2.4–2.8 billion m³ (Comair et al. 2013). An earlier study by the DSI gives the annual discharge as 3.4 billion m³ (DSI 1958). Thus, the annual water potential of the Orontes River system has fallen considerably over the last several decades (Kibaroglu and Sümer 2015). The average annual flow potential at the point of entry onto Turkish soil is estimated at 1.4 billion m³ for the Orontes, 0.6 billion m³ for the Afrin and 0.4 billion m³ for the Karasu (Scheumann et al. 2011). However, during the summer months, the Orontes dries up before reaching Turkey due to extensive water use in Syria's Al-Ghab region (Baran et al. 2006).

Water Diplomacy Background: Competitive Water Usages in the Basin

While water resources of the Orontes River and its tributaries are used intensively for irrigation purposes by all riparians, Syria and Turkey by far take up the lion's share, with demand frequently exceeding the supply of the river system. The Food and Agriculture Organization (FAO) estimates that the total irrigated area of the basin stretches from 300,000 to 350,000 hectares, 58 per cent of which lies in Syria, 36 per cent in Turkey and 6 per cent in Lebanon (FAO 2008). Besides the issue of quantity, one of the most prominent concerns over the Orontes' waters refers to lack of quality caused by pollutant discharge in the Syrian part of the basin, creating significant problems downstream for

Turkey. Thus, water development and use in the Orontes basin constitutes one of the main bones of contention regarding the water diplomacy agenda of any pair of the three riparians.

Despite having the headwaters, utilization of water resources of the Orontes in Lebanon is hitherto mostly confined to small-scale farming, fish farms and tourism activities (UN-ESCWA and BGR 2013), with an annual total use of 21 million m³. While the biggest use is agricultural, at 77 per cent of total use, domestic water use accounts for 23 per cent. According to FAO estimates, 18,000–21,000 hectares are irrigated in the Lebanese part of the Orontes basin. These figures are to rise with the operationalization of the Assi scheme. The two phases of the Assi scheme include the construction of two dams with a total capacity of 64 million m³, a number of pumping stations and irrigation networks which will irrigate an additional 6800 hectares in the regions of Hermel and Al Qaa. The Assi scheme also aims at creating 50 MW of hydroelectricity and providing water for domestic use in Baalbek and Hermel. Syria objected to the project at the beginning, but later conceded. Nonetheless, the project failed to be implemented due to a lack of finance (Canatan 2003). After the signing of the 2002 agreement between Lebanon and Syria, Lebanon started the construction of the diversion dam near Ain Zarqa Spring, of the pumping stations, and of the irrigation network (phase 1); a dam near Hermel Bridge and a hydroelectric power plant in the Hermel and Al-Qaa areas (phase 2). A Chinese company, contracted for phase 1, started working on the dam in 2005, but the works had to be stopped the following year when Israel bombed the site during the 2006 war. This led to a dispute between the Lebanese government and the contractor on compensation for losses. After a special committee was formed in 2011 to address the issue, the Lebanese Council of Ministers renegotiated the work terms to meet the contractor's demands, and a new contract was finalized (Fanack Water 2016). Water quality in the Lebanese part of Orontes is relatively good, given the low level of pollutants originating from agriculture, industry or domestic water use (Kibaroglu and Sümer 2015).

Syria has been using 90 per cent of Orontes' annual flow which amounts to 1.2 billion m³ at Syria-Turkish border (FAO 2008). Unlike the rest of the country, harnessing the water of the Orontes started during the French Mandate in the 1930s. In 1937, reconstruction of the ancient Qattineh Dam was initiated in order to regulate the flow and increase the irrigation capacity of Orontes (FAO 2008). In terms of water use, the Orontes River constitutes the second most important river in Syria after the Euphrates, providing 20 per cent of the country's total estimated water use volume. Agriculture is the largest water user, consuming about 1,977 million m³ per year (77 per cent of total water use), followed by domestic water use at 9 per cent and industry at 8 per cent.

Since the 1950s, Syria has intensively developed water resources in the Orontes basin. The first large dams built in Syria were constructed along the Orontes, at Rastan and Mhardeh, in 1960 (FAO 2008). This was further accelerated with Decree No. 3 of 1972, which launched the construction of multipurpose dams. Syria has built 41 dams in the basin. The total reservoir capacity of all dams in the basin had reached around 950 million m³ per year by 2006. The Rastan, Qattineh, Zeita and Mhardeh Dams are the largest in terms of storage capacities (FAO 2008).

Two main agricultural areas in Syria are supplied with water from the Orontes: the region between Homs and Hama, and the Al-Ghab region. The latter was systematically drained from the 1950s onward to reclaim land for irrigated agriculture. The Orontes river bed was enlarged and deepened, and dams were built to regulate the flow of the river and to provide water for irrigation. The Al-Ghab Project was carried out between 1958 and 1967. An area of around 70,000 hectares has been irrigated as part of this project. The region between Homs and Hama, on the other hand, is partly supplied from Lake Qattineh via the Homs-Hama canal, which provides water to an area of about 23,000 hectares. Since the reservoir does not meet demand, it is supplemented by groundwater wells, which irrigate another 20,000 hectares in this part of the basin. The total irrigated area in the Orontes basin in Syria has increased from approximately 155,000 hectares in 1989 to 200,000 hectares in 1992 and to 215,000 hectares in 2008, while occasionally exceeding 250,000 hectares between 2004 and 2008 (FAO 2008). On average, an area of about 97,000 hectares (43 per cent) is irrigated by surface water and 130,000 hectares (57 per cent) by groundwater. Part of the groundwater use is from fossil aquifers, with the pressure over these resources, particularly in the Ghab region, risking the sustainability of water resources over the Orontes river basin as a whole (Hamade and Tabet 2013). Another region where groundwater use in irrigation has risen significantly is the Province of Idlib (FAO 2008).

The intensification of water use in the Orontes basin in Syria has raised the question of long-term water sustainability. Water tables in some parts of the western Orontes basin have dropped by as much as 57 meters in 10 years (FAO 2008). The total need of water for irrigation in Syrian part of the Orontes basin is given as 3,536 billion m³ (Wakil 1993), a number well above the annual discharge capacity of the river. The Orontes basin is considered one of the country's most disturbed hydrological ecosystems. Apart from agriculture-based nitrate and phosphate pollution, industrial wastewater is discharged into the streams with limited or no treatment. Water quality is also threatened by domestic wastewater discharge in many parts of the basin (UN-ESCWA and BGR 2013).

On the other hand, by adopting remote sensing technology, recent research analyzed the impact of the Syrian civil war on irrigated agriculture and summer crop production within conflict-affected agricultural lands in the Orontes basin (Jaafar et al. 2015). Their findings indicated that irrigated agricultural production dropped between 15 per cent and 30 per cent in the Syrian portion of the Orontes basin in 2000–13, with hotspots identifiable in Idlib, Homs, Hama, Daraa and Aleppo regions of Syria. The remote sensing approach proved effective in identifying and locating losses in agricultural productivity due to conflict, rather than drought.

In Turkey, the Orontes River system is the main watercourse for the country's eastern Mediterranean provinces, namely Hatay and Kilis. The Amik Plain in the Hatay province is a significant agricultural area in the Turkish part of the basin. Because of the occurrence of frequent floods in nearby towns and villages due to insufficiency of natural drainage canals, authorities decided to drain Lake Amik in early 1940s. The draining of Lake Amik was actually started in 1950s by DSI and was completed in early 1970s. The Amik Plain, covering an area of 31,000 hectares, thus became an important agricultural area of Turkey's eastern Mediterranean region. However, due to problems in the drainage works, particularly those constructed in the 1970s, flooding, and increased soil salinity – negatively affecting agricultural productivity – have become two major concerns (Kibaroglu et al. 2005).

The two most noteworthy dams in the Turkish part of the Orontes basin are the Yarseli and Tahtakopru, both located on tributaries of the Orontes (Kibaroglu et al. 2005). Recently in the Amik Plain, a clay core sand-gravel filling type dam, namely the Reyhanli Dam has been constructed in order to irrigate 60,000 hectares area and to protect 20,000 hectares area from flood (*Habertürk* 2020).

Irrigated agriculture in the Turkish part of the basin covers an area of more than 125,000 hectares, according to the Ministry of Agriculture and Rural Affairs (2004). According to exploratory surveys by DSI, the total area that can be irrigated with Orontes River system is around 225,000 hectares (DSI 1958).

Water Diplomacy Practices: Claims-Counter Claims, Negotiations and Treaties

There are a number of bilateral water agreements involving Turkey, Syria and Lebanon, the earliest of which dates back to the French mandate (over Lebanon and Syria) in the early 1920s. The issue of supplying water for irrigation is the biggest priority in the basin which is reflected in the agreements. However, to date, there is no agreement involving all three riparians.

Negotiations between Lebanon and Syria on the Orontes began as early as 1940. In 1962, a Syrian-Lebanese joint committee was established to deal with the Orontes which allocated 100 million m³ per year for Hermel and Ka'a regions in Lebanon. In 1968, the committee decided to reconsider the annual water needs of both countries. Syria and Lebanon decided in 1972 to allocate 80 million m³ per year to Lebanon, this agreement never became operative (Salha 1995; Comair et al. 2013). Finally, on 20 September 1994, the Bilateral Agreement Concerning the Usage and Sharing of the Waters of the al-Asi River (Orontes) between the Syrian Arab Republic and the Lebanese Republic was signed, which formally allocated 80 million m³ per year to Lebanon, and 340 million m³ per year to Syria. In case of a fall in annual discharge of the Orontes below 400 million m³ per year, Lebanon's share would be proportionately reduced. The management of the headspring and river's flow was agreed upon. This agreement also outlined the formation of a technical committee charged with controlling and managing the headwaters of Orontes in Lebanese part of the river basin, which would be composed of experts from both countries. These works, however, were to be financed solely by Syria. This agreement is also noteworthy for having recognized the Orontes as 'common waters' (Canatan 2003).

Downstream, meanwhile, Turkey was totally excluded from this agreement, causing condemnation from Turkish officials and the general public alike. Turkey was neither notified nor consulted in the process of negotiations (Salha 1995). As Comair et al. (2013) notes, on the judicial level, the agreement does not comply with the frameworks of international water law, including the 1997 UN Convention, failing to regard basic principles. Hence, the agreement was renegotiated in 1997, by which time Lebanon had begun to recover from the effects of the civil war and lessen its dependence on Syria (UN-ESCWA and BGR 2013). In 1997, an addendum was made to the 1994 agreement, envisioning the exclusion of five sub-basins of the Orontes River from the Lebanese share of 80 million m³ per year. According to the addendum, these five sub-basins were to be considered 'closed' basins and not common sources; in other words, as are located within Lebanon, and are not part of any transboundary basins, they would thus be excluded from the 1994 agreement. This amendment de facto increased the allocation of the basin's water to Lebanon (Comair et al. 2013). Given the country's increasing detachment from the Syrian influence, and the fact that both the Lebanese and Syrian governments signed the 1997 UN Convention on the non-navigational uses of international watercourses, they decided to form a committee to revise the 1994 agreement and the 1997 addendum. A new bilateral agreement reached in 2004 then enabled an 80 million m³ per year share to Lebanon plus 16 million m³ from wells, and the construction of a diversion dam and of a storage dam to allow Lebanon to expand its agricultural activities (Comair et al. 2013).

So far, disputes over the use of the Orontes' waters occurred mainly between Turkey (downstream) and Syria (upstream). From the Turkish perspective, the agricultural water demand and planned irrigation projects of both countries are a source of issue, not to mention the quality parameters of the water as it enters Turkey (Scheumann et al. 2011). Syria, for a long time, did not recognize Hatay as Turkish territory, and thus rejected any discussions over the waters of the Orontes that flowed through that province. For Syria, the main objective was rather to control the headwaters of the Orontes in Lebanon – which appears to be one of the factors that largely contributed to Syria's lengthy military involvement in Lebanon.

There were several agreements with clauses relevant to Orontes waters signed between Turkey and the French mandate of Syria during the 1920s and 1930s (Caponera 1993). The first agreement between independent riparians was the Final Protocol to Determine Syria-Hatay Border Limitation in 1939 between Syria and Turkey, which stipulated that the waters of the rivers (i.e. Orontes, Karasu and Afrin), where they constitute the boundary between Syria and Turkey, will be utilized in an equal manner. Apart from this, there were no stipulations over the nature of the use of these water resources.

In 1950, Syria approached the World Bank to obtain funding for the Al-Ghab Project. An agreement was signed between the two parties in the same year. The World Bank assumed that water usage in the Orontes River basin would not be jeopardized as a result of the project, and that the control of winter floods would be beneficial for all riparians, while the summer flow would provide enough water to irrigate all areas in the region (Scheumann et al. 2011). However, the World Bank also considered the concerns of the Turkish side and organized a meeting between Turkish and Syrian experts in Syria. On this occasion, the Turkish representatives claimed that Turkey would face frequent floods during construction, and that the project would leave no water for Turkey during irrigation seasons (Caponera 1993).

In 1962, Syria assigned the development of the Orontes River project to the Dutch company NEDECO. As Caponera (1993) noted, this plan focused solely on the projects in Syria without mentioning the 'requirements, interests, and acquired rights of Turkey'. In response to this plan, the Turkish delegation, during a meeting involving experts from both riparians, offered a draft protocol calling for a river basin development plan for the whole basin to be developed in order to determine measures to mitigate flood hazards, to study the feasibility of a dam on the border to irrigate the Amik Plain and to install early warning systems for flood protection. This proposal was not welcomed by the Syrian delegation, and no agreement was reached (Caponera 1993; Kibaroglu et al. 2005).

It soon became evident that transboundary water talks between Turkey and Syria appeared to be more difficult than the negotiations between Syria and Lebanon. One of the reasons for this related to conflictual views over the subject of negotiations. From 1983 onwards, water-related talks between Syria and Turkey continued mainly under the mandate of a Joint Technical Committee (JTC). Turkey and Syria adopted conflicting strategies with regard to the subject of negotiations. While Turkey insisted that negotiations would encompass all regional transboundary waters, including the Orontes, the Euphrates and the Tigris, Syria refused to formally discuss the Orontes River with Turkey. Since Syria claimed the Turkish province of Hatay – through which the Orontes River flows and discharges into the Mediterranean – as Syrian territory, Syria regarded the Orontes River as a 'national river' which flows on Syrian territory and drains into the Mediterranean Sea without crossing Turkey. Any negotiation would have been tantamount to acknowledging Turkey's sovereignty over the Hatay region.

Beginning from 1995 onwards, Turkey's complaints about the quantity of water entering into Turkey became vociferous. According to Turkish Ministry of Foreign Affairs, the quantity was reduced from 1.55 billion m^3 to 140 million m^3. Syria, on the other hand, advocated that the fall in the quantity released to Turkey was predominantly caused by the drought conditions, not by an increase in Syrian use (Shapland 1997).

Friendship Dam: A Benefit-Sharing Approach to Water Diplomacy

A change of tide occurred when the two countries signed the Adana Security Protocol in October 1998, which was followed by reciprocal visits of Syrian president to Turkey, and Turkish prime minister to Syria, as well as the signing of the Agreement on Avoidance of Double Taxation and Agreement on Reciprocal Promotion and Protection of Investment (FTA 2004). This trade agreement, with corresponding assurances to open Syrian trade missions in the province of Hatay, was considered by Turkish authorities to de facto imply recognition of the international border, including the province of Hatay. It was also in 2004, during the Turkish prime minister's visit to Damascus, that the first proposal for a joint dam project on the Orontes was made by the Turkish authorities. Both sides agreed in principle to proceed with the joint dam development project. After a number of technical studies on the topographical and geological characteristics of the region, a number of sites were identified for the construction of the dam (Scheumann et al. 2011).

Finally, on 23–24 December 2009, the MoU between the Government of the Republic of Turkey and the Government of the Syrian Arab Republic for the Construction of a Joint Dam across the Orontes River under the Name 'Friendship Dam' was reached at the first meeting of the High-Level Strategic Cooperation Council (HSCC) in Damascus, which also resulted in the signing of 50 MoUs between Turkey and Syria – four of which related to water issues (MoU 2009a).

Scheumann and Shamaly (2016) describe how positively Turkey perceived the Friendship Dam by citing the statements made by then-Turkish Minister of Environment and Forestry, Veysel Eroglu: 'The Friendship Dam will provide benefits to both countries, since Turkey and Syria will make use of the dam in a 50-50 model'.

The benefit-sharing approach essentially pertains to the idea that riparian countries should consider a river as a productive resource and focus on the benefits they can share from its use rather than conceptualizing water use in quantitative terms. Benefits could include energy production to meet energy needs, the expansion of irrigated agriculture to meet food demands, the mitigation of hazardous floods and droughts. Dam projects hold various such benefits, but not without external impact. Turkey supported this project in the hope of reaping the rewards of such benefits, with an economic incentive for construction of the dam pressed by a need to control floods, offered the sharing of hydro-electricity to make the idea more attractive for Syria. Moreover, Turkey was willing to bear a greater share of the costs, which is reasonable given the benefits desired would have a greater significance for Turkey in terms of flood control, irrigation, and hydropower, compared to Syria, which would only benefit from hydropower alone (Scheumann and Shamaly 2016). This being the case, while Turkish and Syrian politicians at high levels pushed for the planning and laying of the foundations for the construction of the Friendship Dam within a very short time, the subsequently signed MoU (23 December 2009) did not entail technical specifications, such as the location of the dam axis, the maximum storage volume in the reservoir or the maximum water level – during flood periods (Scheumann and Shamaly 2016). Both sides agreed to form a joint technical delegation to study the technical issues pertaining to the construction of the joint dam. When negotiations came to a halt due to the onset of the Syrian crisis, major technical issues were yet to be specified and agreed upon.

The dam was expected to be approximately 15 meters high with a capacity of 110 million m^3. Of this, 40 million m^3 would be used for flood protection, while the rest would be utilized for energy production and irrigation. Costs of construction would be shared by two riparians. It was also decided that both countries would install and operate flow-measuring stations in the area to serve as early warning system for flood protection. The foundation of the dam was laid on 7 February 2011. Although the initial plan was to finish the main body of the dam in one year, and the hydroelectrical plant and irrigation systems in two years, the outbreak of internal unrest in Syria, later accompanied by a total deterioration of Turkish-Syrian relations, caused the cessation of the project.

Notwithstanding the fact that any chance of the Friendship Dam project's continuation will only be possible after a resolution of the Syrian conflict, the 2009 signing of an official protocol on the waters of Orontes had been considered a real breakthrough in Turkish-Syrian hydropolitical and even broader political relations. For decades, Syria failed to recognize the Turkish-Syrian political border, through which the Orontes flows, by claiming territorial rights over the Turkish province of Hatay. According to some analysts, negotiations on the Friendship Dam and the signing the MoU meant Syria's unofficial yet effective recognition of Turkish sovereignty over Hatay (Jörum 2014). For decades, again, Turkey had demanded the right to regulate the waters of the Orontes River, which had often fluctuated, causing severe floods and droughts in downstream towns and villages in Turkey. Yet, Syria never agreed to build water development structures on the border, on the basis that the Orontes constituted a national river. In this respect, with the Protocol (MoU) of December 2009, a drastic change in the Syrian attitudes could be acknowledged. In fact, one can point to flourishing cooperation between otherwise hostile riparian states following the joint dam pledge.

Turkey's water diplomacy practices in the Orontes basin have been essentially shaped and directed by the country's overall foreign policy orientation towards Syria. The principles and practices of water diplomacy have been consistent – not to mention creative, particularly when overall political relations have been conducive for cooperation. Since the early 1980s, within the framework of the JTC meetings, Turkish diplomats adopted a regional approach regarding transboundary waters. Thus, throughout the water talks, Turkish diplomats insisted on negotiating over Euphrates-Tigris together with the Orontes river basin. The main issues, which were prioritized by Turkish diplomatic circles during the negotiations, were the needs for water development projects for flood protection, hydropower generation and irrigation development, as well as the sustained and increased application of efficiency in use throughout the entire region.

While Syria and Lebanon had agreed on detailed water allocations in 1994 and 2002, Turkey and Syria had only settled the demarcation of their border – and this going back to 1939. However, in December 2009, Turkey and Syria signed the MoU for the construction of a joint dam on the Orontes. Both countries focused on developing water resources for irrigation, hydropower, drinking water and infrastructure for flood control. However, as perceived by the Turkish side, the persistent issues to agree on the Orontes' water stems from agricultural water demand, planned irrigation projects in both countries and the quality of the water which arrived in Turkey. There is a need for reliable data on the water resource potential and the actual use in both riparian countries. Yet, challenges over water use and management at the transboundary level can only be addressed, and joint projects only realized, when peace is restored in the region.

Euphrates–Tigris River Basin

The Euphrates and the Tigris originate in one particular climatic and topographic zone and end up in quite a different one. The basin is characterized by high mountains to the north and west and extensive lowlands in the south and the east (Kibaroglu 2002). In conformity with the expert judgments of geographers, the Euphrates and the Tigris rivers can be considered as forming one single transboundary watercourse system. They are linked not only by their natural course when merging at the Shatt Al-Arab, but also by a man-made Thartar Canal which links the Tigris to the Euphrates through the Thartar Valley in Iraq (Anderson 1986; Beaumont 1992; Bilen 1994; Kliot 1994).

The Euphrates flows from a point in the eastern highlands of Turkey, between Lake Van and the Black Sea, and is formed by two major tributaries, the Murat and Karasu. It enters the Syrian territory at Karkamis, downstream from the Turkish town of Birecik. It is then joined by its major tributaries, the Balik and Khabur, which also originate in Turkey, and flows southeast across the Syrian plateaus before entering the Iraqi territory near Qusaybah (FAO 2008).

Of the Euphrates basin, 28 per cent lies in Turkey, 17 per cent in Syria, 40 per cent in Iraq, 15 per cent in Saudi Arabia and just 0.03 per cent in Jordan. The Euphrates River is 3,000 km long, divided between Turkey (1,230 km), Syria (710 km) and Iraq (1,060 km) (FAO 2008).

The Tigris, also originating in eastern Turkey, flows throughout the country until it reaches the border city of Cizre. From here, it forms the border between Turkey and Syria over a short distance and then crosses into Iraq at Faysh Khabur. The River Tigris is 1,850 km long, with 400 km in Turkey, 32 km on the border between Turkey and Syria and 1,418 km in Iraq. Of the Tigris basin 12 per cent lies in Turkey, 0.2 per cent in Syria, 54 per cent in Iraq and 34 per cent in Iran. Within Iraq, several tributaries flow into the river coming from the Zagros Mountains in the east, thus all lie on its left bank (FAO 2008).

The Shatt Al-Arab is the river formed by the confluence downstream of the Euphrates and the Tigris as it flows into the Persian Gulf after a course of 180 km. The Karun River, flowing from Iranian territory, has a mean annual flow of 24.7 billion m^3 and flows into the Shatt Al-Arab just before it reaches the sea carrying a large amount of freshwater (UN-ESCWA and BGR 2013).

The mean annual flow of the Euphrates is 32 billion m^3 per year of which about 90 per cent is drained from Turkey, whereas the remaining 10 per cent originates in Syria. As for the Tigris, the average total discharge is determined as 52 billion m^3 per year, of which approximately 40 per cent comes from Turkey, whereas Iraq and Iran contribute 51 per cent and 9 per cent, respectively. Estimates for the total flow of the Tigris–Euphrates and their tributaries vary between 68 billion m^3 and 84.5 billion m^3 (Kolars and Mitchell 1991; Kolars 1994; Belül 1996; Altinbilek 2004).

The upper parts of the ET basin are characterized by a cold continental climate, whereas the lower parts are classified as hot desert or hot semi-arid (Bozkurt and Sen 2013). The rivers overflow in spring when the snow melts, augmented by seasonal rainfall, which is at its heaviest between March and May. The summer season is hot and dry, resulting in extensive evaporation and low humidity during the day. Evaporation increases water salinization and water loss in major reservoirs throughout the three riparian countries (Naff and Matson 1984; Kliot 1994)

Initial Water Diplomacy Mechanisms

Friendly relations continued between the riparian states from the early 1920s until the late 1950s, when each country's priority was the establishment of state bureaucracies and all had similar concerns and the same need for socio-economic development. Throughout this period, planning was done largely on a country-by-country basis. None of the relevant countries engaged in major development projects which would have resulted in utilization of water by each to the detriment of the others, and thus there was little cause for conflict. Essentially, the Euphrates and Tigris linked the communities in the river basin as they had done for thousands of years, and the newly established riparian states had yet to clash over the use of the water (Kibaroglu and Ünver 2000).

At a transboundary level, harmonious water relations reigned in the basin under a series of bilateral political treaties. The first legal arrangement among the riparians was an agreement signed by France and Turkey in Ankara on 20 October 1921, with a view towards promoting peace between the two countries. Under Article XII of that treaty concerning the 'Distribution and Removal of Waters', it was agreed that 'the city of Aleppo may also organize, at its own expense, a water-supply from the Euphrates in Turkish territory in order to meet the requirements of the district'. Article 109 of the 1923 Lausanne Peace Treaty covers another legal aspect of the issue, stating that, if the fixing of a new frontier results in the river system of one state being dependent on facilities that were established before the war and are now located within the borders of another state, the parties concerned must conclude an agreement that is capable of safeguarding their respective interests and sovereign rights and that, in the absence of an agreement, the dispute will be settled by arbitration.

One of the most important legal agreements between Iraq and Turkey concerning water resources is the protocol annexed to their 1946 Treaty of Friendship and Good Neighbourly Relations (Treaty 1946). This protocol establishes a framework that sets out the two parties' respective rights and obligations in the Euphrates and Tigris River system. Above all, it emphasizes the urgency of installing flood control works on the rivers and underlines the positive impact that storage facilities sited on Turkish soil would have for both. The parties agreed that, if the most suitable sites were on Turkish territory, the entire cost would be met by Iraq. Permanent observation stations would be built, operated and maintained by Turkey, with Turkey and Iraq sharing the costs equally. Turkey agreed to inform Iraq of its construction plans and, in the event that it determined that it needed water for irrigation and hydropower purposes, assured that separate negotiations would be held in this regard. In recognizing the rights and obligations for both the upstream and downstream states, this seems peculiarly enlightened, and not only for its time, since contemporary bilateral water treaties such as the 1987 Protocol between Turkey and Syria and the 1990 Protocol between Syria and Iraq (described in detail in the following related section) seem less balanced in their recognition of upper and lower riparian rights and obligations.

During this initial period, the riparian countries were mainly concerned with water supply for urban and rural populations. Bureaucracies with technical expertise were busy with the initial organizational setup and the planning of irrigation systems and dam construction. Transboundary waters were the subject of domestic planning and development exercises and had little to do with the foreign policy agenda. Those involved in transboundary water relations at the time were therefore mainly medium-level technocrats – advisers and professionals who prepared the technical ground for the drafting of the water-related clauses of the treaties in whose conclusion the riparian diplomats acted as brokers (Kibaroglu and Scheumann 2013).

Water Diplomacy during the Era of Competitive Water Development Projects

As the riparian states further consolidated their regimes between 1960 and 1980, they began to pay more attention to socio-economic developments in terms of water and land resources. Thus, transboundary water relations saw a hub of competitive activities taking place in an uncoordinated and unilateral fashion across the region.

Turkey has long been dependent on oil imports. Having been hard hit by the oil crises in the 1970s, the government embarked on a program of indigenous resource development that particularly emphasized hydropower and lignite schemes with the aim of minimizing the national economy's dependency on imported oil (Kibaroglu 2002).

The Syrian economy has traditionally been dominated by agriculture. Exploration for oil did not begin until the early 1980s. Even though oil made a significant contribution to export earnings in the following decades, as world oil prices fluctuated, Syria focused on agricultural development with the aim of achieving food self-sufficiency. These considerations were reinforced by political goals which, under the ruling Ba'ath Party, placed the emphasis on the development of rural areas and the organization of peasants as a political power base (Richards and Waterbury 1990).

Since 1958, Iraq transformed itself from an agrarian economy exporting wheat, rice and other crops to an oil-producing, semi-industrial nation forced to import most of its own food. Yet, after the Iraqi government nationalized its oil companies in 1972 and began to receive more income from oil, the focus also turned to agricultural production. This led to an expansion of irrigated areas, with the aim of achieving food security for the Iraqi people (Allan 1990; McLachlan 1991).

The central water agencies of all riparian countries have been founded for the oversight of large-scale development projects. In Turkey, the state agencies' main objectives were to irrigate the fertile lands in southeastern Anatolia, which make up one-fifth of the country's irrigable land, using the huge water potential of the Tigris and Euphrates river basin, a basin which accounts for 28.5 per cent of the country's surface water supply. It was to this end that Turkey implemented the Lower Euphrates Project, initially a series of dams designed to increase hydropower generation and expand irrigated agriculture. Subsequently, however, in the late 1970s, the Lower Euphrates Project evolved into a larger, multisectoral development project, which encompassed the Tigris waters and became known as the Southeastern Anatolia Project (GAP in Turkish acronym). This extended to 21 large dams, 19 hydropower plants and irrigation schemes spanning over 1.7 million hectares of land (Ünver 1997; Tigrek and Kibaroglu 2011).

The Euphrates River basin provides 65 per cent of Syria's surface water supply and accounts for 27 per cent of total land resources. Syria's Ba'ath Party launched the Euphrates Valley Project to achieve a number of object-ives, namely, the ability to provide irrigation over an area spanning as much as 640,000 hectares; the construction of the large, multipurpose Tabqa or Al-Thawra Dam to generate the electricity needed for urban areas and industrial development; and regulation of the flow of the Euphrates to prevent seasonal flooding (Bakour 1992).

The main channels and tributaries of the Euphrates and the Tigris rivers account for almost the entire supply of freshwater for Iraq, which pioneered and built its first dams in the 1950s: the Euphrates Dam in 1955–56 to divert water to Lake Al-Habbaniya; and the Samarra Dam on the Tigris, completed in 1954, to protect against otherwise catastrophic floods. The Ba'ath Party, which came to power under Saddam Hussein's presidency in 1968, adopted the slogan 'food security for the Iraqi people', which was to be accomplished through the development of irrigation. The Revolutionary Plan was developed to this end, entailing the establishment of a Higher Agriculture Council attached to the presidency, the Soil and Land Reclamation Organization attached to the Ministry of Irrigation, and many other new departments charged with carrying out studies, creating designs, and constructing and maintaining water projects (Allan 1990; Kibaroglu 2002).

Owing to the competitive and uncoordinated nature of these water devel-opment projects, disagreements over transboundary water uses surfaced in the late 1960s. Over this period, transboundary water issues were regarded by each country's political leadership as falling within the sphere of economic and technical aims and could be handled by official technical delegations. Hence, water negotiations were held by technocrats from the riparians' cen-tral water agencies, accompanied by diplomats who advised and monitored the negotiations, particularly when international legal and political aspects came under discussion (Kibaroglu and Scheumann 2013). The main theme of these technical negotiations was the impact of the construction of the Keban Dam in Turkey and the Tabqa Dam in Syria on Iraq's historical water use patterns. While Turkey suggested the establishment of a JTC to determine the water and irrigation needs of the riparians, Iraq insisted on a guarantee of specific flows and a water-sharing agreement. While Turkey released certain flows during the construction and impounding of the Keban Dam, no final allocation agreement was reached, even after numerous technical meetings.

These meetings failed to achieve their expressed aim of coordinating the water development and use patterns of the three riparians. Consequently, a political crisis occurred in the region in 1975. Turkey began impounding the Keban reservoir at the same time that Syria was completing the construction of the Tabqa Dam – during a period of severe drought. The impounding of the two reservoirs triggered a crisis in the spring. Iraq accused Syria of reducing the river's flow to intolerable levels. Meanwhile, Syria blamed Turkey for the problem. The Iraqi government was not satisfied with the Syrian response, and the mounting frustration resulted in mutual threats that brought the parties to the brink of armed hostility. A war over water was averted when, thanks to Saudi Arabia's mediation, Syria released additional quantities of water to Iraq. The main cause of this crisis was the mounting political rivalry and tension between the two Ba'athist regimes. In other words, it was not a water-sharing crisis per se, but rather the beginning of the use of water as a political lever in non-riparian issues (Scheumann 1998, 2003).

Emergence of Water Diplomacy Institutions during the Period of Political Confrontations

From the 1980s until the late 1990s, political tensions among the parties insinuated itself into every aspect of their relationship and thus, inevitably, water issues moved into the realm of high politics. Bilateral relations between Turkey and Syria had long been strained. Two principal sources of friction were Syria's extensive logistical support for the Kurdistan Workers' Party (PKK), a separatist terrorist organization, and Syrian irredentist claims to the province of Hatay in Turkey. Despite official denials in Damascus, Syria's support for subversive activities against Turkey was widely known and can be shown to have existed since the early 1980s (Kibaroglu and Scheumann 2013).

Although the regional political environment was not conducive to water cooperation in the early 1980s, the growing exploitation of the Euphrates through the construction of the Ataturk Dam in Turkey led to fresh calls for cooperation. Because the issues triggered by water development schemes along the Tigris and Euphrates are so complex and far-reaching, the three riparians had to find ways to structure their discussions. To this end, Iraq took the initiative in the formation of a permanent joint technical body. The first meeting of the JTC between Turkey and Iraq in 1980 led to its official establishment in 1983, with membership including participants from all three riparians assigned to lay down methods and procedures that would lead to the definition of a reasonable and adequate quantity of water for each country from both rivers (Kibaroglu 2002). However, the JTC was unable to agree on any substantial resolution even after sixteen meetings.

Negotiations were suspended in 1993. A careful examination of the records of the negotiations among the riparian states, and their failure, shows that non-water issues, more precisely, the overall pattern of relations between the three countries, played a decisive part in the growth of tension and disputes.

The use of transboundary rivers was only one factor in their complex web of relations and interactions (Scheumann 1998).

The major issues that led to deadlock within the JTC were related to both the subject and the object of the negotiations: should the Euphrates and the Tigris be considered a single system, or could discussions be confined to the Euphrates river alone? The wording of the JTC's ultimate objective – establishing a common terminology – was also problematic: should there be a proposal for the 'sharing' of the 'international rivers', or should there be a tri-lateral regime for determining the 'utilization of transboundary watercourses'? Iraq and Syria considered the Euphrates an international river and insisted on an immediate sharing agreement under which its waters would be shared on the basis of the needs of each country. Turkey, on the other hand, regarded the Euphrates and Tigris as forming a single transboundary river basin from which water should be allocated according to objective needs (Kut 1993).

International customary law on transboundary watercourses acted as the point of reference throughout the negotiation process at the JTC meetings. The principles of equitable and reasonable utilization, of the optimum use of water resources between states, and of the avoidance of transboundary harm to both nature and human usage were evoked by diplomats representing the three riparians. By their nature, the principles of international customary law do not constitute enforceable rules, nor are they subject to what concepts such as 'equity' might mean in concrete situations. In this way, while interpreting the principles of international law concerning equitable utilization, the riparians adopted opposing and rigid positions, with Turkey insisting on its water needs being met, and Syria and Iraq demanding their unilateral shares and respect for water rights.

Turkey's needs-based approach was expressed in the Three-Stage Plan put forward by the technocrats from its central water agency. According to the plan, inventory studies of water and land resources comprising the territories of the various states throughout the region would be undertaken and jointly evaluated. On the basis of these studies, the means and measures needed to attain the most reasonable, optimum utilization of resources would be defined. Although founded on principles of scientific rationality, the likely result of the acceptance of Turkey's proposal as a basis for tripartite negotiations would be to reveal the lesser viability of Syria's and Iraq's irrigation expansion plans – which would, of course, be unacceptable to them. On the other hand, Syria and Iraq insisted on an immediate agreement under which the waters of the Euphrates would be shared on the basis of the water rights claimed by each country. Both countries asserted that, as the annual average flow of the Euphrates River was around 1,000 m^3 per second, Turkey should keep only one-third of the flow for itself and allow the remaining two-thirds to be shared by Syria and Iraq (Kibaroglu 2002).

The JTC meetings, which provided a platform by which claims and counterclaims concerning the use of the rivers and the nature of customary international water law could be voiced, did not make an effective contribution to the settlement of the regional water dispute. The JTC did not provide a platform for delineating the riparians' priorities and needs as a basis for addressing regional water problems. In this respect, water use patterns and the riparians' related legislation and institutional structures never had a chance of being discussed. National management and allocation policies were like 'black boxes', and water management practices within the various countries simply could not be debated during these negotiations (Kibaroglu and Scheumann 2013).

However, the role of the JTC should not be underestimated. Although its meetings were infrequent and appear to have made little substantive progress on the question of water allocation, it was a useful channel for water diplomacy in the ET basin.

Neither of the treaties signed in the late 1980s prove a useful means of managing the transboundary river system equitably. In 1987 and 1990, two bilateral accords – acknowledged by all the riparian states as constituting interim agreements – were signed following a number of high-level meetings of top officials in the region. In 1987, the Turkish-Syrian Protocol on Economic Cooperation was the first formal bilateral agreement reached on the Euphrates River. With this protocol, Turkey promised a water flow of up to 500 m^3 per second, or around 16 km^3 per year, at the Turkish-Syrian border (Protocol 1987). Meanwhile, the Syrian-Iraqi water accord of 1990 designated Syria's share of the Euphrates waters as 42 per cent and the remaining 58 per cent was allocated to Iraq as a fixed annual total percentage (Law No. 14 1990).

However, the existence of these bilateral accords, both relating to the Euphrates alone, could not be accepted as evidence of cooperation. Each agreement was bilateral and predominantly concerned with water quantity issues. The riparians could not agree on more comprehensive forms of cooperation that would adopt an integrated approach to the various aspects of water use and needs (quality, quantity, flood protection, preservation of ecosystems and prevention of accidents) and might potentially facilitate negotiations by linking water management issues. The agreements lacked effective organizational backup, at least in the form of joint monitoring. Most critically, both treaties failed to address fluctuations in flow, meaning that they contained no clauses referring to the periods of drought and flooding that occur frequently in the basin and cause drastic changes in the flow regime that require urgent adjustment to the use of the rivers.

During that period, water relations among the riparian states were mostly handled at the diplomatic level through the exchange of curt diplomatic notes. When diplomacy failed to ease the tensions, meetings were held at the highest level where the driving rationale was the pursuit of Turkey's, Syria's and Iraq's strategic national objectives. Yet these strategic interests lacked sound and scientific foundations, particularly when they were most needed as water shortages grew and water quality deteriorated. Instead, rhetoric prevailed and all parties stressed the need to achieve food self-sufficiency, food security or other social and regional development objectives, claiming them as strategic national goals. Consequently, the riparians' negotiating strategies were incompatible and, unsurprisingly, favoured national claims (Kibaroglu and Scheumann 2013).

Water Diplomacy during High-Level Political Rapprochement

In the first decade of the 2000s, transboundary water policy relations began to take place in a cooperative environment. Political will expressed at the highest decision-making levels was most decisive in building these cooperative frameworks. However, water bureaucracies also had a role in the turnaround. In 1998, Turkish-Syrian relations became tense, when Turkey threatened Syria with military measures to prevent the country from providing ample support to the PKK. War was prevented by the mediation of then Egyptian president Hosni Mubarak and Iranian foreign minister Kamal Kharrazi. Syria decided not to risk war and expelled the head of PKK, namely Abdullah Ocalan, who was subsequently captured by Turkish security forces in February 1999. This event paved the way for the conclusion of the Turkish-Syrian Adana/Ceyhan Security Agreement in October 1998. Shortly after signing, Syria requested the resumption of the JTC meetings to enable the water issue to be considered. The Ceyhan Security Agreement (Adana Accords) marked the beginning of a new era based on more cooperative initiatives of interest to both sides (Scheumann 2003). One of the first initiatives came in the form of the 2001 Joint Communiqué between the Southeastern Anatolia Project Regional Development Administration (GAP RDA) under the Turkish prime minister and the General Organization for Land Development (GOLD) under the Syrian Ministry of Irrigation (Joint Communiqué 2001). The GAP RDA–GOLD partnership was based on the common understanding of the importance of the sustainable utilization of the region's land and water resources through joint rural development and environmental protection projects, joint training programs, exchanges of experts and technology, and study missions. Syrian and Turkish delegations visited one another's development project sites. Over the course of these visits, the two sides were given the opportunity to exchange their experiences of positive and negative impacts of water and land resource development projects going back several decades. Once again, the water issue was relegated to the technical level, as in the 1960s, and left to intergovernmental networks composed of technocrats. However, unlike the technical negotiations held in the 1960s, the GAP RDA-GOLD dialogue covered such disparate issues as urban and rural water quality management and rural development (participatory irrigation management and agricultural research). Even though the dialogue between these two leading institutions has not resulted in concrete project implementation or regular exchange programs, it has served as a semiformal consultation mechanism and paved the way for initiatives taken by other government departments and agencies in 2008 and 2009 with the similar objective of solving transboundary water problems within a broader framework of political, economic and social development.

In 2008, the Turkish government embarked on a number of cooperative foreign policy initiatives involving its southern neighbours, Syria and Iraq in particular. The political reasons behind these initiatives can be analyzed at contextual, regional, bilateral and domestic levels, although that analysis is beyond the scope of this chapter. However, the political will expressed and sealed at the highest level in Turkey for broader cooperation with its southern neighbours was also reflected in official statements and cooperative transboundary water development and management initiatives in the Euphrates, Tigris and Orontes river systems. In this context, Turkey and Iraq signed a Joint Political Declaration on the Establishment of the HSCC on 10 July 2008. The first ministerial meeting of the HSCC, a forum for joint meetings of the Iraqi and Turkish cabinets, was held in Istanbul on 17–18 September 2009. The Turkish foreign minister was accompanied by seven executive members of the cabinet, including the ministers of trade, energy, transport, agriculture and the environment (water), while the Iraqi minister was accompanied by nine executive cabinet members, the counterparts of the Turkish ministers, and their deputy ministers.

According to the strategic partnership agreement signed between Turkey and Iraq, the HSCC was to meet at least once a year, with the prime ministers of the two countries chairing the meetings. Ministerial meetings, on the other hand, would be held at least three times a year and technical delegations would come together four times a year. Decisions made by the HSCC would be implemented within the framework of an action plan (Kibaroglu and Scheumann 2013).

On the other front, the first Turkish-Syrian HSCC meeting took place in Damascus on 22–23 December 2009. These cooperative initiatives taken at the highest political level made it possible to resolve a number of outstanding disputes between Turkey and Syria. Thus, under the chairmanship of two ministers, Syria's minister of irrigation and Turkey's minister of the environment and forestry, a commission composed of technocrats and diplomats from the two countries met in Ankara on 8 December 2009 to prepare the framework and contents of the series of protocols, MoUs, on the modalities of development, management, and use of the waters of the Euphrates, the Tigris and the Orontes Rivers. This period of rapprochement showed that, when led by politicians at the highest level, the riparians preferred functional cooperation and a benefit-sharing approach.

Water Diplomacy in Its Heydays: Water Protocols of 2009

At the Turkey–Iraq HSCC meeting, 48 MoUs were signed by the two countries on 15 October 2009, one of them concerning water (Memorandum of Understanding between Turkey and Iraq, 2009). Although the river is not referred to by name in the title, the text of this MoU explicitly states that it concerns the waters of the Euphrates and the Tigris Rivers. In line with the envisaged functional approach, the MoU was signed by Iraq's Ministry of Water Resources and Turkey's Ministry of the Environment and Forestry (MEF) – the government departments responsible for all technical matters relating in particular to water development and management and the protection of water resources. The MoU identified particular issues requiring urgent transboundary cooperation, including assessment of water resources, which are tending to diminish because of increases in water use and climate change; assessment and calibration of existing hydrological measuring stations; modernization of existing irrigation systems; prevention of water losses from domestic water supply systems and provision of safe water; construction of water supply and water treatment facilities in Iraq, with the participation of Turkish companies; development of mechanisms to solve problems arising during the dry period; and joint investigation, planning and projects for flood protection.

The modalities of cooperation are also outlined by the MoU. The parties agree to transfer knowledge, experience and technology on water management practices by developing cooperative projects and conducting research and development activities. It is interesting to note that, rather than arguing over only their respective water shares, as happened at previous JTC meetings, the Iraqi and Turkish authorities focused on common issues over transboundary water management and use. Those issues are directly related to water development, use and management practices at national level, which actually have direct impacts on transboundary water policies and practices. The protocol also specifically addresses emerging regional (and global) issues, such as the effects climate change might have on regional water resources – an issue which had been neglected for decades. Another distinct characteristic of the MoU is that it envisages involving such non-governmental entities as academic institutions, private firms and non-governmental organizations in the activities that it covers.

At the first meeting of their HSCC held in Damascus on 23–24 December 2009, Turkey and Syria signed 50 protocols, 4 of which concerned regional waters (i.e. those of the Euphrates, Tigris and Orontes). In this context, Turkey and Syria signed a protocol on the Tigris under which Turkey agreed that Syria could withdraw an annual $1.25\ km^3$ of water, provided that the flow of water is within the average. The withdrawals are based on monthly flows and are to be made at appropriate times and places. This protocol is further evidence of a change in the positions of the water and diplomatic bureaucracies, particularly in Syria. When the hydropolitical tensions were at their peak in the 1980s, Syria had never agreed to discuss the waters of the Tigris, considering it to be insignificant because of its geographical location in the basin: the Tigris forms the boundary between Turkey and Syria and between Syria and Iraq for about 40 km. At that time, Syria focused almost exclusively on the Euphrates, prioritizing the completion of the Euphrates Valley Project. As Syrian technocrats eventually encountered technical and social difficulties in reclaiming land in the Euphrates Valley, their attention turned to northeastern Syria where it was possible to expand the amount of irrigated land.

The other two protocols signed by Turkey and Syria cover issues that have only recently come to the agenda of transboundary water negotiations among the technocrats and diplomats concerned (MoU 2009b, 2009c). In this respect, it is interesting to note that this was the first official agreement concluded by the two countries regarding protection of the environment, water quality management, water efficiency, drought management and flood protection with a view towards addressing the adverse effects of climate change. Unlike the bilateral protocol concluded in 1987 on sharing the waters of the Euphrates, these protocols focus on how the riparian states were to use, manage, protect and develop the diminishing water resources of the Euphrates and the Tigris Rivers. An analysis of the wording of these two protocols reveals that the water bureaucracies had a chance to open up the countries' black boxes.

On the basis of the political will expressed at the highest level of the HSCC, water technocrats have together concentrated on the urgent problems of the acute shortage and deteriorating quality of water resources. Gone are the days when the two countries adopted reserved and rigid positions on their water shares and rights: now they openly discuss new and efficient methods and procedures for managing the supply of and demand for water for agricultural, industrial and domestic purposes. The protocols cover a range of issues. These include various forms of supply management such as cloud seeding (artificial rain) to increase precipitation, the installation of early flood warning systems and flood protection measures, and agricultural practices with drought-resistant crops. They also include various forms of demand management such as sharing of knowledge and experience about modern irrigation techniques; prevention of water losses in domestic water supply; organization of training programs relating to the operation of dams and the efficient utilization of water resources; sharing of knowledge and technology pertaining to wastewater storage and the reuse of treated wastewater in agriculture and industry; and cooperation on the development of land use techniques to increase the amount of soil and water saved.

The general approach and the content of the protocols also reveal that Turkey's first-hand experience with the EU water policy and approach to water management has been broadly translated into the principles envisioned in the protocols. Therefore, the staff of Turkey's MEF, in particular, supported these protocols vigorously because they felt that their implementation would be a useful practice for the implementation and extension of the new water legislation in Turkey transposed from the EU's water legislation. The EU's 'river basin level' water management approach in the form of the WFD of 2000 will thus be applied not only in Turkey's national river basins but also in such transboundary river basins as the Euphrates, Tigris and Orontes. Moreover, common standards for measuring (gauging) quantities of water and monitoring the quality of transboundary water are among the MEF's main objectives in its cooperation with Syria and Iraq. In this context, one of the main aims of the Turkish bureaucracy is to establish environmental quality standards and to implement the polluter-pays and cost-recovery principles at transboundary level, as the relevant MoU stipulates (Kibaroglu and Scheumann 2013).

These bilateral MoUs could not be put into practice due to regional instability and increased political tensions between the riparian states. The MoUs also faced the ever-present challenges of incompatibilities in national, institutional and legal frameworks, complex national water management systems and uncoordinated water management practices among the basin countries. The existing water protocols, therefore, can only be properly implemented when the riparians' institutional capacities are upgraded and harmonized in more conducive political circumstances (Kibaroglu 2019).

Flexible Water Diplomacy at the Ministerial Level

On 22 March 2007, at the opening of an international conference in Antalya, Turkey, the Turkish minister of the environment and forestry invited the Syrian minister of irrigation and the Iraqi minister of water resources to join him in discussing how to set up a cooperative framework to deal with regional water issues. These ministers decided that the periodic meetings of the JTC, which had been held between 1982 and 1992 before being completely abandoned, should be resumed. Thus, a series of JTC meetings have been held since – the first in Damascus, Syria, on 7–11 May 2007 – which was followed by a tripartite ministerial meeting in Damascus, on 10–11 January 2008, at which it was agreed that training programs on irrigation water management and efficient utilization of water resources would be conducted. At the second JTC meeting held in Istanbul on 23–24 February 2009, officials decided that the next ministerial meeting would be held in Baghdad, opportunities for developing joint projects would be seized and a JTC bylaw stating its mission and responsibilities would be adopted. On 3 September 2009, both a tripartite ministerial meeting and the third meeting of the JTC took place in Ankara. The three sides decided to cooperate in initiating water training programs and in monitoring and exchanging information on climate change and drought conditions in the three countries. They also agreed to erect new water flow gauging stations and to modernize the existing ones. After talks between the Iraqi foreign minister and the Turkish environment minister, Turkey further agreed to provide 550 m^3 per second of water from the Euphrates River during the dry season in the autumn of 2009 (Kibaroglu and Scheumann 2013).

In March 2008, the Turkish, Iraqi and Syrian ministers agreed to establish a joint water institute in Turkey, with each riparian appointing 15 water engineers to conduct studies on water use efficiency and improved water management in the region. The institute was to map water resources in the region and draw up a report on measures that the respective countries should take to ensure effective management of those resources. Engineers from the three countries met to exchange information and know-how. The first training activity in this context concerned modern irrigation practices in the region and the second focused on dam construction and safety. The group also developed an interest in studying climate change and its impacts on regional waters. The training institute in Istanbul hosted the third training program for experts in that field. The ministers' initiative in reconvening the JTC facilitated the drafting of a series of MoUs, putting an official seal on cooperation. Moreover, their network also led to a series of training programs that have helped water bureaucracies, in particular, achieve a certain level of common understanding and discourse. Furthermore, the ministerial network proved capable of flexibility and spontaneity in addressing acute water shortages in the region by making swift decisions to adjust flows to meet the needs of downstream riparians (Kibaroglu and Scheumann 2013).

Current and Emerging Challenges for Water Diplomacy Frameworks

Notwithstanding the failures in interstate water cooperation and the shortcomings and loopholes in the existing water agreements, the present overarching challenge in the ET basin is to coordinate water resources management and establish good transboundary water governance in the midst of the current state of affairs. The Syrian civil war and overall political instability, which have had deep impacts and spillover effects in the region, demonstrate that, while the genesis of the conflict is a complicated narrative, water is certainly part of it.

Given the continuation of violence and instability in the region, a lack of interstate coordination and poor security schemes along the rivers themselves, violent non-state actors such as 'Islamic State' (IS) have been able to use water both as a resource and as a weapon. Not only have such groups destroyed water-related infrastructure, such as pipelines, sanitation plants, bridges, and cables connected to water installations, but they have also used water as an instrument of violence by deliberately flooding towns, polluting bodies of water and ruining local economies by disrupting electricity generation and agriculture (Vishwanath 2015). In 2014, for instance, when IS shut down Fallujah's Nuaimiyah Dam, the subsequent flooding destroyed many Iraqi fields and villages. In June 2015, they closed the Ramadi barrage in Anbar Province, reducing water flows to the famed Iraqi Marshes and forcing locals to flee. The capture of the Mosul Dam, while in the group's possession for a few weeks in August 2014, gave IS control of nearly 20 per cent of Iraq's electricity generation (Von Lossow 2016). Since the civil war erupted in Syria, furthermore, IS has seized the opportunity to control territory in the conflicted region by joining the fight against the Assad regime (Hashim 2014).

IS subsequently lost control of all dams, but not before using them to flood or starve downstream populations in order to pressure them to surrender. At the same time, governments and militaries have used similar tactics to combat IS, closing the gates of dams or attacking water infrastructure under their control, causing the surrounding population to suffer. The Syrian government has been repeatedly accused of withholding water, reducing flows or closing dam gates during its battles against IS or other rebel groups, and of using the denial of clean water as a coercive tactic against many Damascus suburbs thought to be sympathetic to rebels. Water contamination is widespread, disastrously increasing incidences of deadly water-borne diseases.

The emergence of IS as a non-state violent actor in the region meant that riparian states must be thoroughly prepared for and responsive to possible attacks on the region's water supply and development infrastructure. This should also convince the riparian states of the need to establish regional security arrangements to preserve and protect their resources. With collaborative management underpinning collective protection, water – often a source of competition and conflict – could become a facilitator of peace and cooperation (Waslekar 2017).

Tignino (2010) analyzes the link between water and international peace and security by focusing on the impact of armed conflict on water. She concludes that ensuring access to water, along with protecting water resources, contributes to the prevention of conflicts and transition to peace in post-conflict states. The Global High-Level Panel on Water and Peace, which was launched in Geneva in 2015 to develop a set of proposals for strengthening the global architecture to prevent and resolve water-related conflicts, also produced recommendations for protecting water during and after armed conflict (Geneva Water Hub 2016).

As the Syrian civil war pushes riparian states to develop new water governance principles and practices in conflict and post-conflict situations, the riparian states in the ET basin must improve their understanding of the strategic role that water and water supply infrastructure play in armed conflicts and to reflect on possible ways to improve the protection of water under international law during and after armed conflicts. The linkage between international humanitarian law (Additional Protocols of 1977 to the Third and Fourth Geneva Conventions of 1949) and the law on transboundary water resources (Article 29, UN Watercourses Convention 1997) may ensure better protection of water during armed conflict. Riparian states should also envisage joint ways of dealing with transboundary water resources over the course of reconstruction and rehabilitation efforts in the post-conflict phase.

Enduring Water Diplomacy Frameworks: Turkey–Iraq Track

Years after having been suspended, JTC meetings were revitalized in 2007. This launched the beginning of a series of meetings held on a bilateral and trilateral basis, however irregularly, until the civil war erupted in Syria. After years of deadlock in transboundary water relations, due to uncertainties imposed by the Syrian civil war, Turkey and Iraq decided, at a ministerial level, to reopen dialogue on their transboundary water resources. In this context, the Minutes of the Bilateral Cooperation Meeting between Turkey and Iraq signed by the deputy undersecretary of the Ministry of Forestry and Water Affairs (MFWA), Turkey, and the head of the unit for Neighboring Countries and Law of the Ministry of Foreign Affairs, Iraq on 15 May 2014 includes the principles, modalities and issues of bilateral water cooperation. According to this official document, both sides agreed in principle to continue to hold meetings aiming to further develop transboundary water relations. Both sides agreed to advance technical collaboration, to further develop and diversify technical training, and to engage in technical cooperation on issues relating to irrigation systems. It was decided to establish a joint working group with a mandate to prepare for projects on the Hacibey Stream and the Lesser Zab (Tigris River tributaries). This working group would prepare a report to be presented to the ministers of both countries. Turkey agreed to notify the Iraqi side six months prior to impoundment of the Ilisu Dam and further agreed to provide an impoundment plan to the Iraqi side. A visit by the Iraqi delegate to the Ilisu Dam site was planned for a later date under appropriate conditions. It was agreed that the Iraqi side would extend official demands to the Turkish side concerning technical help for the prevention of water losses in the Mosul Dam. It was also decided that bilateral cooperation should be established on environmental matters relating to the Tigris River and agreed that each side would provide technical support to the other if the need arose.

On 25 December 2014, furthermore, the 2009 Turkish-Iraqi MoU on Water (Memorandum of Understanding between Turkey and Iraq 2009) was revisited, and Article 2 (paragraph 'a') was amended. It was decided that,

> Cooperation on joint projects on the water resource management of the Euphrates and Tigris shall further be developed. This cooperation will include the assessment of water resources and the increase in water use (agricultural, industrial, municipal and drinking water) and climate change. Turkey will release equitable and reasonable river waters to Iraq according to the above assessment. Over the course of joint studies, the current situation of the water resources in respect to the meteorological and hydrological conditions in the Euphrates and Tigris will be determined. (Saatci 2015)

As a follow-up activity, water experts from relevant ministries in Turkey and Iraq met in Istanbul in 2016. They discussed the enhancement of water cooperation between Turkey and Iraq, joint technical studies on climate change and the organization of technical training programmers. Both parties agreed to complete the legislative processes required to put the Memorandum of Understanding (2009) into force. Parties also agreed to form a joint expert committee to study and investigate the proposed Hacibey and Karadag friendship dam projects on the Turkish-Iraqi border.

The Turkish Water Institute (SUEN in Turkish acronym) conducted training programmes for the Iraqi experts. A delegation of 10 experts from the Ministry of Water Resources of the Republic of Iraq attended a short course at SUEN in 27–31 March 2017, with a programme of lectures covering the planning of water resources, water and wastewater treatment, water quality management and river basin planning. Field trips were made to the drinking water and wastewater treatment plants in Istanbul (SUEN 2017b).

Thanks to the enabling political atmosphere created by the state institutions concerned, various other actors in transboundary water governance had taken measures to foster cooperation between Turkey and Iraq. The Strategic Foresight Group (SFG), a Mumbai-based think tank, facilitated dialogue between Iraq and Turkey, involving policymakers and experts from the two countries. With the support of the Swiss Agency for Development and Cooperation, the SFG organized a series of meetings in 2013–14, with stakeholders from both countries deciding to focus on the Tigris River, as the situation in Syria did not allow any basin-wide cooperation on the Euphrates River. As a culmination of its efforts, the SFG organized a meeting between senior representatives from Iraq and Turkey in June 2014. The delegations, comprised senior advisors from the prime ministers, former cabinet ministers, members of parliament, officials of water ministries and water authorities and experts from Iraq and Turkey, established consensus on a Plan of Action to promote exchange and calibration of data and standards pertaining to Tigris River flows. The plan was expected to contribute significantly to transforming water from a source of crisis into an instrument of peace. Such a change in the role of water in a region as challenging as the Middle East requires institutional arrangements. On several occasions, the governments of Iraq and Turkey have agreed in principle to promote exchange and harmonization of water data. The SFG initiative has been intended to help both countries take the agreement to the next level of an operative plan of action (Kibaroglu 2019).

The Center for Middle Eastern Strategic Studies (ORSAM in Turkish acronym), a non-profit research centre in Ankara, organized a workshop called Water Issues in Turkey-Iraq Relations on 15 March 2017 in cooperation with the Nahrain Center, Iraq, and the Iraqi Embassy in Ankara. The Iraqi water resources minister also attended as the keynote speaker. The workshop drew a number of diplomats, bureaucrats and academics from both countries and addressed several issues pertaining to the importance of water in bilateral relations; the importance of the Tigris and Euphrates Rivers to the Iraqi people; inefficient water policies in Iraq before 2003; the impact of the presence of IS on water management in Iraq; the situation of the Iraqi water infrastructure and reconstruction projects; and the management of irrigation waters in Iraq. The Turkey–Iraq track, involving official as well as non-official contacts, demonstrates that, when multilateral negotiations became impossible, riparians can continue talks on their transboundary waters at a bilateral level even in volatile times. Turkish and Iraqi government officials as well as water professionals have made sustained efforts to create new areas for water cooperation, such as developing projects for building joint dams on the border (Kibaroglu 2019).

Yet, the Turkey–Iraq track fell short of adopting joint strategies for response the actions of violent non-state actors and could not build a basin-wide understanding for protecting water resources during and after conflict. New water cooperation frameworks, therefore, should address these thorny issues. The existing transboundary water institutions, such as the JTC, could act as a multilateral platform for implementing water cooperation frameworks. Compared to bilateral water sharing treaties, moreover, the existing MoUs, with their broader outlook, can provide useful guidelines for comprehensive transboundary water cooperation. However, these bilateral MoUs should be synthesized into a multilateral protocol involving all of the riparian states and all of the stakeholders concerned, including civil society organizations and private companies in the energy, agriculture, environment and health sectors as well as relevant development-related sectors. Whenever there is an opportunity to do so, transboundary water cooperation should be resumed from a variety of perspectives that may provide opportunities for regional cooperation. These should include, among other things, joint initiatives for collecting reliable data on surface and groundwater resources. In fact, water technocrats drafting the MoUs have already emphasized this aspect by referring to the issue of the assessment of water resources and the calibration of existing hydrological measurement stations in the bilateral protocols. Such objective and consistent knowledge of the river system would allow joint projects to be conducted in water-related development fields, such as energy, agriculture, the environment and health (Kibaroglu 2019).

Turkey's Harmonization with the European Union and Transboundary Water Policy

Turkey's water policies and role in its neighbourhood, namely Europe, the Middle East and Caucasus have evolved considerably. Among these evolving relations, those enjoyed with the EU within the framework of accession negotiations deserve special attention. The goal of EU accession implies that Turkey is obliged to adopt and implement the entire body of European Environmental Law, covering many far-reaching legal requirements, namely the WFD with significant implications for the member states' international water cooperation, and a number of international environmental agreements to which the EU is a contracting party. Turkey's EU accession progress, however, has been strikingly slow, and out of the 35 chapters necessary to complete the accession process only 16 had been opened and only 1 had been completed and closed. Even though accession negotiations have stalled since 2016 due to political differences, Turkish water and environment bureaucracy (i.e. General Directorate of Water Management) has continued to develop new legislation and policies which are in line with EU water policies.

Against this backdrop, cooperation on Turkish transboundary rivers becomes an important issue in accession negotiations and demands careful analysis of achievements and shortcomings to date. In the EU–Turkey accession partnership, the transboundary water issue has already been identified as a priority which demands short-term considerations and progress (Kibaroglu et al. 2011).

The official discourse in Turkey's water diplomacy underlines that Turkey and the EU have had diverging approaches to water development, management and protection (Rende 2013). In the official contention, while Turkey considers water resources as a major driving force for sustainable development, the EU gives priority to the protection of the environment and water ecosystems.

The focus of the EU water management understanding is, in general, to deal with the impacts of water resource use and to mitigate the negative impacts thereof. The reason for this is that the EU member states have completed their major water development projects and shifted to the next phase of water management, that is, the effective and efficient use of existing resources, practicing demand management and eliminating the negative impacts of water use (Kibaroglu and Sümer 2007).

Turkey, in pursuing socio-economic development, has yet to complete its construction of water development structures in order to meet the increasing demands of domestic, irrigation and energy sectors. Contrary to EU water policies, Turkey still follows a 'hydraulic mission' that is mainly focused on water quantity and increase of supply. Nevertheless, Turkey has also experienced the negative impacts of water resource development. Hence, Turkey too, had to adopt methods such as demand management and assessments of environmental impacts.

Within the context of integrated basin management, the WFD gives priority to the completion of river basin management plans, together with identifying detailed negative impacts on ground and surface water in river basins, as well as measures and sanctions that will be put into practice for mitigating those impacts. However, among the factors that play a crucial role in making the river basin management plans, the existing situation and impacts and the mitigation of these impacts come to the forefront, while socio-economic development needs, which are deemed essential and strategic by Turkey, receive the least attention in the WFD (Grontmij Consulting Engineers 2004). Whereas the EU defines future uses of water as risks, Turkey does not regard the building of new infrastructures (dams and irrigation systems) for water resources development as such. On the contrary, the building of new infrastructures is designed to have positive effects on socio-economic development. Conducting river basin management plans in isolation from a macroeconomic analysis is not an appropriate policy within the integrated water resources management framework. Hence, the WFD has a narrow approach concerned solely with impacts and measures. One may argue that the Turkish case points to a number of gaps in the general principles of the WFD. Regardless, Turkey has to carry out water resources development painstakingly, by taking into consideration environmental, social and economic impacts (Kibaroglu and Sümer 2007).

The EU adopts a 'limited territorial sovereignty' doctrine with regard to transboundary water resources management and utilization. While, on the one hand, Turkish diplomatic discourse has emphasized that Turkey would begin adopting the EU water- and environment-related legislation, it adds that it would be extremely costly. The official discourse also underlines that full harmonization with EU water policy and legislation, namely the EU WFD as well as accession to the regional conventions such as the UNECE Helsinki, Aarhus and Espoo Conventions, could only be realized when Turkey becomes a full member of the EU (Rende 2004).

The MFA has overseen the efforts and accomplishments of the MFWA in terms of passing legislation related to integrated water resources management, river basin level planning and management, and water quality management. However, the MFA authorities have been strict in directing the MFWA to defer the adoption of EU water legislation provisions related to the transboundary waters to a date after Turkey becomes EU member. Thus, although EU WFD stipulations were meticulously studied for adoption, the articles related to transboundary water management, such as article 13, have not been looked at within the scope of Turkey's harmonization process with EU legislation. On the other hand, Turkey has continued to receive repeated criticisms from the EU regarding water quality and has stressed several times in the progress reports that further efforts are needed to transpose and implement the EU *acquis*, including a new framework law on water resources, and to bring drinking water and wastewater discharge standards in line with the *acquis*.

Water diplomacy networks, particularly at a governmental level, have developed a doubtful understanding of the EU authorities' approach to Turkey's transboundary water policy. This has essentially been due to the release of an EU Commission Report (2004), which contains controversial comments related to the 'international management' of the Euphrates and Tigris rivers (EU Commission 2004).

> A key issue in the region has been access to water for development and irrigation. Water in the Middle East will increasingly become a strategic issue in the years to come, and with Turkey's accession, one can expect international management of water resources and infrastructures (dams and irrigation schemes in the Euphrates and Tigris river basins, cross-border water cooperation between Israel and its neighboring countries) to become a major issue for the EU. (EU Commission 2004)

The MFA expressed serious concerns over the report, first of all under-lining that, contrary to Turkish stance, in the report, the Euphrates and Tigris were considered as two separate river basins. The MFA interpreted the linkage made in the report between 'international management of water resources and infrastructures' and 'Turkey's accession' as a sign of the possibility that EU authorities would ask Turkey to make commitment for harmonization with regional and global environment and water conventions to which EU is party as a performance criterion/precondition in order to launch EU mem-bership negotiations. Moreover, inclusion of 'Israel and its neighboring coun-tries' in the issue gives the impression that the waters of the ET basin could be considered as a regional source from which all regional countries other than the riparians could also benefit.

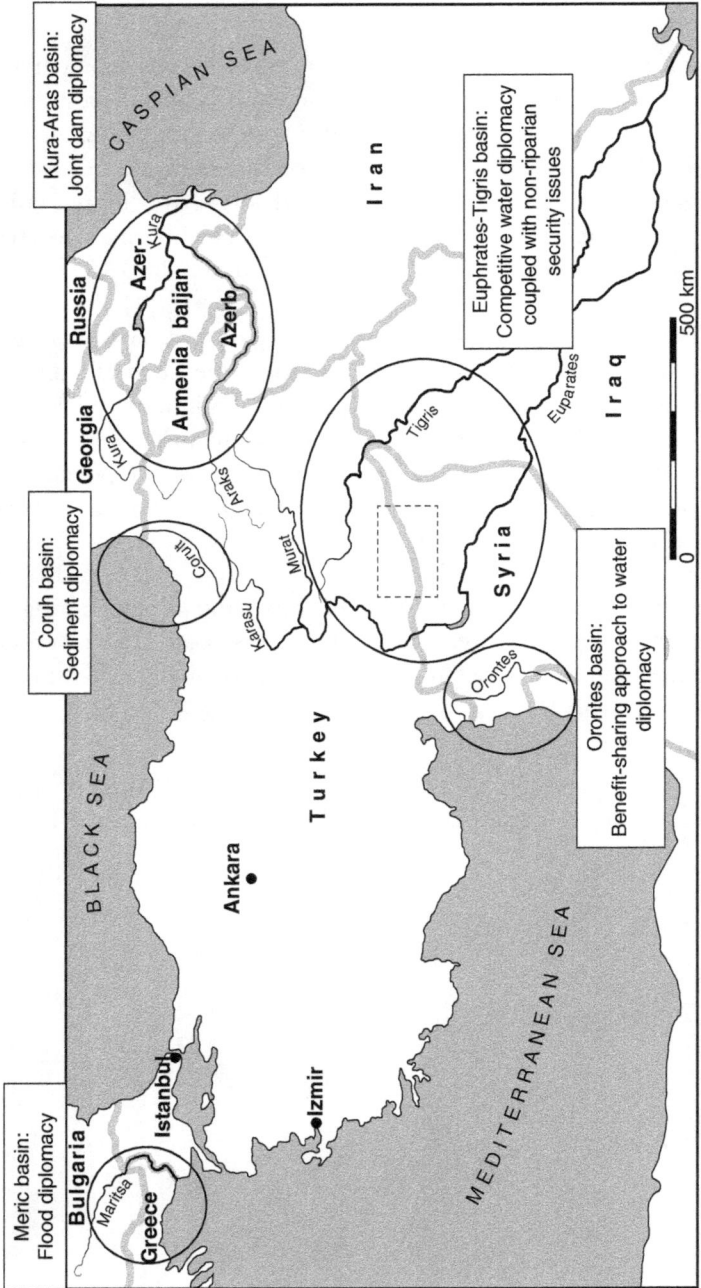

Figure 2. Water diplomacy frameworks in Turkey's transboundary river basins Source: Kibaroglu et al. 2005, p. 4.

Chapter 5

ANALYZING NON-STATE ACTORS AND PROCESSES IN TURKEY'S WATER DIPLOMACY FRAMEWORK

Overview

Water diplomacy covers a complex array of water management problems that can be best understood as a product of competition, feedback and interconnectivity between natural and societal variables within a political context (Islam and Susskind 2013). Although we currently observe the emergence and increasing presence of non-state actors within the framework of water diplomacy, states are nonetheless pivotal in its practice. Hence, previous chapters of this book have expounded upon the discourses and practices of water diplomacy as have been implemented by the Turkish state, analyzing its institutional foundations in the context of the country's historical and geographical realities.

Broadening the view, however, this chapter offers a look at the role non-state actors play in Turkey's water diplomacy framework (WDF); investigating if and how epistemic communities, academia and civil society contribute to transboundary water policymaking. Particular attention has been paid to a Track II initiative, namely the Euphrates-Tigris Initiative for Cooperation (ETIC), which was established in 2005 by a group of scholars and professionals from Turkey, Syria and Iraq in the Euphrates-Tigris (ET) river basin.

The chapter concludes with a presentation of the best practices and lessons learned from the history of Turkey's water diplomacy. Keeping an open dialogue with its neighbours over transboundary water issues as well as signing of several bilateral water agreements (i.e. best practices) can be seen as achievements in Turkish water diplomacy. Yet, lack of a comprehensive river basin treaty and Turkey's (non-party) position towards global and regional (European) conventions still constitute stumbling blocks from which lessons should be drawn. The chapter offers a non-zero-sum approach to water negotiations in making policy-relevant recommendations for tackling with future challenges in Turkey's water diplomacy.

Non-State Actors in Turkey's Water Diplomacy Framework

*Track II Water Diplomacy: Euphrates–Tigris Initiative for Cooperation**

The international arena is no longer the exclusive domain of foreign ministries and diplomats. Aside from the efforts of official diplomats, civil society and academia play an important role in establishing connections and building trust between various parties (Huntjens and de Man 2017).

Track I diplomacy is typically carried out by government officials, who use bargaining, negotiation and other peaceful means to negotiate treaties, trade policies and other international agreements – including those aimed at preventing, limiting, managing or settling conflict. Track II diplomacy (unofficial or nonofficial), meanwhile, refers to the use of non-traditional diplomatic agents, including academics, professionals, NGOs, business executives and other private citizens who are typically conducting dialogue and problem-solving activities (Snodderly 2011).

In addition to state actors, 'networks of professionals' may also take the initiative in facilitating cooperation. In this context, as a Track II diplomacy initiative in the Euphrates–Tigris (ET) basin, the ETIC was established in May 2005 by a group of scholars and professionals from the three major riparian countries: Turkey, Syria and Iraq. The overall goal of the initiative was to promote cooperation among the three riparians to achieve technical, social and economic development throughout the ET river basin (Kibaroglu 2008).

The establishment of a coordinated approach to the ET basin represents a challenging endeavour. As has been seen, each of the riparians have adhered to stringent positions that changed little over the course of three decades leading to the suspension of the negotiations in the early 1990s. Since the 1960s, mostly state officials, whether technocrats, diplomats or legal advisers, have achieved little over the course of lengthy negotiations. While political issues surrounding the river basin are perceived as relevant and complex in each of these delegates' eyes, those related to water and development are more complicated, albeit this may not seem evident.

---

* Discussion in this section is largely drawn from Aysegül Kibaroglu. 2008. 'The Role of Epistemic Communities in Offering New Cooperation Frameworks in the Euphrates-Tigris Rivers System'. *Journal of International Affairs* 61, no. 2: 183–98.

The composition and role of the ETIC fits remarkably well into the epistemic community theory, especially in terms of its role in institutional bargaining. Epistemic communities are a 'network of professionals with recognized expertise and competence in a particular domain and an authoritative claim to policy-relevant knowledge within that domain or issue-area' (Haas 1990).

The ETIC provides a test of propositions drawn from epistemic community literature from the discipline of international relations, which posits that non-governmental experts can influence governmental decision making. The epistemic community approach regards scientists and scientific knowledge as the key elements in explaining and analyzing international reality. The conflict and uncertainty inherent in interstate negotiations generate the need for expertise in developing each country's policy positions. Insofar as epistemic communities develop common understandings of problems and solutions cross-nationally, they may help their respective governments reach convergent solutions.

From the perspective of constructivist theory, this may entail new learning and discourse. Peter M. Haas (1990) argues that epistemic communities function as promoters of cooperation by decreasing, or sometimes by completely eradicating, the uncertainty factor that otherwise tends to hinder cooperation over international resources. Thus, by spreading knowledge and facilitating the learning processes, these communities consequently motivate states to reconsider their positions. Members of these communities share common beliefs in the causal structure of the issue area, in the possible technological solutions to the problem, and in the policy applications of these technologies. Epistemic communities help define the problem and narrow the range of options available to decision makers. They help integrate environmental concerns into economic and political decision making.

Epistemic communities think outside the box. They address issues that are not yet on governmental agendas, serving as a kind of early warning mechanism. Additionally, they may provide fresh approaches to problems that seem to be at an impasse in deliberations among officials. Epistemic communities can function very well across national boundaries due to the scientific community's largely transnational tradition – another factor which serves as a good base for conducting negotiations on transnational problems.

Resource politics demand an interdisciplinary approach and a balance between the scientific study of the problem, the subsequent generation of solutions and application of scientific solutions to society through the political process. As a multi-riparian initiative, the ETIC has been unique in that it looks beyond water rights, per se, to themes related to environmental protection, development and gender equity, water management and governance, and grassroots participation in a holistic, multi-stakeholder framework. The origin of the ETIC may be traced to early meetings between scientists concerned from Iraq, Syria, Turkey and the United States in 2004. This group of dedicated scholars convened multiple times, albeit irregularly.

At the first stage of these gatherings, participants shared information concerning their country's own national water policies and raised the significance of water issues in regards to socio-economic development targets. Within a short period of time, members of the group were able to develop a common understanding of existing conditions, pressing problems and needs of the region. Thanks to this, these scientists decided to turn their expertise and experience into the joint initiative of the ETIC.

The ETIC is a Track II diplomacy effort, meaning that it is voluntary, unofficial, non-binding, non-profit seeking and entirely non-governmental. Although not affiliated with any government, it aims to contribute positively to the efforts, official and unofficial, that will enhance dialogue, understanding and collaboration between the riparian states of the ET region. Although the setting up of the ETIC was initiated from within the region, its establishment benefitted from collaboration with two universities in the United States – namely Kent State University and the University of Oklahoma.

The members of ETIC have backgrounds in either academic or professional institutions. Thanks to their common scientific tongue, shared concerns and involvement with social and developmental issues pertaining to water, the group's founding members managed to rather smoothly agree upon the vision and the mission of the initiative in 2005.

The ETIC's objectives and guiding principles display a blend of lowest common denominator statements and some creative efforts to move beyond existing national positions. The ETIC focuses on the conditions, needs and opportunities for development and cooperation in the ET region. It embraces a holistic, development-focused, multisectoral approach as opposed to one simply aimed at sharing river flow, as the latter has proven divisive and unproductive. The ETIC does not promote any particular model of cooperation or formula for water sharing. Instead, it envisages itself as representing a platform through which the right one of these might be conceived.

The ETIC program areas were delineated with the active participation of stakeholders over the course of a series of meetings that took place in 2005 and 2006. The areas pertain to the three pillars of sustainable development developed at the 2002 World Summit on Sustainable Development in Johannesburg, namely, economic development, social development, and environmental protection as they relate to the development of water and land resources in the region. Development is a unifying issue that creates multiple opportunities for win-win alternatives for regional cooperation. Cooperation which is based around development provides synergy and added value to individual efforts. It also helps catalyze progress and enrich other processes.

The ETIC's overall mission, as well as its program areas, is more comprehensive than the earlier attempts at cooperation made by the Joint Technical Committee (JTC) in the 1980s (see Chapter 4). The ETIC focuses on the key concepts of sustainable regional development, namely water quantity and quality management, health issues, agricultural development, energy production, infrastructural development and environmental protection. Moreover, the ETIC action takes the form of focused meetings, expert exchanges, training programs, curriculum development, joint projects, site visits and stakeholder meetings. The JTC was endowed with a limited mandate compared to the ETIC, which was not particularly effective in creating innovative solutions for water-based social and economic development in the region. Whereas JTC meetings assembled only diplomats and legal advisors, ETIC gatherings have been more inclusive and are marked with the attendance of academics, professionals, representatives of civil society organizations and business circles, as well as representatives of various relevant international agencies. This broad range of stakeholders has defined the urgencies, needs and action modalities for regional cooperation under the leadership of the ETIC.

The ETIC intends to open the cooperation process beyond government circles and the academic community, extending participation to NGOs and society at large. The ETIC intends to lead dialogue not just around resolving narrow bilateral water disputes, however important such efforts may be, but to create a regional context through which important socio-economic development issues affecting the region can be discussed and addressed. During the years 2005, 2006 and 2007, ETIC founding members and riparian officials participated in international meetings in India, Sweden, Japan and Mexico. In 2006, ETIC organized a training program on dam safety in collaboration with the United Nations Educational, Scientific and Cultural Organization (UNESCO) aimed at training up professionals from Iran, Iraq, Syria and Turkey. The ETIC organized a stakeholder workshop and conference on Technical Cooperation for Regional Development in the Euphrates and Tigris region in September 2007. The ETIC's prospects were discussed and collaboration in ETIC activities by international agencies, such as the United Nations Development Program (UNDP), the Food and Agriculture Organization of the United Nations (FAO), Swedish International Water Institute (SIWI) and the Blue Revolution Initiative of the United States Agency for International Development (USAID) were explored with representatives in attendance. The ETIC has striven to mobilize faculty members and students from regional universities to get involved in developing joint research activities focused on development. Moreover, the ETIC intends to promote dialogue and networking among stakeholders from water-based development sectors and foster implementation of collaborative activities (ETIC 2019).

The ETIC's founding members outlined the concepts that would serve to define the scope of its objectives. ETIC members contend that awareness of the concepts surrounding socio-economic development is essential in understanding the real dynamics of the region. Hence, the vision of the ETIC is defined by its founders as a means for 'the quality of life for people in all communities, rural and urban areas, [to be] improved, and harmony between countries and in line with the natural life of the ET region [to be] achieved', contributing to the overall goal of the ETIC, namely the promotion of cooperation on technical, social and economic development over the ET region. In line with its vision and overall goals, the ETIC will continue to prepare and implement joint training and capacity-building programs as well as research and implementation projects with the aim of responding to the common needs and concerns of people across the region. In building confidence and trust among riparians, the ETIC will act toward decision makers in a responsive and cooperative manner and be transparent in all actions. The ETIC aims to enhance the consciousness of decision makers and the wider public for the facilitation of a broad range of policy issues in the region (ETIC 2019).

However, the ETIC is faced with many challenges, including the need to establish an institutional structure – that is, a legally binding, tangible status, which is deemed necessary to formalize relations with institutions regionally and internationally. Moreover, the ETIC needs to secure funding for the implementation of projects. The ETIC has prepared a project portfolio comprising research projects, assessments and evaluations, as well as developmental interventions. The academic community, government institutions, farmer organizations, municipalities and other relevant civil society organizations are determined major partners in conducting these projects.

The general regional security environment can affect calculations about whether such efforts as those embarked upon by the ETIC can be introduced to a larger audience. Thus, in more favourable regional security environments, there is a greater chance for the development of such epistemic communities, allowing greater exposure and therefore acceptance at the broader societal level. Conversely, high levels of regional conflict and tension make the transmission of cooperative ideas to official policymakers and the wider public more difficult. The ET region still lacks an institutionalized framework of political and economic cooperation. Border insecurity, terrorism and the prolonged effects of wars in Iraq and Syria inhibit the development of trust and confidence between the states. The ETIC is trying to detach collaborative activities from political conflicts in such a volatile region. Against all the odds, the region still hosts a web of cultural, social and economic interactions, and bilateral political relations are improving, particularly between Iraq and Turkey. The ETIC is trying to seize such opportunities for cooperation to carry out water-based development activities in the region (McClimans 2016).

Non-Governmental Organizations and Water Diplomacy

When the Integrated Water Resources Management Paradigm (IWRM) was introduced as the most contemporary and expedient paradigm in the early 2000s, stakeholder involvement was highlighted as an essential component in IWRM achieving equitable and effective water administration and protection on a basin-wide scale. However, subsequent debates over global water management paradigms did not substantially elaborate on how stakeholders, namely water users, local authorities, NGOs and civil society organizations, could be included in consultation and decision-making processes at transboundary level. In due course, while the absence, or rather exclusion, of the local population and authorities from transboundary water resources negotiations and decision-making processes have been emphasized by research, only scattered analysis has been given to the roles played by NGOs in water diplomacy (Petropoulos and Valvis 2011). This subsection is an attempt, in this context, to delineate the role of NGOs in Turkey's WDF.

The National Water Plan adopted by the Water Management Coordination Council as recently as 29 May 2019 particularly referenced the need for the increased participation of NGOs in policy development in Turkey (Ministry of Agriculture and Forestry 2019). The National Plan stresses the importance of government working together with NGOs to coordinate public awareness campaigns for water conservation. The plan also emphasizes the vital role played by NGOs in increasing public awareness of the responsible use of water, stating that water management in Turkey can only be conducted effectively by involving all relevant agencies, institutes, basin commissions and other NGOs in the policymaking process.

Since the 1990s, NGOs have steadily gathered more and more experience and knowledge regarding the practical implementation of sustainable water management initiatives in Turkey and have played a key role in demanding more participatory forms of river basin management, while further developing good practices on the ground (Divrak and Demirayak 2011). Especially when well-staffed with qualified personnel, NGOs have the advantage of being better able to implement participatory water management practices on the ground. Many NGOs, in order to pursue their objectives, have established good relationships with the public and developed skills to mobilize public support. Second, NGOs – as compared to public administrations, academia or the private sector – are more flexible and better poised to respond quickly to emerging needs. Furthermore, they show high commitment to the planning and implementation process as a whole, with a good sense to coordination and are able to act as a catalyst by bringing various parties together (Divrak and Demirayak 2011).

Over the course of the last decades, conservation activities have led to the emergence of many national and regional environmental NGOs, whose objectives comprise proposing efficient solutions and encouraging public participation in dealing with various environmental issues. Their strategies include boosting public awareness and providing a basis as a pressure group in decision-making processes. In Turkey, there are 10–15 national NGOs (e.g. Turkish Foundation for Combating Soil Erosion; Reforestation and Protection of Natural Habitats (TEMA); Regional Environment Center (REC Turkey); Greenpeace International; The Nature Association; Birdlife International; Turkish Environmental and Woodlands Protection Society (TURCEK); Water Foundation) dealing with environmental issues. The spirit of cooperation through international relations having gained momentum with Turkey's European Union (EU) accession process, most of the Turkish NGOs have developed partnerships with international organizations such as with World Wide Fund for Nature (WWF), Greenpeace, Birdlife and so on, in order to benefit from their experience and increase fund-raising opportunities. In fact, these partnerships have provided a good basis for the evolution of Turkish environmental NGOs, many of which have broadened their focus from specific species-oriented conservation efforts towards involving environmental concerns in the management of natural resources (Divrak and Demirayak 2011).

Representatives of the Nature Association were invited to join a team of officials and experts from the Southeastern Anatolia Project Regional Development Administration (GAP RDA) at the 3rd World Water Forum (WWF3) to discuss the economic benefits and social and environmental impacts of the large-scale water and land resources development project implemented over the Turkish portion of the ET river basin (Secretariat of the WWF3 2003). The Nature Association joined in discussions alongside representatives from academia and multipurpose community centres from across the GAP region, and evaluated the environmental impact of water-based development, informing international attendees about environmental protection projects in which the association had acted jointly with state institutions in Turkey. GAP RDA and the State Hydraulic Works (DSI) organized several sessions and side-events at the WWF3 which gathered various stakeholders in discussion, namely NGOs, academics and representatives from the private sector. These initiatives could be analyzed as a symbol of proactive water diplomacy and increased recognition of the need to inform international public opinion about the much-criticized GAP regarding its possible implications for transboundary water use along the ET river basin.

WWF Turkey attended the Middle East Seminar: Cooperation Prospects in the Euphrates-Tigris Region that was organized by the ETIC alongside a number of international development and aid agencies at the World Water Week in Stockholm in 2006 (SIWI 2006). The seminar included a panel discussion on the role of civil society in transboundary water management, with the WWF Turkey chair sharing her experiences on the role of civil society in the peaceful settlement of water disputes, as well as sustainable development and protection of water resources in the ET region. The seminar was attended by senior diplomats and officials from the relevant Turkish, Iraqi and Syrian ministries (SIWI 2006).

Standing as a different kind of NGO, the Union of Chambers of Turkish Engineers and Architects (TMMOB in Turkish acronym) is a corporate body and a professional organization defined as a public institution in line with Article 135 of the Turkish Constitution. An umbrella organization, it has 23 Chambers and about 300,000 members. As the major pressure group in the political system, the Chambers of Electrical, Mechanical, Civil, Environmental and Agricultural Engineers under TMMOB have developed major critiques against privatization initiatives launched by the government in hydroelectricity and the irrigation sector in Turkey, with lawsuits filed leading to numerous declarations and organized public meetings, briefings and national water conferences with the main objective being to halt neoliberal attempts to shift water policy and management to the private sector. The TMMOB has also shown a keen interest referring to the international dimensions of water, holding various roundtables meetings, seminars and national conventions on issues related to the politics of pivotal transboundary river basins, namely the Euphrates–Tigris, Meric and Orontes river basins (Baran et al. 2006). Through such events, the TMMOB has managed to bring together officials from the country's various ministries, as well as diplomats, academics, NGOs and representatives from the private sector, forming a broad platform for debate among stakeholders in Turkish water policy and management.

The Center for Middle Eastern Studies (ORSAM in Turkish acronym) was established in 2009 to inform the general public and the foreign policy community on the Middle Eastern issues. ORSAM is a non-partisan and non-profit research centre based in Ankara, which provides information on Middle Eastern affairs, exposing Turkish academia and political circles to the perspectives of researchers from across the region. Water issues constitute a significant area of its research and dissemination and, since the inception of its Water Research Program, ORSAM staff, along with academics, experts and officials from the ministries concerned, have drafted numerous articles in its periodical magazine (Middle East Analysis), as well as analysis reports and policy briefings encompassing up-to-date findings and analyses on Turkey's transboundary relations and discussion papers on emerging concepts and issues in global water policy. ORSAM's qualified staff have also held various interviews with former and active diplomats, academics and foreign and Turkish experts on various aspects of water policy and science (Maden and Kilic 2011). All in all, since 2011, the ORSAM Water Research Program has produced up-to-date information and analysis on various aspects of water policy at both a national and transboundary level that may serve as an input in decision-making in terms of Turkey's WDF.

The Hydropolitics Academy Association, a legally registered association launched in 2014, is organically affiliated with the Water Policies Association and has acted as the successor of the Soil, Water and Energy Working Group, which was introduced with a host of web-based studies back in 2011. The chair of the Hydropolitics Academy leads the activities of the association, and he and other members appear frequently in the national press to report on the Academy's opinions and recommendations regarding Turkey's national and transboundary water policies. The Hydropolitics Academy has placed a special focus on water diplomacy along with its research and advocacy in the area of water security and the water-energy-food nexus (Hydropolitics Academy Association 2015). The Academy advocates that 'Turkey should implement proactive hydro-diplomacy to boost trust among riparian states in the ET region' (Yildiz 2019b). The Academy puts forth that 'the new hydropolitical approach regarding ET basin must focus on efficient sharing of the benefits provided by the water among states through a shared goal, shared vision and unity of effort, rather than allocation of decreasing amount of water' (Ersen 2018).

Dursun Yildiz, chair of the Academy, goes on to argue that 'Turkey should take a leading role in restoring trust among the regional countries and adopt an open policy to implement a new hydro-political paradigm'. Likewise, he states, 'Turkey may lead the preliminary work on the establishment of an organization for cooperation on water management, as part of its proactive hydro-diplomacy particularly in the post-conflict era in Syria. Turkey can help the re-construction of war-torn water management infrastructures in Syria'. The Hydropolitics Academy has praised initiatives taken by the Turkish government such as the organization of short-term training sessions for Iraqi irrigation engineers and technicians at the DSI.

Dursun Yildiz stated that 'water resources in Syria and Iraq will determine the settlement areas and industrial production once the peace is restored. Millions of refugees who will return to their countries will start settlements in areas with water security', adding that, 'without resolving water issue in the Middle East, it is not possible to ensure permanent peace in the region' (Ersen 2018). Hydropolitics Academy has been acting as a pressure group through activities such as convening roundtables to brainstorm on pivotal water policy issues in Turkey and its relations with neighbours and the wider world; participating in national and international events; appearing in various national and local media outlets and producing numerous reports, policy briefs and books on new and emerging concepts and issues in global, regional and national water policy.

Academia and Water Diplomacy

Faculty members and researchers at a number of Turkish universities, particularly those with departments in economics, public administration, political science and international relations, have conducted systematic academic research on water politics – with a special emphasis on Turkey's relations with its neighbours over the transboundary rivers, as well as the links between international water law and water diplomacy. Furthermore, undergraduate and graduate courses on transboundary water policy have been included in the curricula of various programs (Middle East Technical University 2016, 408).

Universities' growing interest in transboundary water policy have culminated in the holding of various international conferences. To illustrate, in 1991, Bilkent University's Department of International Relations convened the International Conference on Transboundary Waters in the Middle East: Prospects for Regional Cooperation, which provided a platform for leading local and international scholars and experts in the field of transboundary water issues to interact with technocrats, diplomats and legal advisers from the Turkey's relevant ministries. The conferences allowed figures from academia and government to have the chance to exchange viewpoints on transboundary water politics as they had evolved in the Middle East. Such conferences further allow academics the opportunity to learn first-hand information from diplomats and policymakers on Turkey's position in transboundary waters, particularly in relation to the Euphrates, Tigris and Orontes Rivers. Likewise, in 1998, Bilkent University held another academic conference on water policy, namely the Bi-National Conference on Conflict and Cooperation in the Middle East with Reference to Water (Bilkent University 1998). At this event, Israeli and Turkish experts had the chance to exchange opinion and knowledge on prospects for water cooperation between the two states, with particular attention to water imports from Turkey's (national) Manavgat River to Israel. The conference coincided with a period when Turkish-Israeli bilateral relations were flourishing politically, militarily, economically and culturally. Water dialogue was seen as integral to then-growing interstate cooperation (Kibaroglu and Kibaroglu 2009).

The Hydropolitics and Strategic Research & Development Center, Hacettepe University, which worked tirelessly for a decade as of 1994 had an overall objective of 'promoting cooperation in all respects among the river basin countries of the Middle East'. It outlined its specific purpose as 'identifying economic, social, political, legal, biological and environmental status of the rivers and the lakes in Turkey; co-operating with public and private institutions and organizations; organizing panel discussions, meetings and conferences with a view to enlighten the public; providing consultancy to public and private institutions and agencies and co-operating with international institutions and organizations for its purposes' (Hacettepe University n.d.).

For more than a decade, the center offered an interdisciplinary MSc program on hydropolitics, whose graduates joined the cadres of leading think tanks and policy institutions in Turkey, namely the ORSAM, Hydropolitic Academy and the Turkish Water Institute (SUEN). Several graduate theses were completed and archived. Moreover, the center organized seminars and workshops that were attended by research and policy community including former and active diplomats.

The center's interdisciplinary curriculum included courses taught by the leading experts, with former high-level technocrats and diplomats joining the ranks of the faculty as part-time instructors to share their knowledge and experience with graduate students (Hacettepe University n.d.). To illustrate, Ozden Bilen, former director general of the DSI, shared his unique experiences of participating in the technical negotiations with Iraq and Syria over the construction and filling of the first dams across the Euphrates. Ozden Bilen contributed extensively to water diplomacy literature in Turkey with his monographs and memoirs on pivotal issues such as Turkey's water relations with Middle Eastern countries (Bilen 2000), as well as Turkey's evolving water agenda through harmonization with EU water policy (Bilen 2008). Bilen indeed managed to build invaluable professional ties in Turkey between water practitioners, and diplomats on the one hand and academia on the other.

The Water Management Institute was established at Ankara University in 2010 with an overall objective of offering new perspectives and suggestions to water-related problems in Turkey and around the world. The Institute is one of the few existing university research institutes in Turkey specializing in water management and policy (Ankara University 2010). The Institute has performed a leading role in the development of new graduate programs. Its interdisciplinary Water Policy and Security Program is embedded in the Graduate School of Social Sciences, along with the initiation of the Integrated Water Management Program in the Graduate School of Natural and Applied Sciences, Ankara University. The institute has underlined that Turkey, which is not a water-rich country, is among those most at risk of the potentially adverse impacts of climate change and global warming. For this reason, all kinds of water-related activities such as research, development, training, policy formulation, coordination, development of legislation and standards have gained urgency and importance in the country. To this end, the institute aims to carry out research, development and educational activities towards creating solutions for water issues on a local, national and international scale. The institute has a targeted mission to train future leaders and specialists in Turkey on water management to overcome social, environmental and technological boundaries, combining information belonging to various disciplines and converting theoretical knowledge into practice (Ankara University 2010).

Furthermore, a small number of foundation universities in Turkey have pursued international cooperation with leading research organizations and think tanks on water diplomacy, international water law and water development cooperation. In this context, the Department of International Relations at Istanbul Okan University partnered with the Max Planck Institute for Comparative Public Law and International Law for the project entitled Water Conflicts in International Law, which essentially focused on the law and politics of the ET river basin. In addition to creating a database for the relevant national and international law applicable to ET river basin dispute, the project inter alia worked to create a network of international as well as regional experts and scholars working on the subject. The work culminated in an international and inter-disciplinary conference on Advancing Cooperation in the Euphrates and Tigris Region: Institutional Development and Multidisciplinary Perspectives, held on the premises of Okan University in Istanbul, Turkey, in May 2012. This conference was jointly organized by the Max Planck Institute for Comparative Public Law and International Law, Okan University, and the ETIC. The conference was attended by a wide-ranging group of participants, including former and active diplomats and technocrats from all riparian states as well as numerous other countries, indicating that the issues which were discussed and that are also mirrored in the follow-up publication, reflect some very crucial questions for the region. The conference culminated in the publication of an edited volume, which unlike many other scholarly works on the subject, not only puts the focus on the governing normative framework but also places it into the wider context of a comparative and interdisciplinary dimension as well (Kibaroglu et al. 2013). As an important product of the two-year-long project, the publication provides an opportunity to examine different aspects of managing and protecting the waters of the Euphrates and Tigris region including the difficulties and the possible solutions within WDFs.

The Department of Political Science and International Relations at MEF University in Istanbul held a High-Level Forum on Blue Peace in the Middle East on 19–20 September 2014. The forum brought together approximately ninety diplomats, policymakers, academics, journalists and opinion-makers from Middle Eastern countries with a view to discuss various aspects of water as a means of promoting peace and cooperation in the region. The forum was convened jointly by MEF University and the Strategic Foresight Group (SFG) in cooperation with the Swiss Agency for Development and Cooperation and the Political Directorate of the Swiss Federal Department of Foreign Affairs. The participants endorsed the diplomatic mechanisms for settling disputes and proposed concrete initiatives at bilateral as well as regional levels to promote cooperation and the sustainable management of water resources in the region. The forum included special presentations on the experience of the Senegal River Basin Authority in collaborative water management and work in progress of the Orontes River Basin Atlas for post-conflict water management in Syria and its neighbouring countries (MEF University 2014). This event was followed-up by another international conference on Women, Water and Peace in the Middle East, convened on 18–19 March 2016 and co-hosted by the Department of Political Science and International Relations at MEF University and SFG with support from the Swedish International Development Cooperation Agency (SIDA) in Stockholm. The meeting brought together 60 thought leaders and female opinion makers from Iraq, Jordan, Lebanon and Turkey as key participants, including former ministers, members of parliament, diplomats, other government officials, academics and editors of newspapers. The international conference explored the role of women in WDFs in the Middle East. The conference resulted in concrete recommendations for the promotion of water cooperation in the Middle East and the role that women could play in this regard (MEF University 2016).

MEF University led the organization of the International Conference entitled Water Resources Management in the Asi (Orontes) River Basin: Assessment of Issues and Opportunities on 13–14 November 2014. The workshop was co-organized by MEF University and the Graduate Institute of International and Development Studies based in Geneva with the support of the Swiss Agency for Development and Cooperation. The ultimate objective of the workshop, which was attended by diplomats, technocrats, water experts and leading academics from Turkey, Syria, Switzerland, Germany and Holland, was to produce a much-needed synthesis of academic works and technical studies that are conducted on the Orontes river basin. The conference was unique in the sense that it also looked into issues pertaining to Orontes river basin water during the conflict in Syria and culminated in the publication of an e-book comprising contributions from Syrian experts with first-hand information on the water situation in Syria before and during the ongoing conflict (Kibaroglu and Jaubert 2013). The book composed of recommendations for actors of water diplomacy, first and foremost for states, but also for the development of activities that could be undertaken by aid and international funding agencies concerning how such actors could work with and support the scientific community and civil society organizations to achieve a peaceful and sustainable transboundary water management of the Orontes basin.

Salient Processes in Turkey's Water Diplomacy Framework

Best Practices

Turkey's WDF encompasses a well-structured institutional setting through which consistent and predictable water diplomacy principles are generated. The central and defining role of the Ministry of Foreign Affairs (MFA) has been solid and has contributed to the development of main principles in water diplomacy since the late 1980s. The fact that the MFA has systematically provided information on Turkey's principles regarding water diplomacy through readily accessible manuals, websites and various other open sources, such as oral presentations and interviews given at national and international media outlets, could be evaluated as part of the best practices in Turkey's WDF. In the same manner, keeping an open dialogue with their counterparts over transboundary water issues, as well as signing several bilateral water agreements could be assessed as some of the main accomplishments of diplomatic and other concerned official circles in the country.

On the other hand, burgeoning water stress in several transboundary river basins around Turkey, and the growing need for stakeholder engagement for equitable and effective water resources management, calls for new perspectives and contributions from non-state actors. Track II diplomacy networks, academia and NGOs in Turkey have built up the necessary skills and experience to enable themselves to provide inputs to realize cooperative arrangements in transboundary water settings. It would be indeed a convenient and rational choice for official (diplomatic or technocratic) mechanisms to make use of the accumulation developed in non-state actors in coping with various water challenges at national and international levels.

At the institutional level, the MFA and DSI, are the two pivotal institutions in Turkey's WDF. The DSI provides all necessary technical inputs to the MFA regarding physical (hydrological) conditions as well as planned and ongoing water development projects in Turkey's transboundary settings. Their long-lasting bureaucratic collaboration could also be assessed as best practices in WDF. In the mid-1980s, this bureaucratic collaboration produced the

Three-Stage Plan as a constructive water diplomacy initiative in the ET basin (see Chapters 1 and 4). However, the Three-Stage Plan was coolly received by downstream riparians, namely Syria and Iraq, and constituted a unique initiative taken up by an upstream country offering joint studies on water and land resources in the basin, followed up by an allocation plan based on these studies.

Furthermore, the DSI has continued to act closely with the MFA in creating the idea and preliminary work on the possibilities of building joint dams on the border with Syria (Friendship Dam across the Orontes River) and Iraq (dams on the Tigris boundary tributaries). The 'joint dam diplomacy' was mainly crafted with the technical contributions from DSI staff and provided various opportunities for sharing (energy, irrigation, flood control) benefits from those long-disputed rivers.

Moreover, since the late 1990s, this style of exemplary bureaucratic collaboration strengthened with further cooperation between MEF (Ministry of Agriculture and Forestry since 2018) and the MFA. MEF led the EU harmonization process in close consultation with the MFA. With its technical competence on water quality management and environmental protection, MEF took charge of scrutinizing EU water law and transposing this body of legislation into national legislation. Within this framework, the MFA underlined Turkey's approach vis-à-vis transboundary rivers, making sure the adopted EU legislation fell in line with Turkey's standpoint and priorities in transboundary waters. Thus, water diplomacy towards the EU was conducted jointly between the two ministries (see Chapter 1).

The SUEN's activities should also be evaluated as best practices in Turkey's WDF. The SUEN has organized several training programs for technocrats from neighbouring countries, which has been significantly contributing to the building up of a cadre of regional water bureaucrats and diplomats who, when need be, could act in a cooperative manner for the realization of possible joint projects along the country's transboundary river basins. The SUEN has also contributed to Turkey's growing role in global and regional water diplomacy by leading the organization of the Istanbul International Water Forum (IIWF), which gathers various players in the global water community in Istanbul every three years one year prior to the World Water Forum to discuss current international water-related issues. Furthermore, the SUEN has built partnerships with international research organizations around knowledge and dissemination projects on transboundary rivers. The SUEN has become a significant partner of the Blue Peace in the Middle East Initiative by holding its coordination office in Istanbul. The Blue Peace Initiative is a pioneering move in terms of regional water diplomacy in the Middle East, having emerged from a series of meetings attended by former politicians, diplomats, academics, journalists and professionals in water management and development sectors from Jordan, Lebanon, Syria, Iraq and Turkey. The initiative was led by a Mumbai-based think tank called the SFG and is sponsored by the Swiss Agency for Development and Cooperation and SIDA (Celik 2018).

Turkey's water diplomacy practices in its neighbourhood demonstrate that whenever transboundary water negotiations, which have been systematically carried out by career diplomats and technocrats, have been stalled, high-level politicians, that is, a minister, the prime minister or head of the state, have taken charge and handled matters over water use and allocation in face-to-face high-level meetings. The involvement of high-level politicians can be evaluated as a best practice since it has prevented the escalation of water disputes and facilitated problem-solving understandings. More importantly, high-level water diplomacy has provided prompt responses to the needs of all riparian states. To illustrate, Turkey completed the construction of the Ilisu Dam across the Tigris River in 2018, and began filling the reservoir behind the dam in mid-2018. Yet, because of increasing needs from Iraq, Turkey and Iraq agreed that Turkey would allow the river's natural flow to continue in a decision which came amid a drought in Iraq. Turkey's measure of goodwill reportedly continued until the autumn 2019. During a press conference, Hassan al-Janabi, Iraq's minister of water resources, said meetings would continue between the two countries on how to ensure enough water would flow to Iraq during and after the filling of the reservoir behind the Ilisu Dam (*Daily Sabah* 2018).

Another best practice of Turkey's water diplomacy has been registered since the civil war broke out in Syria. In the midst of the unrest in Syria and in the process of the worsening of bilateral political relations between Turkey and Syria, Turkey has since never considered water as an instrument of a threat or coercive tool against the Syrian regime. On many occasions Turkish high-level officials have stated that Turkey would never cut off the water supply for Syria regardless of the state of the relations in light of the needs of the Syrian people.

Lessons Learned

Diplomatic mechanisms, that is, negotiations, after all, ought to be conducted sincerely and purposefully with an ultimate aim of reaching agreements. A major drawback in Turkey's WDF appears to be a lack of comprehensive water agreements that bring all riparian states together to accomplish effective and equitable use and management of transboundary river systems. Most of Turkey's transboundary rivers are framed, in terms of governance, by bilateral agreements (Williams 2011). These agreements include clauses on border issues, river bank protection, exchange of data on water quantity, exchange of information on floods, joint studies on infrastructure, water allocation rules, compensation requirements, joint technical organs and the like (see Chapter 4).

However, such bilateral agreements do not represent comprehensive forms of cooperation with an integrated approach that encompasses various aspects of issues pertaining to transboundary water use and management, such as stakeholder involvement, preservation of ecosystems, land use and groundwater quantity and quality management along with surface water management. Agreements which have been made, have in general lacked effective organizational backup, at least in the form of joint monitoring systems. Most critically, these bilateral treaties fail to address fluctuations in flow, meaning that they contain no clauses referring to periods of drought and flooding that occur frequently in the basins and cause drastic changes in the flow regime that require urgent adjustment to the use of the rivers.

The lack of comprehensive agreements providing for a fair and economically sound allocation of water stands as a critical issue in Turkey's WDF. Turkey has a number of rudimentary bilateral agreements (e.g. Kura-Aras river basin, see Chapter 4) which lack the necessary clauses on water quality standards, while exchange of data turns out to be insufficient. Bilateral agreements do not reconcile conflicting interests over pivotal issues such as water quantity allocation, exchange of water quality data and flood protection (e.g. Meric basin, see Chapter 4).

Thus, Turkey's transboundary water cooperation is largely of a bilateral nature and mainly based on bilateral protocols that predominantly tackle technical issues and the allocation of water resources (e.g. The 1987 Bilateral Protocol between Turkey and Syria). While such an approach might indicate the advantage of potential negotiations, due to an apparently limited number of riparians and topics, an enlargement of state cooperation on the issues might offer the countries new mutually beneficial issues and could make the negotiation of linkage issues easier. For instance, an increase in topics for negotiation in regard to the ET basin on the basis of water-related development sectors (e.g. energy, food) could perhaps pave the way for progress in terms of transboundary water cooperation.

On another front, Turkey's non-party position in the global and regional conventions constitutes another drawback in its WDF from which lessons should be drawn. Turkey's position regarding international water legislation has been widely perceived as reluctant, and the fact that Turkey voted against the UN Convention on the Law of the Non-navigational Uses of International Watercourses (1997) illustrates this view. However, Turkey acknowledges several basic principles of international water law. According to the Turkish position, the principle of the equitable and reasonable utilisation of water resources should serve as a guiding rule for the allocation of transboundary waters and the settlement of conflicts.

Consequently, Turkey makes passes towards the promulgation of the doctrine of limited territorial sovereignty. However, the state objects to the doctrine of the co-sovereignty of riparians, which would strengthen down-stream interests (according to the Turkish position) in an asymmetrical manner. However, it seems that Turkey's reservations towards global and regional conventions mainly stem from a reluctance to agree on far-reaching procedural rules (e.g. compulsory mechanisms for dispute settlement, detailed procedures for prior notification). As the analyses of cooperation regarding the rivers show, this does not mean that Turkey rejects transboundary cooper-ation (see Chapter 4). Interestingly, the historical bilateral agreements which have concerned riparians include mechanisms for conflict resolution.

CONCLUSION

This book presents the main institutions and the principles of Turkey's water diplomacy framework. All through the book, the chapters dwell upon and highlight the specific role of the Euphrates–Tigris (ET) river basin in developing water diplomacy principles as well as shaping Turkey's stance vis-à-vis the international water law. One key finding of the book is that Turkey's water diplomacy framework embodies clearly identifiable, well-established formal state institutions. Thus, as Figure 1 demonstrates, the Ministry of Foreign Affairs (MFA) constitutes the central node of water diplomacy institutional framework. In the same vein, the MFA leads the systematic bureaucratic collaboration with water line ministries and relevant institutions, namely the State Hydraulic Works (DSI) and the Ministry of Agriculture and Forestry (former MFWA and MEF). Those state institutions, which are generally responsible for the development, management and preservation of water resources have worked closely with the MFA in the formulation of the fundamental principles of water diplomacy. Moreover, the concerned state institutions that are responsible for different aspects of water policy and management have been diversified in the early 2000s. Thus, the General Directorate of Water Management and the Turkish Water Institute (SUEN) have contributed to water diplomacy discourses and practices under the Ministry of Agriculture and Forestry. Furthermore, as the water diplomacy policies and practices expanded towards new dimensions, like 'humanitarian water diplomacy', DSI and other state institutions, such as Turkish Cooperation and Coordination Agency (TIKA) and Disaster and Emergency Management Presidency (AFAD) as well, have been integrated into Turkey's water diplomacy institutional framework.

Another observation on Turkey's water diplomacy framework entangles the peculiarity of the ET river basin in the formation of water diplomacy institutions and principles. In this context, transboundary (Joint Technical Committee) as well as national (Southeastern Anatolia Project Regional Development Administration (GAP RDA)) institutions are delineated as integral components of institution-building in water diplomacy framework.

The role of non-state actors or informal institutions in transboundary water policymaking is still minimal even though there is ample room to involve them in water diplomacy in particular, with an objective to communicate more effectively across a wide spectrum of scientific disciplines, policymaking bodies and practitioners, and also to strive for integrated approaches to tackle the complex issues like transboundary water cooperation in conflict-laden regions, such as the downstream riparians of the ET river basin.

Another key finding is that the coherence and directness of water diplomacy principles make it possible to find out why Turkey behaved in a certain way in a specific transboundary setting, and also enable one to predict as to how it might behave in transboundary relations in the future. Along with this special focus on the ET river basin, the book also provides a thorough analysis on Turkey's transboundary water relations with its neighbours in all of its main transboundary basins. It is concluded that Turkey's water diplomacy practices in transboundary settings involve issues that are peculiar to each river basin. That is to say, in the Meric river basin, the major issue has been the prevention as well as mitigation of floods. Hence, the book displays how Turkey has pursued 'flood diplomacy' in Meric basin to settle the disputes with its neighbours (Bulgaria, in particular). In the Coruh river basin, on the other hand, Turkey undertook diplomatic negotiations in order to address the concerns of Georgia over sediment losses in downstream parts of the river. Hence, 'sediment diplomacy' has been successfully conducted between the two good neighbourly states with a view to preventing possible economic losses. It is also substantiated in the book that the relations between upstream Turkey and its downstream neighbours along the Kura–Aras basin had been manageable since the 'joint dam diplomacy' has worked smoothly with the building of the Arpacay Dam on the Turkish-Armenian (formerly Soviet Union) border. The ET basin, on the other hand, has generally been the stage of competitive water diplomacy practices that were coupled with confrontational non-riparian security issues. Likewise, in the Orontes basin, strained diplomatic relations were observed, particularly between Turkey and Syria, with the exception of a short period in the early 2000s when Ankara and Damascus agreed on building a joint dam on the border with a benefit-sharing approach to water diplomacy.

Turkey's fundamental foreign policy principles with respect to transboundary waters have been shaped by the physical as well as human geography, and influenced by the global, regional and bilateral political, economic as well as social interactions. In review of these principles, one can observe major influences of core norms of customary international water law (see Chapter 3) and Turkey's upstream dilemma specifically as it relates to the ET basin.

With regard to the treaty practice, there are several transboundary water agreements, which Turkey has signed with its neighbours. However, all of these agreements are at bilateral level and some are outdated, with regulations that would not be relevant to the current-day situation. These agreements predominantly concern issues, such as water quantity and borders. The book underlines that Turkey and its neighbours have not yet agreed on more comprehensive forms of cooperation that can tackle different aspects of water use and needs, such as quality, quantity, flood protection, preservation of ecosystems and prevention of accidents, in an integrated manner that could potentially facilitate negotiations by linking various water management issues. Thus, the book concludes that Turkey's keen interest in keeping up with diplomatic negotiations and signing of several bilateral water agreements, could be assessed as an achievement in water diplomacy framework. Yet Turkey's (non-party) position towards the regional and global conventions limits its chances to draw conclusions from practices in those bilateral transboundary river contexts.

The book chapters, in their order, demonstrate that Turkey's water diplomacy framework embodies, on the one hand, clearly identified institutions (Chapter 1) and principles (Chapter 2) through which Turkey's water diplomacy practices could be delineated. Chapter 4, on the other hand, displays how Turkey's interactions with its neighbours in various river basins end up with complex water challenges with their interconnected, uncertain, unpredictable and boundary-crossing features. In this context, Islam and Susskind's Water Diplomacy Framework (WDF), which embraces a problem-solving approach with divergent disciplinary knowledge and convergent approaches of a strategic collaboration of disciplines, methods, actors and institutions, offers a useful analytical framework (Islam and Susskind 2012). In line with the main premise of the problem-solving approach of Islam and Susskind, this book attempts to combine the observation-based technical (*what is*) dimension with the value-based socio-political (*what ought to be*) dimension of the complex problems in Turkey's WDF. In this respect, Chapter 4 and Chapter 5 include recommendations (i.e. what ought to be) on how Turkey should act to seek consensus and mutual benefits when negotiating resolutions over transboundary water resources as well as achieving equity and sustainability in transboundary river basin management. In this regard, Chapter 4 encompasses analyses on Turkey's major transboundary rivers and underlines that there is a need for finding effective measures to build and then to enhance trust among the riparians. Trust is particularly needed for improved sustainable transboundary water use and management.

Similarly, the Multi-track Water Diplomacy Framework (MWDF) of Huntjens et al. (2016) intends to identify the key determinants for shifting water conflict into cooperation in transboundary rivers. It aims at delineating the key factors affecting current efforts by state and non-state actors to cooperate on transboundary water issues. The MWDF facilitates identification of political actors, institutions and processes that influence, and more often than not, constrains the effectiveness of transboundary cooperation. It also helps to diagnose water problems across sectors and administrative boundaries, and at different levels of governance. To this end, the MWDF identifies intervention points and proposes sustainable solutions that are sensitive to diverse views and values, and it can also accommodate ambiguity, uncertainty as well as changing and competing needs. Even though this book has mainly a country-specific focus, its analysis on Turkey's transboundary river settings is inspired by the MWDF's conceptual framework, which analyses the interaction between the agent (state and non-state actors) and the structure (institutions) as well as the different outputs, outcomes and impacts as a result of that interaction.

Furthermore, Klimes et al. (2019) defines 'water diplomacy as a multidisciplinary concept that draws on technical, political, and socio-economic knowledge; located at the intersect of science, policy, and practice, and including both state and non-state actors'. In line with this broader definition, this book provides an extensive analysis on water diplomacy actors, which comprises formal actors, such as the MFA, water line ministries and other government agencies as well as informal or non-state actors, which have an important role in water diplomacy dialogues as representatives of Track II initiatives, such as the NGOs, academia and think tanks. Since trust is essential in water diplomacy, as argued in Chapter 5, non-state actors have an important role in contributing to improved dialogue among the riparian countries by clarifying misunderstandings and acknowledging ambiguities and uncertainties – information, action and perception – pertaining to water management decisions (Islam and Susskind 2012). The analysis on external actors (third parties), such as bilateral development and credit agencies, also demonstrate that those actors play significant roles in Turkey's water diplomacy framework. Moreover, the analysis on Turkey's transboundary rivers, the Euphrates–Tigris and the Orontes, in particular, entails that water diplomacy is a multidisciplinary field and water conflicts are not about water alone – interest incompatibility can start with water, but it is often embedded in the deeper political context.

Turkey's water diplomacy framework embodies complex transboundary water management problems, which can be best understood as a product of competition and interconnection among various actors in a political context. Thus, with a main goal of understanding, explaining and predicting Turkey's water diplomacy practices, and with certain inspirations from the existing literature (i.e. Islam and Susskind 2012; Huntjens et al. (2016); Klimes et al.

(2019)), this book attempts to clarify the legal and institutional foundations of Turkey's water diplomacy framework. It comprises thorough analyses on Turkey's position towards international water law. Finally, the book delineates the role of non-state actors in Turkey's water diplomacy framework, and comes up with policy-relevant recommendations for tackling with the growing challenges in transboundary water relations.

REFERENCES

AFAD (Disaster and Emergency Management Presidency). 2017. 'Humanitarian Aid for the Syrians in Turkey'. (on file with the author).

Allan, John Anthony. 1990. *Agricultural Sector in Iraq*. London: University of London.

Altinbilek, Dogan H. 2004. 'Development and Management of the Euphrates–Tigris Basin'. *International Journal of Water Resources Development* 20, no. 1: 15–33.

Altingoz, Mehmet, Belinskij, Antti, Bréthaut, Christian, do Ó, Afonso, Gevinian, Suren, Hearns, Glen, Keskinen, Marko, McCracken, Melissa, Ni, Vadim, Solninen, Niko, and Wolf, Aaron T. 2018. *Promoting Development in Shared River Basins: Case Studies from International Experience*. Washington, DC: World Bank.

Ammar, Khalil, and de Chaisemartin, Marguerite. 2014. *The Collaborative Programme Euphrates and Tigris*. Dubai: International Center for Biosaline Agriculture (ICBA). www.biosaline.org/sites/default/files/scientific_poster_-_8-_cpet.pdf. Accessed 20 November 2019.

Anatolian Agency. 2012. 'Turkey Favors Fair Share of Waters of Tigris, Euphrates'. 10 October. https://www.aa.com.tr/en/turkey/turkey-favors-fair-share-of-waters-of-tigris-euphrates/328311. Accessed 10 September 2019.

Anderson, Ewan. 1986. 'Water Geopolitics in the Middle East: Key Countries'. Conference on U.S. Foreign Policy on Water Resources in the Middle East: Instrument for Peace and Development. 24 November. Washington, DC: CSIS.

Angelidis, Panagiotis, Kotsikas, Michalis, and Kotsovinos, Nikos. 2010. 'Management of Upstream Dams and Flood Protection of the Transboundary River Evros/Maritza'. *Water Resources Management* 24, no. 11: 2467–84.

Ankara University. 2010. Water Management Institute. Ankara, Turkey. http://suyonetimi.ankara.edu.tr/en/preface/. Accessed 15 October 2019.

Bakour, Yahia. 1992. 'Planning and Management of Water Resources in Syria'. In *Country Experiences with Water Resources Management, Economic, Institutional, Technological and Environmental Issues*, edited by Guy Le Moigne, Shawki Barghouti, Gershon Feder, Lisa Garbus and Mei Xie, 151–55. Washington, DC: World Bank.

Baran, Turkay, Ozis, Ünal, and Ozdemir, Yildirim. 2006. 'Sınır Asan Asi Havzasi Su Potansiyeli ve Yararlanilmasi'. TMMOB Water Policy Convention. 21–23 March, 571–81. Ankara, Turkey.

Beaumont, Peter. 1978. 'The Euphrates River: An International Problem of Water Resources Development'. *Environmental Conservation* 5, no. 1: 35–43.

Beaumont, Peter. 1992. 'Water: A Resource under Pressure'. In *The Middle East and Europe: An Integrated Communities Approach*, edited by Gerd Nonneman, 183–88. London: Federal Trust for Education and Research.

Beaumont, Peter. 1998. 'Restructuring of Water Usage in the Tigris-Euphrates Basin: The Impact of Modern Water Management Policies'. In *Transformations of Middle Eastern Natural Environments: Legacies and Lessons (Bulletin Series, Yale School of Forestry and Environmental Studies)*, edited by Jeff Albert, Magnus Bernhardsson and Roger Kenna, 168–86. New Haven, CT: Yale University Press.

Belül, Lütfü M. 1996. 'Hydropolitics of the Euphrates-Tigris Basin' (unpublished master's thesis). Ankara: Middle East Technical University.

Bilen, Ozden. 1990. 'Initiation of Atatürk Reservoir's Impounding'. http://ozdenbilen. com/Dosyalar/OzdenBilenYayinlari/MakaleRaporSunum/Report_onthe_ Initiation_of_Ataturk_Dam_Impounding.pdf. Accessed 22 July 2019.

———. 1994. 'Prospects for Technical Cooperation in the Euphrates-Tigris Basin'. In *International Waters of the Middle East: From Euphrates-Tigris to Nile*, edited by Asit Biswas, 96–116. Oxford: Oxford University Press.

———. 2000. 'Turkey and Water Issues in the Middle East'. Republic of Turkey, Prime Ministry. Ankara: Southeastern Anatolia Project Regional Development Administration. http://www.ozdenbilen.com/Dosyalar/OzdenBilenYayinlari/Books/ Turkey&WaterIssuesintheMiddleEast.pdf. Accessed 25 August 2019.

———. 2008. *Türkiye'nin Su Gündemi: Su Yönetimi ve AB Su Politikaları*. [Turkey's water agenda: Water management and EU water policies]. Ankara: DSI. http://ozdenbilen. com/Dosyalar/AbSuCerceveYonergesi/AbSuPolitikalari.pdf. Accessed 12 July 2019.

Bilkent University. 1998. 'Bi-National Conference on Conflict and Cooperation in the Middle East With Reference to Water'. 20–21 April. Ankara: Bilkent University.

Bourne, Charles B. 1996. 'The International Law Association's Contribution to International Water Resources Law'. *Natural Resources Journal* 36, no. 2: 155–216.

Bozkurt, Deniz, and Sen, Omer Lütfi. 2013. 'Climate Change Impacts in the Euphrates-Tigris Basin Based on Different Models and Scenario Simulations'. *Journal of Hydrology* 480: 149–61.

Brunnée, Jutta, and Toope, Stephen J. 1997. 'Environmental Security and Freshwater Resources: Ecosystem Regime Building'. *American Journal of International Law* 91: 26–59.

Caflisch, Lucius. 1998. 'Regulation of the Uses of International Watercourses'. In *International Watercourses, Enhancing Cooperation and Managing Conflict*, edited by Salman M. A. Salman and Laurence Boisson de Chazournes, 3–17. Washington, DC: World Bank.

Canatan, Evren. 2003. 'Türkiye-Suriye Arasinda Asi Nehri Uyusmazligi' (unpublished master's thesis). Ankara: Hacettepe University.

Caponera, Dante. 1993. 'Legal Aspects of Transboundary River Basins in the Middle East: The al-Asi (Orontes), the Jordan and the Nile'. *Natural Resources Journal* 33, no. 3: 629–63.

Case Concerning Gabcikovo-Nagymaros Project (Hungary/Slovakia). 1998. 'Judgment of 25 September 1997'. *International Law Materials* 37: 162.

Celik, Mehmet. 2018. 'Turkish Institute to Coordinate Regional Initiative for Transboundary Water Cooperation'. *Daily Sabah*. 4 September. https://www. dailysabah.com/diplomacy/2018/09/04/turkish-institute-to-coordinate-regional-initiative-for-transboundary-water-cooperation. Accessed 17 March 2019.

Chen, Huiping, Rieu-Clarke, Alistair, and Wouters, Patricia. 2013. 'Exploring China's Transboundary Water Treaty Practice through the Prism of the UN Watercourses Convention'. *Water International* 38, no. 2: 217–30.

Cohen, Saul. 2015. *Geopolitics: The Geography of International Relations*. Third Edition. London: Rowman & Littlefield.

Comair, Georges F., McKinney, Daene C., Scoullos, Michael J., Flinker, Raquel H., and Espinoza-Davalos, Gonzalo. 2013. 'Transboundary Cooperation in International Basins: Clarification and Experiences from the Orontes River Basin Agreement: Part 1'. *Environmental Science & Policy* 31: 133–40.

Convention on the Law of the Non-navigational Uses of International Watercourses. 1997. 21 May. https://legal.un.org/ilc/texts/instruments/english/conventions/8_3_1997.pdf. Accessed 01 July 2019.

Convention on the Protection and Use of Transboundary Watercourses and International Lakes done at Helsinki. 1992. 17 March. https://www.unece.org/fileadmin/DAM/env/water/pdf/watercon.pdf. Accessed 02 February 2019.

Daily Sabah. 2018. 'Turkey, Iraq to Discuss Water Issue on November 2'. 8 June. https://www.dailysabah.com/business/2018/06/08/turkey-iraq-to-to-discuss-water-issue-on-november-2. Accessed 11 May 2020.

Darama, Yakup. 2009. 'Flood Risk Management of Maritza River and Early Warning System'. Presentation held at Workshop on Transboundary Water Resources Management in South-Eastern Europe. 18–20 May. Sarajevo. http://www.unece.org/env/water/meetings/Sarajevo_workshop/presentations/session4/Aegean_Sea/MARITZA.pdf. Accessed 17 March 2019.

Delipinar, Sermin, and Karpuzcu, Mehmet. 2017. 'Policy, Legislative and Institutional Assessments for Integrated River Basin Management in Turkey'. *Environmental Science & Policy* 72: 20–29.

Divrak, Buket B., and Demirayak, Filiz. 2011. 'NGOs Promote Integrated River Basin Management in Turkey: A Case-Study of the Konya Closed Basin'. In *Turkey's Water Policy: National Frameworks and International Cooperation*, edited by Aysegül Kibaroglu, Waltina Scheumann and Annika Kramer, 161–76. Berlin: Springer-Verlag.

Draft Articles, first reading. 1991. *Report of the ILC on the Work of its Forty-third Session*, UNGAOR, 46th Session, UN Doc. A/ 46/ 10.

Draft Articles on the Law of the Non-Navigational Uses of International Watercourses and Commentaries Thereto. 1994. Adopted on the second reading by the International Law Commission at its forty-sixth session. 12 July. A/CN.4/L.493.

DSI. 1958. *Asi Havzası İstiksaf Raporu* [The Exploratory Report on the Orontes Basin]. Ankara: Devlet Su Isleri, Etud Plan Dairesi.

———. 1975. 'Report on the Negotiations among Turkey, Syria, and Iraq on the Euphrates River State Hydraulic Works'. Ankara: Turkish Ministry of Energy and Natural Resources.

———. 2012. 'Water and DSI'.

———. 2017. 'Ülkemizdeki 25 Su Havzasının "Havza Master Planı Raporu" Çalışmaları Devam Ediyor'. [The studies on 'Basin Master Plan Reports' of 25 water basins in our country continues]. 17 March. www.dsi.gov.tr/haberler/2017/03/17/ulkemizdeki-25-su-havzasinin-havza-master-plani-raporu-calismalari-devam-ediyor. Accessed 08 October 2019.

Eleftheriadou, Eleni, Giannopoulou, Ioanna, and Yannopoulos, Stavros. 2015. 'The European Flood Directive: Current Implementation and Technical Issues in Transboundary Catchments, Evros / Maritsa Example'. *European Water* 52: 13–22.

Ersen, Elif. 2018. 'Transboundary Power of Waters: Nature's Leverage over Peace, Stability, and Trust in Euphrates-Tigris Basin'. *Daily Sabah*. 27 July. http://www.dailysabah.com/business/2018/07/28/transboundary-power-of-waters-natures-leverage-over-peace-stability-and-trust-in-euphrates-tigris-basin. Accessed 07 September 2019.

ETIC (Euphrates–Tigris Initiative for Cooperation). 2019. https://euphratestigrisinitiative forcooperation.wordpress.com/. Accessed 15 October 2019.

European Commission. 2007. Directive 2007/60/EC on the Assessment and Management of Flood Risks. http://ec.europa.eu/environment/water/flood_risk/index.htm. Accessed 10 January 2020.

European Communities. 2000. 'Directive 2000/60/EC of the European Parliament and of the Council of 23 October 2000 Establishing a Framework for Community Action in the Field of Water Policy'. *Official Journal of the European Communities* L327, 22.12.2000: 0001–0073.

EU Commission (Commission of the European Communities). 2004. *Issues Arising from Turkey's Membership Perspective: Impact Report.* 6 October 2004 {Brussels, COM (2004) 656 final}.

———. 2005. *Turkey 2005 Progress Report* {Brussels, COM (2005) 561 final}.

Fanack Water. 2016. 'Shared Water Resources'. https://water.fanack.com/lebanon/shared-water-resources/. Accessed 18 May 2018.

FAO. 2008. *Irrigation in the Middle East Region in Figures.* Water Reports 34. Aquastat Survey. Rome: FAO.

FTA. 2004. 'Turkey, Syria Sign Free Trade Agreement'. 23 December. https://www.trade.gov.tr/free-trade-agreements/syria. Accessed 09 March 2019.

Geneva Water Hub. 2016. *The Protection of Water during and after Armed Conflicts.* Think-Tank Roundtable Report. Geneva. https://www.genevawaterhub.org/sites/default/files/atoms/files/gwh_ghlp_roundtable_armedconflicts_rev_march2017nomail_0.pdf. Accessed 21 April 2020.

Ghvinadze, Nino, and Lindermann, Laura. 2013. *Cross-Border Electricity Exchanges: Bolstering Economic Growth in the South Caucasus and Turkey.* Washington, DC: Atlantic Council.

Global Water Partnership. 2000. 'Integrated Water Resources Management'. Technical Advisory Committee Background Papers no 4. Stockholm: Global Water Partnership.

Goldsmith, Jack L., and Posner, Eric A. 2005. *The Limits of International Law.* Oxford: Oxford University Press.

Grontmij Consulting Engineers. 2004. *River Basin Management Plan (draft) Buyuk Menderes.* Houten: Grontmij.

Gürün, Kamuran. 1994. *Akıntıya Kürek Çekmek: Bir Büyükelçinin Anıları* [Rowing against the Flow: Memoirs of an Ambassador]. Istanbul: Milliyet Yayinlari.

Haas, Peter M. 1990. 'Obtaining International Environmental Protection through Epistemic Consensus'. *Millennium: Journal of International Studies* 19, no. 3: 347–63.

Habertürk. 2020. 'Reyhanli Baraji Acildi'. https://www.haberturk.com/reyhanli-baraji-acildi-2823573-ekonomi. Accessed 07 November 2020.

Hacettepe University. n.d. Hydropolitics and Strategic Research & Development Center. http://www.hidropolitik.hacettepe.edu.tr/staff.htm. Accessed 11 September 2019.

Hamade, Sara, and Tabet, Charles. 2013. 'The Impacts of Climate Change and Human Activities on Water Resources Availability in the Orontes Watershed: Case of the Ghab Region in Syria'. *Journal of Water Sustainability* 3, no. 1: 45–59.

Hashim, Ahmed S. 2014. 'The Islamic State: From al-Qaeda Affiliate to Caliphate'. *Middle East Policy* 21, no. 4: 69–83.

Huntjens, Patrick, and de Man, Rens. 2017. 'Water Diplomacy: Making Water Cooperation Work'. *Policy Brief.* The Hague: The Hague Institute for Global Justice.

Huntjens, Patrick, Yasuda, Yumiko, Swain, Ashok, de Man, Rens, Magsig, Bjørn-Oliver, and Islam, Shafiqul. 2016. *The Multi-Track Water Diplomacy Framework: A Legal and Political*

Economy Analysis for Advancing Cooperation over Shared Waters. The Hague: The Hague Institute for Global Justice.

Hurd, Ian. 2015. 'International Law and the Politics of Diplomacy'. In *Diplomacy and the Making of World Politics*, edited by Ole Jacob Sending, Vincent Pouliot, and Iver B. Neumann, 31–54. Cambridge: Cambridge University Press.

Hurriyet Daily News. 2018. President Erdogan Announces Ministers of Turkey's New Cabinet, Ankara. http://www.hurriyetdailynews.com/president-erdogan-announces-ministers-of-turkeys-new-cabinet-134375. Accessed 17 February 2019.

Hydropolitics Academy Association. 2015. Preface. https://www.hidropolitikakademi.org/en/about-us/27435/vision---mission. Accessed 20 June 2019.

International Law Association. 1966. *Report of the Fifty-Second Conference: Helsinki Rules*. London: ILA.

Interview. 1996. Ministry of Foreign Affairs. Ankara.

Islam, Shafiqul, and Susskind, Lawrence. 2012. *Water Diplomacy: A Negotiated Approach to Managing Complex Water Networks*. RFF Press Water Policy Series. Abingdon: Routledge.

Jaafar, Hadi H., Zurayk, Rami, King, Caroline, Ahmad, Farah, and Al-Outa, Rami. 2015. 'Impact of the Syrian Conflict on Irrigated Agriculture in the Orontes Basin'. *International Journal of Water Resources Development* 31, no. 3: 436–49.

Joint Communiqué Between the Republic of Turkey, Prime Ministry, Southeastern Anatolia Project Regional Development Administration (GAP RDA) and the Arab Republic of Syria, Ministry of Irrigation, General Organization for Land Development. 23 August 2001. Ankara, Turkey. (on file with the author).

Jörum, Emma Lundgren. 2014. 'Syria's "Lost Province": The Hatay Question Returns'. 28 January. http://carnegieendowment.org/syriaincrisis/?fa=54340. Accessed 18 June 2019.

Kibaroglu, Aysegül, 1998. 'Designing Institutions for Equitable Allocation of Transboundary Water Resources: The Euphrates-Tigris River Basin'. Bi-National Conference on Conflict and Cooperation in the Middle East with Reference to Water. 20–21 April. Ankara: Bilkent University.

———. 2002. *Building a Regime for the Waters of the Euphrates-Tigris River Basin*. The Hague: Kluwer Law International.

———. 2008. 'The Role of Epistemic Communities in Offering New Cooperation Frameworks in the Euphrates-Tigris Rivers System'. *Journal of International Affairs* 61, no. 2: 183–98.

———. 2015. 'An Analysis of Turkey's Water Diplomacy and Its Evolving Position vis-a-vis International Water Law'. *Water International* 40, no. 1: 153–67.

———. 2019. 'State-of-the-Art Review of Transboundary Water Governance in the Euphrates-Tigris River Basin'. *International Journal of Water Resources Development* 35, no. 1: 4–29.

———. 2020. 'Legal and Institutional Foundations of Turkey's Domestic and Transboundary Water Policy'. In *Water Resources of Turkey*, edited by Nilgun Harmancioglu and Dogan Altinbilek, 493–516. Berlin: Springer.

Kibaroglu, Aysegül, and Baskan, Argun. 2011. 'Turkey's Water Policy Framework'. In *Turkey's Water Policy: National Frameworks and International Cooperation*, edited by Aysegul Kibaroglu, Waltina Scheumann and Annika Kramer, 3–25. Berlin: Springer.

Kibaroglu, Aysegül, and Ünver, Olcay. 2000. 'An Institutional Framework for Facilitating Cooperation in the Euphrates-Tigris River Basin'. *International Negotiation: A Journal of Theory and Practice* 5, no. 2: 311–30.

Kibaroglu, Aysegül, Baskan, Argun, and Alp, Sezin. 2009. 'Neo-Liberal Transitions in Hydropower and Irrigation Water Management in Turkey: Main Actors and Opposition Groups'. In *Water Policy Entrepreneurs. A Research Companion to Water Transitions around the Globe*, edited by Dave Huitema and Sander Meijerink, 287–303. Cheltenham: Edward Elgar.

Kibaroglu, Aysegül, Brouma, Anthi, and Erdem, Mete. 2008. 'Transboundary Water Issues in the Euphrates–Tigris River Basin: Some Methodological Approaches and Opportunities for Cooperation'. In *International Water Security: Domestic Threats and Opportunities*, edited by Nevelina Pachova, Mikiyasu Nakayama and Libor Jansky, 223–52. Tokyo: United Nations University Press.

Kibaroglu, Aysegül, and Jaubert, Ronald. (eds.). 2016. *Water Management in the Lower Asi-Orontes River Basin: Issues and Opportunities*. Geneva: Graduate Institute of International and Development Studies. Istanbul: MEF University.

Kibaroglu, Aysegül, Kirschner, Adele, Mehring, Sigrid, and Wolfrum, Rüdiger. (eds.). 2013. *Water Law and Cooperation in the Euphrates Tigris Region*. Leiden: Brill.

Kibaroglu, Aysegül, Klaphake, Axel, Kramer, Annika, Scheumann, Waltina, and Carius, Alexander. 2005. *Cooperation on Turkey's Transboundary Waters*. (F+E Project No. 903 19 226). Berlin: German Federal Ministry for Environment, Nature Conservation and Nuclear Safety.

Kibaroglu, Aysegül, and Scheumann, Waltina. 2013. 'Evolution of Transboundary Politics in the Euphrates-Tigris River System: New Perspectives and Political Challenges'. *Global Governance* 19: 279–307.

Kibaroglu, Aysegül, Scheumann, Waltina, and Kramer, Annika. (eds.). 2011. *Turkey's Water Policy: National Frameworks and International Cooperation*. Berlin: Springer-Verlag.

Kibaroglu, Aysegül, and Sümer, Vakur. 2007. 'Diverging Water Management Paradigms between Turkey and the European Union'. *Water International* 32, no. 5: 728–38.

Kibaroglu, Aysegül, and Sümer, Vakur. 2015. 'Turkey's Foreign Policy Orientation in the Water Context and the Orontes Basin'. In *Science Diplomacy and Trans-Boundary Water Management. The Orontes River Case*, edited by Roberta Ballabio, Fadi Georges Comair, Mario Scalet and Michael Scoullos, 57–78. Venice, Italy: UNESCO.

———. 2016. 'Transboundary Water Relations in the Asi Basin: The Case of Turkey-Syria Relations'. In *Water Management in the Lower Asi-Orontes River Basin: Issues and Opportunities*, edited by Aysegul Kibaroglu and Ronald Jaubert,139–50. Geneva: Graduate Institute of International and Development Studies. Istanbul: MEF University.

Kibaroglu, Aysegül, Sümer, Vakur, and Scheumann, Waltina. 2012. 'Fundamental Shifts in Turkey's Water Policy'. *Journal of Mediterranean Geography (Journal Méditerrané)* 119: 27–34.

Kibaroglu, Mustafa, and Kibaroglu, Aysegül. 2009. *Global Security Watch-Turkey: A Reference Handbook*. Westport: Praeger.

Kimence, Taner, Altunkaya, Cavus, and Cankaya, Burhan F. 2017. 'Türkiye'de Su Yönetimi'nin Değişimi' [Evolution of Turkey's Water Management] Ankara: MFWA.

Kirschner, Adele, and Tiroch, Katrin. 2012. 'The Waters of the Euphrates and Tigris: An International Law Perspective'. In *Max Planck UNYB*, edited by A. von Bogdandy and R. Wolfrum, 16: 329–94.

Kishan, S. Rana. 2011. *21st Century Diplomacy: A Practitioner's Guide*. New York: Continuum International.

Klaphake, Axel, and Kramer, Annika. 2011. 'Kura-Aras River Basin: Burgeoning Transboundary Water Issues'. In *Turkey's Water Policy: National Frameworks and International Cooperation*, edited by Aysegül Kibaroglu, Waltina Scheumann and Annika Kramer, 263–75. Berlin: Springer-Verlag.

Klaphake, Axel, and Scheumann, Waltina. 2011. 'Coruh River Basin: Hydropower Development and Transboundary Cooperation'. In *Turkey's Water Policy: National Frameworks and International Cooperation*, edited by Aysegül Kibaroglu, Waltina Scheumann and Annika Kramer, 251–61. Berlin: Springer- Verlag.

Klimes, Martina, Michel, David, Yaari, Elizabeth, Restiani, Phillia. 2019. 'Water Diplomacy: The Intersect of Science, Policy and Practice'. *Journal of Hydrology* 575 (August): 1362–70.

Kliot, Nurit. 1994. *Water Resources and Conflict in the Middle East*. New York: Taylor & Francis.

Kolars, John F. 1994. 'Problems of International River Management: The Case of the Euphrates'. In *International Waters of the Middle East – from the Euphrates-Tigris to Nile*, edited by Asit K. Biswas, 44–94. Oxford: Oxford University Press.

Kolars, John F., and Mitchell, William A. 1991. *The Euphrates River and the Southeast Anatolia Development Project*. Carbondale: Southern Illinois University Press.

Korkmaz, Hüseyin, and Karatas, Atilla. 2009. 'Asi Nehri'nde Su Yonetimi ve Ortaya Cikan Sorunlar [Water Management in the Orontes and Emerging Problems]'. *Mustafa Kemal Universitesi, Sosyal Bilimler Enstitusu Dergisi* [Mustafa Kemal University Journal of Social Sciences Institute] 6, no. 12: 18–40.

Kramer, Annika, and Kibaroglu, Aysegül. 2011. 'Turkey's Position towards International Water Law'. In *Turkey's Water Policy: National Frameworks and International Cooperation*, edited by Aysegül Kibaroglu, Waltina Scheumann and Anikka Kramer, 215–28. Berlin: Springer.

Kramer, Annika, and Schellig, Alina. 2011. 'The Meric River Basin: Transboundary Water Cooperation at the Border between the EU and Turkey'. In *Turkey's Water Policy: National Frameworks and International Cooperation*, edited by Aysegul Kibaroglu, Waltina Scheumann and Annika Kramer, 229–49. Berlin: Springer-Verlag.

Kut, Gün. 1993. 'Burning Waters: The Hydropolitics of the Euphrates and Tigris'. *New Perspectives on Turkey* 9: 1–17.

Law No. 14, 1990. 'Ratifying the Joint Minutes Concerning the Provisional Division of the Waters of the Euphrates River'. http://www.cawater-info.net/bk/water_law/pdf/euphrates_e.pdf. Accessed 06 July 2019.

Leb, Christina. 2019. 'Implementation of the General Duty to Cooperate'. In *Research Handbook on International Water Law*, edited by Stephen C. McCaffrey, Christina Leb and Riley T. Denoon, 95–108. Cheltenham: Edward Elgar.

Leummens, Harald J. L., and Matthews, Mary. 2013. *Updated Transboundary Diagnostic Analysis for the Kura Ara(k)s River Basin: Reducing Transboundary Degradation in the Kura Ara(k)s River Basin*. UNDP-GEF Project, Tbilisi, Baku, Yerevan https://iwlearn.net/resolveuid/cd0c2a7a3d9d5df250024d394743f3d1. Accessed 12 October 2020.

Lipper, Jerome. 1967. 'Equitable Utilisation'. In *The Law of International Drainage Basins*, edited by A. H. Garretson, R. D. Hayton and C. J. Olmstead, 15–88. Dobbs Ferry, New York: Oceana.

Maden, Tugba, and Kilic, Seyfi. 2011. ORSAM Su Söylesileri [ORSAM water interviews]. https://www.orsam.org.tr/tr/orsam-su-soylesileri-2011/. Accessed 22 May 2019.

Malanczuk, Peter. 1997. *Akehurst's Modern Introduction to International Law*. Seventh Revised Edition. London: Routledge.

McCaffrey, Stephen C. 1986. 'Second Report on the Law of the Non-Navigational Uses of the International Watercourses'. *Yearbook of the International Law Commission* 2, no. 1: 103–33.

———. 1987. 'Third Report on the Law of the Non-Navigational Uses of International Watercourses'. *Yearbook of the International Law Commission* 2, no. 1: 24–28.

———. 1991a. 'The Evolution of the Law of Transboundary Rivers'. International Conference on Transboundary Waters in the Middle East: Prospects for Regional Cooperation. 2–3 September. Ankara: Bilkent University.

———. 1991b. 'International Organizations and the Holistic Approach to Water Problems'. *Natural Resources Journal* 31: 139–65.

———. 1998. 'The UN Convention on the Law of the Non-Navigational Uses of International Watercourses: Prospects and Pitfalls'. In *International Watercourses, Enhancing Cooperation and Managing Conflict*, edited by S. M. A. Salman and Laurence Boisson de Chazournes. Washington, DC: World Bank.

———. 2018. 'The Customary Law of International Watercourses'. In *Research Handbook on Freshwater Law and International Relations*, edited by Mara Tignino and Christian Bréthaut, 147–75. Cheltenham: Edward Elgar.

McClimans, Melinda. 2016. 'Foreword'. In *Euphrates-Tigris Water Issues: An Introduction*. Middle East Studies Center at the Ohio State University: Ohio State Pressbooks. https://ohiostate.pressbooks.pub/etwr/front-matter/foreward/. Accessed 03 November 2019.

McLachlan, Keith. 1991. *The South-East Anatolia Project (GAP) and Its Effect on Water Supply and Management in Iraq*. London: University of London.

MEF University. 2014. *Blue Peace in the Middle East High-Level Forum*. 19–20 September. Istanbul, Turkey. https://www.strategicforesight.com/conference_inner.php?id=29. Accessed 27 June 2019.

———. 2016. *Women, Water and Peace in the Middle East Conference*. 18–19 March. Istanbul, Turkey. http://www.mef.edu.tr/en/news.read/id/52. Accessed 18 July 2019.

MoU (Memorandum of Understanding between Turkey and Syria). 2009a. *Memorandum of Understanding Between the Government of the Republic of Turkey and the Government of the Syrian Arab Republic for the Construction of a Joint Dam on the Orontes River Under the Name 'Friendship Dam'*. 23 December. (on file with the author).

———. 2009b. *Memorandum of Understanding between the Government of the Republic of Turkey and the Government of the Syrian Arab Republic in the Field of Remediation of Water Quality*. 23 December. (on file with the author).

———. 2009c. *Memorandum of Understanding between the Government of the Republic of Turkey and the Government of the Syrian Arab Republic in the Field of Efficient utilization of water resources and coping with drought*. (on file with author).

Memorandum of Understanding between Turkey and Iraq. 2009. *Memorandum of Understanding between the Ministry of the Environment and Forestry of the Republic of Turkey and the Ministry of Water Resources of the Republic of Iraq on Water*. 15 October. (on file with the author).

Middle East Technical University. 2016. 'IR 461 Politics of Water Resources in the Middle East'. In *General Catalog: 2015–2017*, 408. Ankara: Middle East Technical University. https://www.metu.edu.tr/tr/system/files/2015-2017_general_catalog_final.pdf. Accessed 30 May 2019.

Ministry of Agriculture and Forestry. 2019. *Ulusal Su Plani 2019–2023* [National Water Plan 2019–2023]. https://www.tarimorman.gov.tr/SYGM/Belgeler/NHYP%20 DEN%C4%B0Z/ULUSAL%20SU%20PLANI.pdf. Accessed 18 December 2019.

MFA (Ministry of Foreign Affairs Department of Regional and Transboundary Waters). 1995. *Water Issues between Turkey, Syria and Iraq*. Manual. Ankara.

————. 1996. 'Water Issues between Turkey, Syria and Iraq'. *Perceptions: Journal of International Affairs* 3, no. 2: 1–15. https://dergipark.org.tr/en/download/article-file/817266. Accessed 07 December 2019.

————. 2010. Personal communication with the officials. Ankara.

————. 2014. *Turkey's Policy on Water Issues.* http://www.mfa.gov.tr/turkey_s-policy-on-water-issues.en.mfa. Accessed 05 April 2019.

————. 2018a. *Turkey's Policy on Water Issues.* Ankara. http://www.mfa.gov.tr/turkey_s-policy-on-water-issues.en.mfa. Accessed 17 January 2020.

————. 2018b. *Sustainable Water Management.* Ankara. http://www.mfa.gov.tr/sustainable-water-management.en.mfa. Accessed 18 December 2019.

Ministry of Forestry and Water Affairs. N.d. Uluslararası Su Hukuku, Su Politikasi, One Cikan Sözlesmeler ve Diger Belgeler [International Water Law, Water Policy: Main Conventions and Others]. Ankara: Ministry of Forestry and Water Affairs. (on file with author).

MFWA (Ministry of Forestry and Water Affairs). 2017. 'Turkey's Water Aid Perspective: A Vision for Practical International Water Fund'. Ankara: Ministry of Forestry and Water Affairs.

MFWA (Ministry of Forestry and Water Affairs) National Consultation Council on Forestry and Water. 2013. *Report by the Working Group on Basin Management and Water Information Systems.* 21–23 March. Ankara: Ministry of Forestry and Water Affairs. (on file with the author).

Minutes of the Meeting among Turkish, Syrian and Iraqi Delegations. 1972. *Annex 6 to the Report on the Negotiations among Turkey, Syria, and Iraq on the Euphrates River, State Hydraulic Works.* Ankara: Turkish Ministry of Energy and Natural Resources. (on file with the author).

————. 1973a. *Annex 9 to the Report on the Negotiations among Turkey, Syria, and Iraq on the Euphrates River, State Hydraulic Works.* Ankara: Turkish Ministry of Energy and Natural Resources. (on file with the author).

————. 1973b. *Annex 8 to the Report on the Negotiations among Turkey, Syria, and Iraq on the Euphrates River, State Hydraulic Works.* Ankara: Turkish Ministry of Energy and Natural Resources. (on file with the author).

Minutes of the Fifteenth Meeting of the Joint Technical Committee. 1990. Ankara: DSI. (on file with the author).

Mylopoulos, Yannis, Eleftheriadou, Elpida, and Kampragou, Eleni. 2004. 'The Transboundary Catchment of River Nestos and the Bilateral Agreement between Greece and Bulgaria'. Conference on Integrated Water Management of Transboundary Catchments: A Contribution from TRANSCAT. Venice, Italy, 24–26 March.

Mylopoulos, Yannis, Kolokytha, Elpida, Vagiona, Dimitra, Kampragou, Eleni, and Eleftheriadou, Eleni. 2008. 'Hydrodiplomacy in Practice: Transboundary Water Management in Northern Greece'. *Global NEST Journal* 10, no. 3 (November): 287–94. https://journal.gnest.org/sites/default/files/Journal%20Papers/287-294_451_MYLOPOULOS_10-3.pdf. Accessed 10 July 2019.

Naff, Thomas, and Matson, Ruth. C. 1984. *Water in the Middle East: Conflict or Cooperation?* Boulder: Westview Press.

ORSAM. https://www.orsam.org.tr/en/desks/water-/. Accessed 21 September 2019.

Ozbay, Ozdemir. 2006. 'Turkiye Su Mevzuatinin Gecirdigi Evreler' [Evolution of Turkish Water Legislation]. Haber Bulten. *Chamber of Geology Engineers* 3: 37–39.

Ozis, Ünal, Ozdemir, Yalcin, Baran, Turkay, Turkman, Ferhat, Fistikoglu, Okan, and Dalkilic, Yildirim. 2002. 'Türkiye'nin sinir asan sularinin su hukuku ve su siyaseti acisindan durumu' [Status of Turkey's transboundary waters from international law and international politics perspectives]. In *Sinir Asan Sularimiz* [Our Transboundary Waters], edited by Zekai Sen, Ünal Ozis, Ilhan Avci, Ozden Bilen, Cemal Zehir and Mehmet Emin Birpinar, 36–37. Istanbul: Su Vakfi Yayini.

Papayannis, Thymio. 2004. *Shared Catchments and Wetlands – Increasing Transboundary Cooperation*. 5th European Regional Meeting on the Implementation and Effectiveness of the Ramsar Convention. 4–8 December. Yerevan, Armenia. https://www.ramsar.org/sites/default/files/documents/library/mtg_reg_europe2004_docs1d1.pdf?. Accessed 03 November 2019.

Personal correspondence with Judge Mehmet Güney. 1997. Former member of the Appeals Chamber, International Criminal Tribunal for Rwanda; chief legal adviser at the MFA and Ambassador, member of International Law Commission (1991–1995). Personal correspondence during his speech in the Turkish Association of the UN on 24 October.

Personal correspondences with officials at the MFA. June 2002; February 2010; April 2011; January 2014; March 2018.

Petropoulos, Sotiris, and Valvis, Anastasios. 2011. 'International Relations and Environmental Security: Conflict or Cooperation? Contrasting the Cases of the Maritza-Evros-Meriç and Mekong Transboundary Rivers'. In *Transboundary Water Resources Management: A Multidisciplinary Approach*, edited by Jacques Ganoulis, Aureli Alice and Jean Fried, 253–61. Weinheim: Wiley VCH Verlag & Co KGaA.

Polat, Mustafa H. 2004. 'Aras-Kura Havzasinin Hidropolitik ve Stratejik Degerlendirilmesi' [A Hydropolitical and Strategical Survey of Aras-Kura Basin]. (unpublished master's thesis). Ankara: Hacettepe University Hydropolitics and Strategic Research & Development Center.

Protocol on the Meeting of the Turkish-Soviet Joint Commission Pertaining to the Joint Construction of a Dam on the Arpacay (Ahuryan). 1964. (on file with author).

Protocol on Matters Pertaining to Economic Cooperation Between the Republic of Turkey and the Syrian Arab Republic. 1987. United Nations Treaty Series 87/12171, 17/7/1987.

Rende, Mithat. 2002. 'The Looming Global Water Shortage and Turkey's Water Management in a Transboundary Context'. NATO Parliamentary Assembly 48th Annual Session. 16–19 November. Istanbul.

———. 2004. 'Turkey's Water Resources Management and Transboundary Waters Policy'. 4th Biennial Rosenberg International Forum on Water Policy. Ankara.

———. 2013. 'International Law and Turkey's Transboundary Waters Policy'. Presentation Delivered at the Water Politics In-house Training, Ministry of Forestry and Water Affairs. General Directorate of Water Management, Department of Water Law and Political Development. 17–19 September.

Republic of Turkey. 2009. *Plan for Setting up Necessary Administrative Capacities at National, Regional and Local Level and Required Financial Resources for Implementing the Environmental Acquis*. Ankara. (on file with the author).

Revenga, Carmen, Murray, Siobhan, Abramovitz, Janet, and Hammond, Allen. 1998. *Watersheds of the World: Ecological Value and Vulnerability*. Washington, DC: World Resources Institute.

Richards, Alan, and Waterbury, John. 1990. *A Political Economy of the Middle East*. Boulder: Westview.

Salha, Samir. 1995. *'Turkiye, Suriye ve Lübnan Iliskilerinde Asi Nehri Sorunu'* [The Orontes River Problem in Relations between Turkey, Syria and Lebanon]. Ankara: Dis Politika Enstitusu Yayinlari & Hacettepe Universitesi.

Salman, M. A. Salman. 2013. 'Misconceptions Regarding the Interpretation of the UN Watercourses Convention'. In *The UN Watercourses Convention in Force*, edited by Flavia Rocha Loures and Alistair Rieu-Clarke, 28–35. London: Routledge.

Saner, Erol. 2006. 'Türkiye, Su ve Uluslararası Boyutu'. The Union of Chambers of Turkish Engineers and Architects – Proceedings of Congress of Water Policies. Ankara: The Union of Chambers of Turkish Engineers and Architects.

Scheumann, Waltina. 1998. 'Conflicts on the Euphrates: An Analysis of Water and Non-Water Issues'. In *Water in the Middle East*, edited by Waltina Scheumann and Manuel Schiffler, 31–45. Berlin: Springer.

———. 2003. 'The Euphrates Issue in Turkish-Syrian Relations'. In *Security and Environment in the Mediterranean: Conceptualising Security and Environmental Conflicts*, edited by Hans Günter Brauch, Peter Hearns Liotta, Antonio Marquina, Paul Rogers and Mohammad El-Sayed Selim, 745–60. Berlin: Springer.

Scheumann, Waltina, Sagsen, Ilhan, and Tereci, Ece. 2011. 'Orontes River Basin: Downstream Challenges and Prospects for Cooperation'. In *Turkey's Water Policy: National Frameworks and International Cooperation*, edited by Aysegul Kibaroglu, Waltina Scheumann and Annika Kramer, 301–12. Berlin: Springer-Verlag.

Scheumann, Waltina, and Shamaly, Omar. 2016. 'The Turkish-Syrian Friendship Dam on the Orontes River: Benefits for All?'. In *Water Management in the Lower Asi- Orontes River Basin: Issues and Opportunities*, edited by Aysegul Kibaroglu and Ronald Jaubert, 125–37. Geneva: Graduate Institute of International and Development Studies. Istanbul: MEF University.

Scheumann, Waltina, and Tigrek, Sahnaz. 2015. 'Regional Energy Trading: A New Avenue for Resolving a Regional Water Dispute?'. *International Journal of Water Governance* 3, no. 1: 49–70.

Secretariat of the 3rd World Water Forum. 2003. *The 3rd World Water Forum: Final Report*. Kyoto, Japan: Secretariat of the 3rd World Water Forum. https://www.worldwatercouncil.org/en/publications/analysis-3rd-world-water-forum. Accessed 16 March 2019.

Shapland, Greg. 1997. *Rivers of Discord International Water Disputes in the Middle East*. New York: St. Martin's Press.

Skias, Stylianos, Kallioras, Andreas, and Pliakas, Fotis. 2011. 'Basic Problems and Prerequisites Regarding Transboundary Integrated Water Resources Management in South East Europe: The Case of the River Evros/Maritza/Meric'. In *Transboundary Water Resources Management*, edited by Jacques Ganoulis, Alice Aureli and Jean Fried, 80–85. Weinheim: Wiley-VCH Verlag & Co. KGaA.

Snodderly, Dan. 2011. *Peace Terms: Glossary of Terms for Conflict Management and Peacebuilding*. Washington, DC: United States Institute of Peace.

SIWI (Stockholm International Water Management Institute). 2006. Beyond the River, Sharing Benefits and Responsibilities: Final Programme. World Water Week. 20–26 August. https://www.yumpu.com/en/document/read/24632793/final-programme-beyond-the-river-world-water-week. Accessed 12 February 2019.

SUEN (Turkish Water Institute). 2016. 'Technical Experts Meeting between Turkey and Iraq'. 18–19 August. https://suen.gov.tr/Suen/en/catdty.aspx?val=281. Accessed 19 April 2019.

SUEN (Turkish Water Institute). 2017a. Outcomes of 4th Istanbul International Water Forum. Istanbul.

———2017b. Experts from Iraq at SUEN. 31 March. https://suen.gov.tr/Suen/en/catdty.aspx?val=296. Accessed 18 July 2019.

———. 2018. About Us. http://suen.ormansu.gov.tr/suen/AnaSayfa/AboutUs.aspx?sflang=en. Accessed 22 April 2019.

Sümer, Vakur. 2011. *The European Union water framework directive and Turkey's water management policy: An analysis.* (unpublished PhD dissertation). Ankara: Middle East Technical University.

———. 2013. 'Legal Context of Water Management Policy in Turkey'. In *Water Law and Cooperation in the Euphrates-Tigris Region*, edited by Aysegül Kibaroglu, Adele Kirschner, Sigrid Mehring and Rüdiger Wolfrum, 229–57. Leiden: Brill.

Tastekin, Fehim. 2018. 'Turkey, Iraq Trade Blame as Concern Rises over Low Water'. *Al-Monitor.* 28 June. https://www.al-monitor.com/pulse/originals/2018/06/turkey-iraq-ilisu-dam-water-crisis.html. Accessed 19 December 2019.

Technical Delegation Report. 1973. *Technical Delegation Report on the Visits to Syria and Iraq.* Ankara: State Hydraulic Works.

The Statement of Turkey. 1997: UN GAOR, 51st Session, 99th Plenary Meeting, UN Doc. A/51/PV.99.

Tignino, Mara. 2010. 'Water, International Peace and Security'. *International Review of the Red Cross* 92, no. 879: 647–74.

Tigrek, Sahnaz, and Kibaroglu, Aysegul. 2011. 'Strategic Role of Water Resources for Turkey'. In *Turkey's Water Policy: National Frameworks and International Cooperation*, edited by Aysegul Kibaroglu, Waltina Scheumann and Annika Kramer, 27–42. Berlin: Springer-Verlag.

Treaty of Friendship and Good Neighbourly Relations between Iraq and Turkey, Protocol on Flow Regulation of the Tigris and Euphrates Rivers and of Their Tributaries. 1946. United Nations, Legislative Texts and Treaty Provisions Concerning the Utilisation of International Rivers for Other Purposes than Navigation. 1946. N/Doc. ST/LEG/SER. B/12.

Tuncok, Ismail Kaan. 2015. 'Transboundary River Basin Flood Forecasting and Early Warning System Experience in Maritza River Basin between Bulgaria and Turkey'. *Natural Hazards* 75: 191–214.

Turan, Ilter. 2011. 'The Water Dimension in Turkish Foreign Policy'. In *Turkey's Water Policy: National Frameworks and International Cooperation*, edited by Aysegul Kibaroglu, Waltina Scheumann and Annika Kramer, 179–97. Berlin: Springer-Verlag.

Türk Mühendis ve Mimar Odaları Birliği. 2006. *Water Policies Congress.* 21–23 March. Ankara, Turkey. http://www.imo.org.tr/ekutuphane/index.php?yayinkod=277&belgeadi=TMMOB%20Su%20Politikalar%FD%20Kongresi%20-%201.%20Cilt. Accessed 08 January 2019.

The Turkish Government's Observations on the Draft Articles on the Law of the Non-Navigational Uses of International Watercourses. 1997. *Report Sent to the United Nations General Assembly, Sixth Committee, as Member-States Opinions on the Draft Articles.* U.N. Doc. A/C.6/51/SR.61.

UNECE. 2012. 'Report of the Meeting of the Parties on its sixth session in Rome'. UN Doc. ECE/MP.WAT/37/Add.2. 28–30 November. http://www.unece.org/fileadmin/DAM/env/water/meetings/Implementation_Committee/1st_meeting/Documents/ECE.MP.WAT.37.Add.2_decisionVI.1_01.pdf. Accessed 13 April 2019.

UN-ESCWA and BGR (United Nations Economic and Social Commission for Western Asia; Bundesanstalt für Geowissenschaften und Rohstoffe). 2013. *Inventory of Shared Water Resources in Western Asia*. Beirut: ESCWA.

UN General Assembly.1994. *Res 49/52 Draft Articles on the Non-Navigational Uses of International Watercourses*. UN Doc A/Res/49/52.

UNECE Helsinki Convention. 2003. Amendments to Articles 25 and 26 of the Convention on the Protection and Use of Transboundary Watercourses and International Lakes. Madrid. 28 November. http://treaties.un.org/Pages/ViewDetails.aspx?src=TREATY&mtdsg_no=XXVII-5-b&chapter=27&lang=en. Accessed 30 June 2018.

UN Treaty Collection. 2019. Status Chapter XXVII Environment, Convention on the Protection and Use of Transboundary Watercourses and International Lakes. http://www.unece.org/env/water/status/legal1.html. Accessed 22 March 2018.

Ünver, Olcay. 1997. 'Southeastern Anatolia Project (GAP)'. *International Journal of Water Resources Development* 13, no. 4: 453–84.

———. 2001. 'Institutionalizing the Sustainable Development Approach– Coordination across Traditional Boundaries'. *International Journal of Water Resources Development* 17, no. 4: 511–20.

UN-Water. 2018. *Water Facts*. http://www.unwater.org/water-facts/. Accessed 11 July 2018.

USAID. 2012. *HIPP Report on Georgia/Turkey Cross Border Electricity Trade Agreement*. Washington, DC: USAID. http://hydropower.ge/user_upload/Report_on_CBETA_Feb2012.pdf. Accessed 31 July 2019.

Vishwanath, Ambika. 2015. 'The Water Wars Waged by the Islamic State'. 25 November. https://www.stratfor.com/weekly/water-wars-waged-islamic-state. Accessed 14 August 2019.

Von Lossow, Tobias. 2016. 'Water as a Weapon: IS on the Euphrates and Tigris'. German Institute for International and Security Affairs. https://css.ethz.ch/en/services/digital-library/publications/publication.html/195767. Accessed 09 June 2019.

Wakil, Mikhail. 1993. 'Analysis of Future Water Needs for Different Sectors in Syria'. *Water International* 18, no. 1: 18–22.

Waslekar, Sundeep. 2017. 'Wars Will Not Be Fought over Water – Our Thirst Could Pave the Way to Peace'. *The Guardian*. https://www.theguardian.com/global-development-professionals-network/2017/jan/19/water-wars-infrastructure-isis-peace. Accessed 02 June 2018.

Williams, Paul. 2011. 'Turkey's Water Diplomacy: A Theoretical Discussion.' In *Turkey's Water Policy: National Frameworks and International Cooperation*, edited by Aysegul Kibaroglu, Waltina Scheumann and Annika Kramer, 197–214. Berlin: Springer-Verlag.

Wiseman, Geoffrey, and Sharp, Paul. 2012. 'Diplomacy'. In *An Introduction to International Relations*, edited by Richard Devetak, Anthony Burke and Jim George, 256–267. Second Edition. Cambridge: Cambridge University Press.

Wolf, T. Aaron. 1998. 'Conflict and Cooperation along International Waterways'. *Water Policy* 1, no. 2: 251–65.

Working Group of the Whole. 1997. Documents A/51/624 and A/51/869.

World Bank. 2017. *Georgia Trade Summary 2017 Data*. https://wits.worldbank.org/CountryProfile/en/Country/GEO/Year/2017/Summary. Accessed 15 November 2019.

Wouters, Patricia. 1999. 'The Legal Response to International Water Conflicts: The UN Watercourses Convention and Beyond'. *German Yearbook of International Law* 42: 293–336.

———. 2013. 'Sovereignty Revisited – Examining the Rules of International Law that Govern Transboundary Water Resources with a Focus on Upstream/downstream State Practice – Possible Lessons Learned for the Euphrates-Tigris'. In *Water Law and Cooperation in the Euphrates-Tigris Region*, edited by Aysegül, Kibaroglu, Adele Kirschner, Sigrid Mehring and Rüdiger Wolfrum, 373–403. Leiden: Brill.

Wouters, Patricia, Vinogradov, Sergei, and Jones, Patricia. 2003. *Transforming Potential Conflict into Cooperation Potential: The Role of International Water Law*. Paris: UNESCO.

The Yearbook of the International Law Commission. 1987. Volume II, Part 2, A/CN.4/SER.A/1987/Add.1 (Part 2).

Yildiz, Dursun. 1999a. 'Sinir Olusturan ve Sinirasan Su Kaynaklarimiz ve Kiyidas Ulkeler Arasinda Teknik Isbirliği Gereksinimi. *Cevre ve Mühendis* 18: 28–35.

———. 1999b. 'Coruh Havzasinin Hidropolitigi Üzerine'. *Cevre ve Mühendis* 18: 57–63.

———. 2014. *Can We Do It with 1997 UN Watercourses Convention*. https://www.hidropolitikakademi.org/en/article/4862/can-we-do-it-with– 1997-un-watercourses-convention. Accessed 11 April 2019.

———. 2015. *The Failure of Transboundary Water Management in the Maritsa River Basin*. http://www.globalwaterforum.org/2015/05/04/the-failure-of-transboundary-water-management-in-the-maritsa-river-basin. Accessed 07 October 2019.

———. 2019a. 'Climate Change-Transboundary Maritsa River Basin Case'. *UNECE Meeting on Climate Change Adaptation on Transboundary River Basins*. 14–15 February. http://www.hidropolitikakademi.org/en/unece-meeting-on-climate-change-adaptation-on-transboundary-river-basins-in-geneva-concluded.html. Accessed 16 October 2019.

———. 2019b. 'Why innovative hydro-diplomacy?'. *World Water Diplomacy & Science News*. Hydropolitics Academy Center. 1–4 January. Ankara.

Zeitoun, Mark, and Warner, Jeroen. 2006. 'Hydro-Hegemony – a Framework for Analysis of Transboundary Water Conflicts'. *Water Policy* 8, no. 5: 435–60.

INDEX

a Significant Portion of the Turkish–
Greek Thracian Border' 74
'Protocol on the Joint Construction of
the Arpacay Dam' 86–87

Qattineh Dam 92, 93

Ramsar Convention 73
Rastan Dam 93
regional water negotiations 71
remote sensing approach 94
Rende, Mithat 13, 35, 42–43, 60
Report on Basin Management and Water
Information Systems 34
Revolutionary Plan 104
Reyhanli Dam 94
river basin management plans (RBMPs)
16, 23, 25–26, 74, 119–20

Saatci, Ahmet 116
salient processes
best practices 137–39
lessons learned 139–41
Samarra Dam 104
Sarikaya, Hasan 39–40
Scheumann, Waltina 98
Second World War 52
sediment dispute 71, 80–84, 144
Senegal River Basin Authority 136
Serdarabad Regulator 43, 87, 88
Shamaly, Omar 98
shared resource, transboundary water
as 57–58
Shatt al-Arab 41, 101
Soil, Water and Energy Working
Group 132
Soil and Land Reclamation
Organization 104
Southeastern Anatolia Project (GAP) 3–4,
9, 12, 15, 20, 33, 103
Master Plan 29
Regional Development Administration
(GAP RDA) 2, 10, 28–30, 108–9,
130, 143
'sovereign right to the use of water' 37
sovereignty 51–52
sovereignty paradox 37
Soviet Union 70, 80, 81, 86–87, 89, 144

Soviet Union (USSR) 10, 82, 86–87, 89
State Hydraulic Works (DSI) 4, 9, 10, 14–22,
27, 36, 45, 76, 94, 130, 137, 138, 143
coordination with private sector 15
dam projects 20–22
and Keban Dam 17–18
legal experts 16–17
Master Plans 16, 29
and MFA 16–17
mission of 14–15
responsibilities 14–15
riparians crises 20
role in humanitarian water
diplomacy 21–22
role in transboundary water relations 21
technocrats of 17–20
and Three-Stage Plan 18–19
state practice 4–5
Stockholm Environment Institute (SEI) 40
Stockholm International Water Institute
(SIWI) 40, 43
Strategic Foresight Group (SFG) 38–39,
117, 136, 139
Suakacagi Dam 43, 78
SUEN. See Turkish Water Institute (SUEN)
Susskind, Lawrence 145
sustainable water management 31
Sweden 40, 127
Swedish International Development
Cooperation Agency (SIDA) 39,
136, 139
Swedish Meteorological and Hydrological
Institute (SMHI) 40
Swiss Agency for Development and
Cooperation (SDC) 39, 117, 136, 139
Switzerland 40
Syria 2–3, 4, 10, 35–36, 38, 41, 132,
134, 139
benefits sharing 42–43, 57–58
civil war 21, 94, 95, 114–15, 139
and ET basin 14, 30, 67, 100–115,
117, 131
and Euphrates-Tigris Initiative for
Cooperation (ETIC) 123, 124, 126,
127, 128
French mandate of 92, 94, 96
and Iraq 19–20
and Keban Dam 17, 37

www.ingramcontent.com/pod-product-compliance
Lightning Source LLC
Chambersburg PA
CBHW030651270326
41929CB00007B/316